Contents

Abbreviations

AC	Africa Confidential
CMI	Chr. Michelsen Institute
EC	European Community
ECA	Economic Commission for Africa
ERP	Economic Recovery Plan (Tanzania)
FAO	Food and Agricultural Organisation
forex	foreign exchange
Frelimo	Frente de Libertação de Moçambique
FT	Financial Times
GDP	Gross Domestic Product
GLSS	Ghana Living Standards Survey (1987)
IFI	International financial institution(s) [i.e. the World Bank and IMF]
ILO	International Labour Organisation
IMF	International Monetary Fund
MHT	Mosley, Harrigan, and Toye study (see references)
NAI	Nordiska Afrikainstitutet (the Scandinavian Institute of African Studies)
NGO	Non-Governmental Organisation
OAU	Organisation of African Unity
PCP	petty commodity production
PNDC	Provisional National Defence Council (Ghana)
PRE	Economic Rehabilitation programme (Mozambique)
RSC	rent-seeking capitalism
SAL	Structural Adjustment Loan
SAP	Structural Adjustment Programme
SECAL	Sectoral Adjustment Loan
SSA	Sub-Saharan Africa
TCP	transnational capitalist production
UNDP	United Nations Development Programme
UNESCO	United Nations Educational, Scientific, and Cultural Organisation
UNICEF	United Nations Children's Fund
UNIP	United Nations Independence Party (Zambia)
UNRISD	United Nations Research Institute for Social Development

Preface

This book arose from an international symposium on "The Social and Political Context of Structural Adjustment in Sub-Saharan Africa" held at the Chr. Michelsen Institute (CMI), Bergen, Norway in October 1990. The symposium was jointly organised by Nordiska Afrikainstitutet, (the Scandinavian Institute of African Studies), CMI and the United Nations Research Institute for Social Development (UNRISD). Each of these organisations is active in the field of structural adjustment research.

The Scandinavian Institute of African Studies was established in Uppsala in 1962 as a research and documentation centre on Africa for the Nordic countries. It is an independent agency, since 1980 responsible to the Swedish Ministry for Foreign Affairs. Traditionally research activities at the Institute reflected the interests of visiting Nordic researchers, but under the recent directorship of Anders Hjort af Ornäs the Institute has initiated a series of specific research programmes. The most recent of these, dating from 1990, is "The Political and Social Context of Structural Adjustment in Sub-Saharan Africa". Currently, the programme's main components are support to a network of African researchers working on adjustment issues and collaborative work between the programme coordinator and other Scandinavian scholars. The main areas of research being pursued are the political economy of agrarian change under adjustment, women as informal sector workers and household structures under adjustment, developments in the social sector, changing relations between the state, donors, and the non-governmental organisations (NGOs), and the politics of adjustment in adjusting and donor countries.

Chr. Michelsen Institute is an independent research institution located in Bergen. A development research programme (DERAP) has been a major part of CMI's Department of Social Science and Development since the 1960s, and consists of 15–20 researchers. The DERAP programme undertakes basic research as well as commissioned research and consultancies, and the research staff spend a substantial part of their career on long-term assignments in developing countries. The present research areas are economic policies and management, local government and organisation, basic studies on gender relations, population and resources, and democratisation and regional cooperation in Southern Africa. The geographic focus is mainly on Eastern and Southern Africa and South Asia. A programme of human rights studies concentrating on the developing countries was added in 1983.

CMI research on Southern and Eastern Africa has approached the problems of economic and political reforms and restructuring under the Structural Adjustment Programmes (SAPs) from various angles. Studies have been conducted on the economic effects of the SAPs in Mozambique and in Malawi, and ways of measuring the effects are being developed in Uganda. Another set of research projects concern the role of organised interest groups in the introduction and implementation of SAP in Zimbabwe and Zambia. A third and more micro approach is used in studying the impact of and responses to structural adjustment among women in agriculture in Zambia, and among fishermen and fish traders in the region. One objective of these research projects is to develop viable alternative policies to overcome the present crisis.

The United Nations Research Institute for Social Development (UNRISD) is an autonomous research organisation based in Geneva. It specialises in research on key aspects of contemporary social development. UNRISD selects its own research themes and is advised by an independent Governing Board of prominent scholars in the field of international development. Among its current research activities is the project "Crisis, adjustment and social change", which supports field research by multi-disciplinary teams in Africa and Latin America on livelihood strategies and the dynamics of social change.

The Editors
November 1991

Adjustment, Authoritarianism and Democracy: An Introduction to Some Conceptual and Empirical Issues

Yusuf Bangura and Peter Gibbon

The great majority of countries in Sub-Saharan Africa* have adopted—more or less involuntarily—programmes of economic reform designed by the international financial institutions. These "structural adjustment programmes" have included producer price reforms, removal of subsidies, liberalisation of internal and external trade, new foreign exchange regimes usually involving severe devaluations, the introduction of "cost sharing" for state-supplied services, privatisation, restructuring of government institutions and more recently, legal reforms aimed at supplying an "enabling environment". Structural adjustment has been devised by the international financial institutions on the assumption that economic growth in Sub-Saharan Africa will only be resumed through a contraction of state activity and the development of liberalised markets.

The adoption of structural adjustment programmes by governments in Sub-Saharan Africa has usually (but not always) occurred in a context of economic crisis. This crisis has had exogenous and endogenous aspects and causes. While its origins are subject to fundamental dispute, there is broad agreement that its most important result has been African governments' increasing balance of payments and budgetary management difficulties, arising from diminishing export earning, an increasing burden of debt servicing and inappropriate domestic policies. Structural adjustment lending by the international financial institutions has consisted of transfusions of foreign exchange with the primary intention of "buying" conditions under which domestic imbalances can be corrected and export earnings can be increased (and hence debt serviced).

* The term is used throughout to mean all the countries in Africa south of the Sahara, except the Republic of South Africa and Namibia.

Both the economic crisis which preceded adjustment and the process of adjustment itself have meant the erosion of the economic assumptions on which most African governmental politics rested during the first two decades of independence. How to to characterise the content of these politics, as well as to interpret their meaning, is also subject to dispute but most commentators share the view that their central element was an expansion of state responsibility and regulation in the service of *developmentalist* objectives. Mostly, these politics were cast in an authoritarian mould, although they also had strong consensual features (sometimes expressed democratically). A fundamental characteristic of the present period in Africa has been an increasing *differentiation* of authoritarian and democratic political tendencies, in the context of the demise of this developmentalism.

Such complex, and often contradictory, developments have encouraged a number of scholars to study the political dynamics of structural adjustment. A lot of the political theorising on adjustment, particularly as it relates to Africa, is however highly speculative and of uneven quality. As it becomes increasingly difficult to keep track of the rapid changes unfolding in the continent, analysts have come to rely mainly on deductive logic to construct what they believe the political dynamics ought to be. But deductive logic can be sterile when the social structures that formed the basis for the construction of the original theoretical frameworks are themselves undergoing fundamental change, posing new conceptual problems that can only be understood with the generation of fresh empirical data.

This volume has a dual purpose. On the one hand, it embodies and develops a critique of what are becoming the principal trends in the analysis of the politics of adjustment. These trends have emerged from within conventional political science and reflect both certain of its traditional theoretical orientations as well as its equally traditional close relationship to dominant political forces or ideologies. On the other hand, on the basis of this critique it seeks to define a revised research agenda, and address it through new empirical work. It is not attempting to inaugurate a new "school", however. The contributions to be found here share less a common theoretical or political standpoint than a commitment to concrete investigation and an implicit or explicit rejection of what is rapidly becoming the orthodoxy.

CONVENTIONAL POLITICAL SCIENCE AND THE POLITICS OF ADJUSTMENT

Two major perspectives can be identified in the current literature on the politics of adjustment. The first seeks to understand political processes on the basis of the public choice theory's postulation of the likely distribution of gains and losses among competing social groups. Political dynamics and their outcomes are deduced from a framework that assumes a transition from a structure of incentives based on state interventions to one where markets are believed to be fully liberated and competitive. It fails to analyse the social and institutional processes that link economic change with political behaviour, and opts instead for a short-term technocratic view of politics, which is concerned with the modalities for creating the necessary political framework to successfully implement reform programmes.

The second perspective is less tied to functionalist concerns with political order and recognises two significant processes of change in contemporary African societies, informalisation and the rise of civil society. However, it ignores the broad social and political contexts for understanding the dynamics of such changes. This leads to narrow and, at times, romanticised conclusions. A mechanistic link is established between adjustment and a form of democracy inaugurated by movements arising from the informal sector. In the process, organised urban-based groups tend to get written off prematurely, as the complexity of change in which the formal and informal interact in new ways fails to be addressed. Furthermore, both perspectives understand the politics of adjustment purely in relation to the recipient countries. The politics of the international financial institutions themselves escape problematisation.

The public choice theory approach to politics

Central to the public choice theory approaches to adjustment is a picture of gainers and losers that is derived from the types of commodities individuals produce and consume and the nature of factor mobility between different sectors of the economy. As a general rule, individuals and households that produce tradeables* and consume

---

* Tradeables are goods and services for which there is an international, as well as a national market.

non-tradeables are expected to benefit from the reforms, which seek to change the macro-economic structure of incentives in favour of tradeables. Conversely, it is assumed that households that consume tradeables and produce non-tradeables will be penalised by the reforms. If the factors of production are immobile and, therefore, will not earn the same rate of return as in the sectors they are currently employed (which is often the case for African economies), an accurate picture of gainers and losers can only be obtained by grouping individuals sectorally.

Work being done on agriculture thus examines the likely benefits that will accrue to various groups in rural areas as a result of specific adjustment policies. Social groups are divided into several categories, i.e. producers of tradeables and non-tradeables, hired farm workers, and net food buyers. These are further sub-divided depending on whether producers are in the export or domestic food sector, or whether farm workers are engaged in the production of tradeables or non-tradeable goods (FAO, 1990). Bienen recommends a similar model that takes into account the wide variety of urban groups based on the same principles of relative price changes, factor mobility and economic activity lines (Bienen, 1990).

Several observations can be made about this. Although public choice theory should ordinarily be agnostic on the concrete groups that would benefit or lose from adjustment, since the focus is actually on lines of activities groups are engaged in, most writers have linked activity lines with specific groups and have proceeded to construct a picture of gainers and losers and their likely responses to the reforms. One reason for the open identification of groups with activity lines could be related to the need to prove that adjustment programmes actually benefit the majority of the population. Secondly, those who use the model assume that gainers are honourable and should be defended, since their gains are derived from productive activities which add real value to the national product. Losers, in this context, have no moral right to prevent the gainers from maximising the returns to their efforts. Thirdly, adjustment is asserted to lead to a redistribution of income in favour of groups that have been historically discriminated against. The reforms therefore supposedly give voice and economic security to the oppressed majority.

While these theoretical assumptions have been maintained virtually intact through the adjustment period, from 1980 onwards, it is possible to trace a succession of political stances, on the part both of the international financial institutions and those political scientists sharing with them a commitment to manage the changes activated by the reforms. The first to emerge was an essentially technicist position in which it was assumed that the International Monetary Fund (IMF) and the World Bank were and could remain politically neutral. It was believed that the international economy could be regulated by objective economic techniques in which all member governments shared an interest and which all therefore would adopt (Kahler, 1989; Camdessus, 1988). These techniques served to facilitate the ability of market forces to push economies along the path of sustained growth—in a manner ultimately benefiting every sector and social group.

In the early 1980s, as the crisis in many African countries deepened, a second strand of thought emerged in which the idealised view of the Fund and the Bank as supervising experts standing outside of the political arena gave way to a more interventionist outlook. Reflecting the growing influence of neo-liberal political economy it was now believed that governments and recalcitrant social groups had to be forced to recognise the long-term benefits of a radical realignment of price relationships, since developing countries typically possessed embedded structures favouring state-led industrialisation strategies and certain associated rent-seeking activities. Given that urban groups benefitting from these arrangements were likely to oppose policies aimed at changing the structure of incentives in favour of tradeables, some neo-liberal writers believed authoritarian policies were necessary to secure the adoption of reforms (Lal, 1983). Differences in the performance of regimes in implementing structural adjustment programmes were seen as functionally deriving from governmental courage, will and authority. Toye and Beckman (both this volume) show how Bank thinking in the early 1980s was to financially support authoritarian reform-oriented governments to enable them to overcome the short-term domestic pressures expected from aggrieved "urban coalitions".

A third strand in the development of a political perspective emerged in the late 1980s, following the acceptance of adjustment programmes by most countries and the continuing deterioration of their economic conditions. A World Bank study on the implementation of 51 structural and sectoral adjustment loans (SALs and

SECALs) in 15 developing countries (including five from Africa) between 1980 and 1987 showed that only 60 per cent of the policy changes agreed as conditions were fully implemented, and that "the degree to which the conditions were met differed substantially between policy areas". An interesting finding was that tranche releases of about three quarters of all loans were delayed because of unsatisfactory progress in implementing agreed conditions (McCleary, 1989).

Deeper processes of political resistance thus seemed to be at work, contrary to simplistic notions of the absence of political will. A few empirical studies were now also beginning to question the assumed correlation between authoritarianism and the capacity to implement adjustment programmes (Haggard and Kaufman, 1989). Implied by these studies was the need to take political interests and processes much more seriously into account in implementing adjustment programmes. A major question became how to create the necessary environment for competent and politically legitimate regimes to emerge which would also be fully committed to the goals of adjustment. The World Bank's document *Sub-Saharan Africa: From Crisis to Sustainable Growth* attempted to address this question by focusing on some of the issues that political scientists sympathetic to the goals of adjustment were beginning to identify as necessary for overcoming the crisis in Africa: good governance, political accountability, the rule of law, and grassroots participation in government.

But the mandate of the international financial institutions to develop a liberal and standardised system of trade and payments imposes constraints on their ability to relate objectively with the political forces they seek to understand. This colours the perspective they and their allies bring to bear on issues relating to the politics of adjustment. The instinct for regulation and management dictates the choice of strategy and conceptual framework. As Beckman (this volume) shows, the Bank's political agenda remains primarily concerned with shifting the balance of forces in favour of coalitions that will be capable of sustaining the reform programme.

This functionalist and technocratic view of politics provides the framework for the various perspectives that have dominated the academic debate on the politics of adjustment: those that look at the links between rent-seeking activities and political rigidities, and those that are concerned with the political management of adjustment.

The political case for structural adjustment in Africa was originally developed by writers working on the agrarian crisis and using a neo-liberal/public choice theory political economy framework of analysis. They were concerned to show how the distribution of power in post-colonial Africa effected agricultural growth and rural incomes. They argued that rural poverty was a product of discriminatory trade and pricing policies. Peasants suffered a raw deal because they were not represented in the urban political coalitions that shaped development policies in the 1960s and 1970s. Indeed, peasant interests were said to be contradictory to those of industrialists, workers and the political elites whose profit margins and living standards would fall if farm prices were to be raised (Bates, 1981; Lofchie, 1975). Price controls, food subsidies and state-run marketing boards were therefore primarily means of serving and maintaining urban political coalitions (Pletcher, 1986).

Some writers in this tradition concentrate on key policy instruments, usually trade policy, to discuss the political foundations of adjustment. Bienen, for instance, believes that more targeted and specific policies, such as trade liberalisation, are likely to be less dysfunctional to political systems than the pursuit of a wide range of adjustment policies which tend to undermine the livelihood of too many groups. What is more, liberalisation policies could produce positive results very quickly and thus generate immediate support from the beneficiaries who could then counter the resistance of the losers, i.e. the military, politicians and civil servants (Bienen, 1990:719).

Those who focus on the political implications of the adjustment package as a whole tend to link rent-seeking activities with the question of political survival (Herbst, 1990; Bienen and Gersovitz, 1985; Sandbrook, 1991). Herbst, for instance, links distortions in trade policy, agricultural prices and bureaucratic performance with the need to develop local political constituencies. As structural adjustment aims to curtail the rents politicians usually distribute to their clients, the political situation is likely to become very unstable. Herbst rejects the possibility of gainers acting to protect their interests against the state and its traditional allies. Instead leaders would have to repress former clients to implement the adjustment programmes.

Thus, the need for authoritarian forms of rule continues to dominate a lot of the political analysis in works dealing with the transition to market-based incentives. Bienen, for instance, contends that the capacity of regimes to repress and the amount of resources they have devoted to repression is crucial to any assessment of the likely success of the reform policies (Bienen, 1990).

A slightly different strand of argument within the same tradition questions the wisdom of exclusively relying on unrestrained market forces to overcome the recession, and bemoans the failure to recognise the negative consequences of adjustment on groups other than those concerned with administratively derived rents. A large proportion of the losers are poor, often very vulnerable, reside in both urban and rural areas, and lack any access to state power. A policy aimed at repressing the losers could thus be a recipe for political instability, since the losers may well be in the majority.

The pioneering work to defend the weak and vulnerable at the social level was initiated by UNICEF whose programmes are specifically targeted at women and children, two important but politically inactive social groups. Some very useful studies by UNICEF have aimed at influencing both national and international policy makers in the allocation of public resources at the macro and meso levels. The macro level deals with levels of expenditure, the nature of taxes and the question of budget deficits, whilst the meso level is concerned with the distribution of revenues among groups, the allocation of public expenditure between and within sectors, and the way different types of expenditures benefit different social groups (Cornia and Stewart, 1990). But the UNICEF studies have failed to articulate a *political* perspective to defend the vulnerable. They have relied instead on humanitarian concerns and the good sense of governments and the international financial institutions.

The need to understand the social and political costs of adjustment, following the initial UNICEF studies in the late 1980s and popular resistance to conditionality in many countries, has encouraged a host of other writers to focus on a wider range of political strategies that states need to adopt in order to push through the economic reforms. The issues of compensation and the pacing and sequencing of policies popularised by some of the authors associated with the work of UNICEF have come to be seen by some political analysts as instruments for overriding resistance to economic reform.

Callaghy calls for a balanced relationship between state intervention and market forces to satisfy both the economic necessity of adjustment and the political logic of domestic stability. In his framework of seeking to "embed liberalism", state power should be used to simultaneously restructure the crisis economies and minimise the domestic social and political costs of adjustment. States need to be effective to manage the economic and political demands which emanate from both the domestic and international systems. Statecraft, improved bureaucratic capability and coercion will be necessary to overcome resistance from groups with historic claims on state resources (Callaghy, 1989, 1990). Similarly, Nelson examines the compensatory schemes necessary to support the poor and the political coalitions governments need to make with the poor and the less poor through compensatory programmes in order for the adjustment process to be sustainable (Nelson, 1989).

Waterbury adopts a more Machiavellian approach to the study of coalition politics. Not only are compensatory payment schemes given an explicitly political role in coalition-building in order to sustain the reforms, but Waterbury further argues that whilst policies aimed at sending the appropriate signals to economic agents to encourage them to adopt new forms of behaviour need to be as visible and consistent as possible, "austerity policies should be uneven, sometimes internally inconsistent, and if possible camouflaged: losses and benefits to various constituencies should not be made clear." (Waterbury, 1989).

How valid is the public choice theory conception of the distribution of gains and losses among competing social groups? Do "gainers" and "losers" act according to the assumptions of the model? Could political responses be directly deduced from the structure of economic interests? Has this in any event been correctly understood? What issues does the political framework raise for an understanding of the social processes of change?

Politics does, indeed, deal with fundamental conflicts of interest and general issues of livelihood. Social groups and individuals act at various levels of society, and within state apparatuses, to influence the allocation of resources . Knowledge of who the gainers and losers are, how various groups lose and gain as a result of shifts in development strategies, is important in understanding the political dynamics of societies going through structural change.

One major problem with the neo-liberal perspective, however, is its limited view of the way structures of incentives operate in concrete African societies. It posits two contrasting models of resource allocation with different structures of opportunities—one based on state interventions leading to price distortions and economic rents for a privileged few; and a second based on free competitive markets which allocate resources optimally. Quite apart from the obvious fact that some of the elements of the statist model never get completely eliminated even in economies with fully developed markets, the rigid distinction between state and non-state, public and private, rent-seeking and market-oriented is misplaced in the African con-text. A fundamental feature of African economies is in fact the predominance of "grey" economic activity in which these sectors become not only blurred but blended. Even before the independence era, it was a characteristic of some locally dominant social classes in Africa that they "straddled" state employment and a *series* of private sector activities (see e.g. Cowen and Kinyanjui, 1977). It should not be surprising therefore, that when such forces gain state power, one should find them using state resources both in their own right and as means of promoting their private sector concerns (some of which in the process undergo "marriages" with the state, or through the state with foreign capital). As a result "rent-seeking groups" are in an ideal position to utilise their accumulated economic resources and political links with the state to manipulate the operation of markets. In fact, in the general competition among various groups to maximise the returns expected to flow from the shifts in policy, the discredited privileged groups often turn out to be the most effective winners.

Studies of (inter alia) Guinea-Bissau, Sierra Leone and Uganda tend to substantiate the above argument. Mamdani's work on Uganda shows that the "state-created and state-protected stratum of big proprietors", popularly known as the *mafuta mingi*, who came into being with the expulsion of the Asian business community in 1972 and assumed national prominence during Obote's second government, have been the main beneficiaries of the liberalisation policies pursued in the 1980s. The *mafuta mingi* have benefited from shifts in bank lending policies and the operation of an Open General Import Licence scheme in the trade sector. This has led to a "movement of capital away from productive investments ... to commercial and even high-risk speculative investments ..." (Mamdani, 1991).

Rosemary Galli's study on Guinea-Bissau also captures the way rent-seeking groups have benefited from the shifts in policy towards liberalisation. In the case of Guinea-Bissau, liberalisation was accompanied by a substantial inflow of foreign loans and grants which the dominant power groups appropriated for their expanding private sector businesses. Major government institutions concerned with finance, trade and tourism are entrusted with the power to determine "who and what gets financed". Many high ranking government officials, including the President, own large plantations and run a variety of commercial businesses. The liberalisation programme of 1987 has simply shifted the economic power bloc from an exclusive "stateclass" to one which now includes merchants and concessionaires (ponteiros), but with direct links with the "stateclass" (Galli, 1990).

Zack-Williams has also shown, in a study of deteriorating economic and social conditions in Sierra Leone, the rise of an ethnically-based political pressure group, Ekutay, which oversees most of the important decisions of the government. Key individuals within this group have flourishing business enterprises which are largely sustained by their links with the state (Zack-Williams, 1990).

Of course, this in no way rules out that these groups may also be threatened in *some of their activities* by adjustment, and as a result might be not only the main beneficiaries but also the main opponents of adjustment. Something of this kind appears to have occurred in Kenya and Malawi, where certain *agricultural* interests of the local ruling class have been threatened by proposals to dismantle marketing boards from which rents or taxes were derived (Mosley, Harrigan and Toye, 1991). But a more general phenomenon is that the repression of "rent-seekers" becomes directed against groups which turn out to have very little representation in the power structure: workers, the urban poor and the increasingly impoverished middle classes. The most important rent-earning groups are, in fact, likely to be at the forefront in themselves repressing (or supporting governments to repress) these poor but sometimes organised and vocal classes, as the former seek to simultaneously consolidate their political position and adjust their business strategies to some of the requirements of the reforms.

An implication of this critique is that it takes more than conventional theoretical assumptions to understand the way gains and losses are distributed among different social groups. Detailed empirical studies are required that will take into account the concrete social and political structures of different countries, and the degree of diversification of the social locations of classes within them. Only an analysis of this kind can provide a basis for understanding the capacities of different groups to respond to the challenges thrown up by major shifts in economic policy.

Knowledge of such processes requires, as a minimum, detachment from the trend of orienting academic research towards short-term policy objectives of "stable adjustment". Since key issues in the package of reforms remain contestable and actually contested, such politically manipulative "research", however Machiavellian its conception, tends to ideologically revert to the simplifying distortions of social reality embodied in neo-classical theory. In the process it becomes blind even to many of the most obvious signs of support for and resistance to adjustment.

From "informalisation" to "civil society"

A second, probably subordinate, perspective within the orthodox political science literature is found in the work of those who see in economic crisis and adjustment a means for the strengthening of "civil society" and thereby for democratisation. Although some see this process occurring through an adjustment-led dynamic growth of private formal sector activity (Diamond, 1988a), a commoner approach is to see economic and political *informalisation* as the main intermediary in this process. Representative writers occupying this position include Bratton (1989a, 1990), Portes et al. (1989), Lemarchand (1991) and, most consistently, Chazan (Azarya and Chazan, 1987; Rothchild and Chazan, 1988; Chazan, 1988).

Writing on the "vitiation of democratic regimes" in Ghana from the 1960s to the present, Chazan (1988) argues that pluralism has been consistently undermined by the residues of undemocratic colonial traditions, the presence of a high degree of economic inequality in the context of the absence of an indigenous capitalist class, ongoing economic dependency, a weak state, inept leaders, corruption and an "extractive and utilitarian political culture at the state level". On the other hand, there are two grounds for optimism that Ghanaian democracy is about to undergo a revival.

The first of these grounds is the survival of a "deeply democratic tradition" which Chazan believes is "esconced in local political cultures" (1988:130). This tradition tends to be asserted rather than demonstrated, however. The second, and more important, is the emergence of "alternative institutions and patterns of interactions separate from those that have developed in the formal arena" (ibid.).

> Ghana has a vast array of voluntary associations and communal networks that are not only autonomous, but actually flourish when access to the centre is denied. These groups, unable to attain or attenuate formal power, have reorganised their activities and established a series of norms to guide their lateral interactions. Led either by disaffected professionals, traditional authorities, independent farmers, students or members of the country's incipiently capitalist group, they have underwritten the parallel economy and laid the foundation for economic survival ... around these institutions, democracy in Ghana is gaining new relevance ...
>
> Economic revival carries the seeds of political renewal. The peculliar brand of capitalism developing ... is indicative in the promise ingrained in the freeing of economic activities from political constraints. Existing coping strategies ... have shown how groups and economic organisations have carved out economic fields in which they can operate. As resources have accumulated and skills honed, these have garnered a modicum of economic—and hence also political—space. The linchpin of any reordering programme is reformulation of the terms of exchange between these groups and government agencies. The disregard for autonomy led to political dissipation in the past. The precondition for revival is protection of this independence ... (Chazan, 1988:130–132).

Hence informalisation has an essentially libertarian impetus. This is linked furthermore to a *democratic* impetus (formation of autonomous civil society) while—by implication—formal politics becomes marginalised in the process. Chazan's only doubt is whether civil society can be "protected" (from the state) while it is still fragile.

Nobody can dispute that a massive process of economic informalisation is underway in Sub-Saharan Africa. The ILO estimates that between 1980 and 1985 employment in the informal sector increased at an annual rate of 6.7 per cent. Formal enterprises absorbed only 6 per cent of new additions to the labour force in this period, whereas the informal sector absorbed 75 per cent (ILO, 1988). The ILO now also estimates that about 60 per cent of the African urban labour force is engaged in the sector (ILO, 1991). Urban households of all social categories, including professional classes formerly enjoying internationally competitive salaries, have been driven by falling real incomes into multiple income-generating activities (Mustapha, this

volume; Asobie, 1991). Amongst the working class, tendencies toward proletarianisation have been reversed for much the same reason (Mustapha, ibid.). Informalisation has also been growing in the
rural sectors (Ng'ethe et al., 1989). Moreover, urban and rural
groups have become even less neatly divisible than before, as urban
groups have taken up growing their own food (Hermele, this volume; Mustapha, this volume).

Neither can anyone dispute that informalisation poses a number
of problems for political systems that hitherto functioned on the assumptions that the formal sector was not only a motor of economic
growth, but an indicator and regulator of economic performance, a
means of satisfying the political expectations of important social
groups, and a means of ensuring that most social and political transactions could be centrally monitored and controlled. The 1980s have
been a period in which informal enterprises and informal organisations have sprung up all over Africa—the former to secure personal
incomes, the latter to protect the welfare and interests of members as
state-provided social provision has deteriorated or collapsed. In the
process of increasing levels of "autonomous" economic activity, provision of services outside the state and the evolution of new mechanisms for popular interaction with law enforcement agencies, the bureaucracy and politicians, a weakening of the African state's authority and influence has been inevitable.

There are nonetheless good reasons to doubt, or at least severely
qualify most of Chazan's main hypotheses. With regard to the "libertarian" and "democratic" character of informalisation, several reservations are necessary. One is that, in part at least, these characteristics
appear to be deduced from a falsely exclusive identification of
power with the state and exploitation with the public/formal sector.
On this reasoning, anything non-state becomes democratic and anything non-public/formal becomes autonomous and self-determin-
ing. But power and exploitation, though indeed located in the state
and the public/formal sector, are by no means exclusively located
there. Power relations are also found within "civil society". The
power of the chief or elders in the community, the household head
in the family, the priest or sheikh in the church or the mosque—all
are more or less authoritarian, just as the "discussion" which accom-
panies the exercise of their authority is always mitigated by a potential threat of exclusion from land, household or religious commu-

nity. Likewise, exploitation is often found in far more severe forms in the informal sector than the formal, if only because the informal sector is by definition unregulated. Here, for example, one can speak of child labour, often unpaid, as a *norm*.

The romantic attribution of essentially democratic and egalitarian properties to both the informal sector and (especially) civil society tends to further downplay the *ambivalence* of many of the characteristics of the latter in Africa (and probably not just in Africa). If the African state embodies a shifting array of secular, national, ethnic, localistic and parochial practices, then this is also true of civil society. A case in point is Ghana. One does not have to share Richard Crook's claims (1990; 1991) that Ghanaian civil society is more convincingly portrayed as an obstacle to democratisation than as a product of its absence and a foundation for its renewal, to accept that some of its institutions—and the well entrenched communal and neo-traditional elites who stood behind them—played a negative historical role, especially after the fall of Nkrumah when they became internalised within the state. Of course, African civil societies also embody (apparently) secular components such as employers' and professional associations, political parties, ecumenical organisations, as well as some non-local NGOs.

Furthermore, there are frequently complex interrelationships and interplays between these and more "traditionalist" and/or "localistic" fora. Professional associations may become the vehicles for the pursuit of ethnic and parochial objectives, while certain localistic and anti-secular forces have the capacity to embody democratic aspirations and demands, particularly where the politics and economics of a society are dominated by one or a few ethnic groups. Consider in this respect the highly variable and ambivalent role played by Islamic fundamentalism not merely in Africa or the "Third World" but even in contemporary Europe. The point is that civil society has no determining essential properties, neither "democratic" nor "undemocratic".

Another, and perhaps central, difficulty of the Chazan position parallels a key deficiency in the public choice theory approach to politics. Just as the latter hypostasises the private/public division, so Chazan does the same with the distinctions between formal and informal and civil society and the state. One problem with this error is that workers and most other social groups hardly impose rigid dichotomies between formal jobs and their involvement in the informal sectors. Informalisation involves spreading risks, and balancing alternative sources of incomes and resources in an integrated structure (Roitman, 1990). Chew's study on the livelihood strategies of civil servants in Uganda shows that although public servants are involved in "sideline" activities, they perceive government employment as secure and expect salaries to rise in the future; government pay is seen as an assured minimum, and the ability to operate effectively in the informal sector may even depend on the "influence, authority and connections derived" from formal jobs (Chew, 1990). Other studies have shown how the livelihood of informal sector groups is inextricably linked with the activities of formal enterprises (Meagher, 1991; Ng'ethe et al. 1989).

Another problem is that many of these same considerations apply to the relation between civil society and the state. For example, many groups which are powerful within civil society (chiefs, priests, sheikhs, etc.) derive a good part of their power from the state itself. This is particularly true of chiefs, who in some countries were a (colonial) state creation and in many others possess "delegated" degrees of state power. More generally, it is incorrect to understand the expansion of non-state activities as an indication of the state's irrelevance in the economic and political calculations of specific groups. Whether as a source of resources (albeit on a reduced scale and subject to new conditions of extraction) or of extra-economic coercion, the state still continues to impinge on the life of the mass of the population in an everyday way.

Finally, a similar point can be made about the supposed elimination of the role of formally-organised groups such as trade unions, political parties, student movements, as a result of informalisation. The view that these lose influence rests on three major assumptions. First, since unions have not been able to protect their members against retrenchment and the massive decline in real wages, workers' interest in union activities may have suffered an acute decline. In any case, since most workers now straddle several jobs, unions may not be that central to their survival strategies. Second, the corporate nature of unions and other formal organisations does not allow for any meaningful contacts to be established between these organisations and informal groups (Sanyal, 1991). Third, informal organisations themselves are sceptical of relating to trade unions and political parties, which are run on corporatist and patron-client lines (de Soto, 1989; Portes et al., 1989; Ghai and Alcántara, 1991).

The political behaviour of informal actors is much more complex than some of the recent studies of informalisation indicate. Sanyal's review of the politics of the urban informal sector shows that informals assess "each event on its merits, with a shrewd eye to protecting and furthering their own interests" (Sanyal, 1991). In the specific case of Latin America, where the most interesting studies on the politics of informalisation have been conducted, informals have supported military rulers at some times and left-wing parties and pro-democracy movements at others. The latter was done because of the military's austerity programmes. Urban informals in Africa are also known to have joined forces with trade unions, political parties and professional organisations to oppose cuts in food and petroleum subsidies and to support calls for multi-party rule. It is difficult to see how informals would be opposed to corporate institutions and patron-client networks if such could be used to enhance their own specific interests.

These last difficulties of informalisation theory derive from a failure to distinguish between the weakness of trade unions in protecting the living standards of their members during crisis situations, and the role which unions, and indeed formal organisations, can and do, play in the survival strategies and politics of both formal and informal groups. Informalisation means less specialisation in terms of what the majority of people do to earn a living, irrespective of whether they are workers, professionals, informals or peasants. Some households, of course, benefit from the crisis or have better ways of minimising the costs of adjustment than others. Most people, however, are forced to combine jobs and change previous patterns of consumption in ways that tend to homogenise large sections of the population. Wage-earners and professionals, as we have seen, grow their own food, and participate as traders, artisans, food distributors or petty transporters in the informal sector. More generally, informalisation has a levelling effect on society, in terms of getting people of diverse backgrounds to experience each others' work situations and social practices. Workers and professionals not only organise separately in unions and associations, they also take part in ethnic, religious and community-based organisations where they come into contact with informal groups. In periods of rapid economic and social change, these organisations become important in helping members to make the right contacts and in providing some badly needed social and, in some cases, financial support. Wage and salary earners may also be active in the numerous self-help projects and occupationally-based informal organisations emerging in these societies. In this kind of dynamic, those groups with a history of organisational work and knowledge of how to relate with state institutions tend to dominate the political process. This partly explains the high profile of trade unions and professional associations in the democracy movement, despite the decline in their membership and their inability to protect their members from the harsh conditions of adjustment. Such organisations provide the forum for both "formal" and "informal" groups to intervene in the political arena as they seek to introduce changes in the political system. A union leader even led to power the democracy movement in Zambia.

AN ALTERNATIVE RESEARCH AGENDA

The first—and overriding—problem of conventional political science-based approaches to the politics of adjustment has been their fidelity to transposing certain of the key categories of neo-classical economics to the political arena, and their use of these categories to designate watertight social institutions and groups of actors. Hence we find rigidly dichotomised divisions between state and market, public and private, state and civil society and formal and informal. The systematic interpenetration of the relations designated by these categories, perhaps one of the defining features of African social and economic formations, is overlooked, and in the process the economic and political effects of adjustment are systematically misunderstood.

The absence of unambiguous social positions in African societies alone makes problematical the transposition of unambiguous "interests" to the political sphere. There are independent methodological reasons for resisting such reductionist transpositions in any event. These are that, even where unambiguous social positions can be identified, their direct transposition into articulated political interests is historically the exception rather than the rule. One important strand of Marxist thought even argues that such transpositions (e.g. in the case of the Russian industrial proletariat in the first twenty years of this century) only occurs under the highly specific circumstances of a generalised economic and political crisis and an active organisation of divided groups around a common set of practices (Althusser, 1969:94-98). Otherwise, social interests are typically not expressed directly, but through the languages of pre-existing political and ideological traditions—which incidentally, have their own rules and rhythms of development.

The reductionism and essentialism of neo-liberal political economy and public choice theory-inspired political science is expressed best in its completely fallacious derivation of unambiguously "pro-adjustment" political positions on the part of private formal sector capital and of unambiguously "anti-adjustment" positions on the part of "rent seeking" capital. It is also expressed, in a slightly different form, in the derivation of an unambiguously democratic import from the informalisation process. Yet informalisation of institutions and economic activities is not an isolated, linear or unidirectional process from which any single political trend directly follows, and "democracy" cannot properly be understood as an expression of the essential nature of any specific social institution, process or group. Conditions for democratisation can only be specified politically, historically and empirically, not tied speculatively to poorly-defined sociological trends.

The refusal to analyse African economic and political reality in terms of a complex set of overlapping and underdetermined structures, forces, alliances, traditions and ideologies also lays at the root of viewing authoritarianism as a "policy" which governments may adopt or dispose of as they please. A more general implication of this view is that political trends in general can be reduced to matters of will. The relation of both authoritarianism and democracy to adjustment can only be properly understood if the former are seen as expressions of complex sets of social and political relations and if the latter is seen as a fundamentally ambivalent phenomenon, conditioned and mediated by existing economic forces and political alliances.

Particularly glaring in the analytical frameworks of the authors reviewed is their general downplaying of issues of ideology. Since interests are articulated in an unmediated form, ideology—if dealt with at all—tends to be understood as a pure mask for such interests, concocted by political leaders for their own ends. The obvious parallel is the Enlightenment conception of religion as a conspiracy of priests and despots. In keeping with this method, nationalism and populism are depicted as merely mobilisatory devices on the part of rent-seeking groups. Meanwhile, extra-state ideologies such as traditionalism and localism are ignored completely and the ambivalence of all such ideologies is not even considered. This has a number of consequences. Analytically these include seeing contemporary democratic political and ideological trends as independent of and even in opposition to all previously dominant ideologies. Politically they include a severe underestimation of popular cynicism about the objectives of adjustment, a cynicism which focuses in large part on its external imposition and design. Such cynicism indicates the ongoing resilience of a diffuse nationalism, even in a context where many of its formalised variants (e.g. "African socialism") have been totally discredited. The continued influence of such a diffuse nationalism is one reason why structural adjustment has so few vocal African supporters.

This leads to a final conclusion about the one-sidedness of most of the literature reviewed here. While African political reality is explored in it in considerable detail (if not particularly productively), the international context of contemporary African economic and political developments is almost wholly neglected by these perspectives. Just as a mainstream feature of World Bank economic texts on Africa in the 1980s has been an effort to absolve itself of any responsibility for African economic policy-making prior to this decade, and just as the economic content of adjustment continues to be presented as a set of technical "truths", so studies of the politics of adjustment typically exclude the changing politics and ideologies of the international financial institutions, the superpowers and other major bilateral donors. This exclusion is purely arbitrary and—in a double sense—ideological. Firstly, it implies that the international financial institutions etc. are merely neutral and disinterested observers of current events, rather than actively shaping them in line with specific faiths and—indirectly—interests. Secondly, it is one of the preconditions of the uncritical and apparently unconscious direct translation into political science terms of some of the key categories of the IMF's and World Bank's economic thought.

What then would an alternative research agenda which avoids these positions look like? Its first priority would be for concrete studies to generate adequate concepts to describe the real forms of accumulation and the real structures of social and political relations currently reproducing themselves or taking root in Sub-Saharan Africa. With regard to authoritarianism and democracy this implies a detailed investigation of the political trends, balance of forces and alliances which these phenomena represent. With regard to the relation of these trends to structural adjustment, the need is for an assessment of what the economic and social changes adjustment entails in reality (as opposed to in theory) and of how these feed into the political and ideological balance of forces. In turn, such an understanding also properly requires an outline of the content and sources of the principal political and ideological trends preceding adjustment in post-colonial Africa, and an assessment of their current state. Finally, it is necessary to supply an international dimension to this account, partly at least through a political economy of the international financial institutions, the superpowers and the main bilateral donors.

THE CONTRIBUTIONS TO THIS COLLECTION

The contributions to this collection share in common a rejection of the main elements of the orthodox research agenda, and embody some initial and provisional answers to the questions posed in the new agenda outlined above. The remainder of this introduction will indicate some of the central claims which the authors in this collection make and areas of agreement and disagreement between them.

The pre-adjustment situation in the African countries

Bangura, Beckman, Gibbon and Toye all make efforts to provide a general characterisation of pre-adjustment economic, political and ideological conditions in Sub-Saharan Africa, while Hermele and Mustapha make detailed comments on particular countries (Mozambique and Nigeria).

Bangura and Beckman highlight the centrality of a developmentalist and welfarist "social contract" between local ruling and subordinate classes in the pre-adjustment situation. The "social contract" took the form of an exchange of popular political allegiance for the supply by the state to the masses of "roads, schools, health stations, pumps, jobs, contracts, etc." (Beckman). In the process a pattern of social and economic expectations became focused on a state-led modernisation process with strong popular dimensions. But while popular, this "contract" was far from democratic. Its principal mechanisms were a mixture of corporatism and clientilism.

Bangura qualifies this argument by emphasising the "social contract's" highly ambivalent relationship to the peasantry and its authoritarian content. According to him, the form of modernisation commonly pursued by post-colonial states involved a complementary intensification of both the role of transnational capital and of state organised extraction of rent from the peasantry. Accumulation from peasant surpluses fed not only into infrastructural and welfare provision but also into an import-substituting sector in which transnational capital occupied a vital role. A resultant feature of the "contract" was that peasants paid the price of high rates of industrial and urban growth through worsening rural terms of trade. "Modernisation" was also commonly depicted by new ruling groups as a battlefield in which democracy was at best an unnecessary luxury and at worst a source of instability. Very considerable efforts were devoted to the regulation of the subordinate social groups who succeeded in making their voices heard during the independence struggle, and to the construction and propagation of ideologies of national homogeneity such as *negritude*, authenticity and *ujamaa*.

Both Beckman and Bangura share the position that in the period immediately prior to adjustment this development model had begun to disintegrate, along with the "social contract" which it supported. Beckman's explanation of this is largely "externalist", however, while Bangura mainly stresses internal sources of breakdown.

Both Gibbon and Toye place less emphasis than Bangura and Beckman on the consensual elements of the post-colonial model. Gibbon characterises this model (following Mamdani) as one of "accumulation from above", emphasises its continuity with colonial forms of accumulation, and argues that within it, economic relationships ultimately backed up by force, consistently predominated over those which were freely entered into. He also places considerable emphasis on the "privatisation" of accumulation by local ruling classes within this system and upon their own class formation in the process. For Gibbon a dictatorial form of rule was a necessary consequence of these economic relations, although this did not exclude either the introduction by government of some popular measures or the survival of civil societies of different complexities and densities.

Toye characterises the nature of post-colonial society and politics more in terms of state forms than particular kinds of economic or ideological relationships. He argues that the central feature of these forms in Africa was *dirigisme*, closely politically linked with a centrally-directed patronage system. Far from responding to popular pressure from below to implement "welfarist" measures, post-colonial politics (though nationalist in many of its preoccupations) mainly took the form of active search for allies in both urban and rural sectors by initially isolated newly emergent ruling groups. Typically, the allies with which most efforts were made were already existing relatively well-organised elites. Prominent amongst these were oligarchic rural elites—in the Kenyan situation for example, the large-scale grain farmers who flourished in the colonial period. The alliance which emerged in this process enabled farmers to bolster their position through new opportunities to earn rents and politicians to become farmers. The strength of this system necessarily rested on an absence of democracy.

Referring to the Mozambican case, Hermele concurs with Bangura that the "welfarism" embodied in post-colonial politics had a more or less exclusively urban focus and that it rested upon—at the very least—a marginalisation of the peasantry. The significance of this in the Mozambican context was that (unlike elsewhere) it represented an active repudiation of the traditional political and ideological base of the new ruling group. Furthermore, it was associated less with the adoption of "welfarism" than with the promotion of a modernisation model whose main components were industrialisation and collectivisation. This implied a high degree of dependence on external as opposed to internal allies. For Hermele it is in this context that an understanding of the "success" of the Renamo's horrific war of destabilisation has to be situated.

Mustapha, writing on Nigeria, examines some of the social correlates of pre-adjustment developments. He contrasts, in this period, the relative continuity in social relations within the cash-crop growing peasantry with significant processes of change in urban areas. Social relations amongst the cash-crop growing peasantry continued to be complex and diffuse, with a high degree of "straddling" between economic activities and with social differentiation emerging mainly in non-agricultural activities such as trade and transport. But in urban areas—especially in the decade prior to 1983—Nigeria witnessed for the first time a process of formal proletarianisation, as widening industrialisation and increased levels of real wages led to a breakdown of the long-established pattern of cyclical involvement in wage labour. As a result, the pre-adjustment era in Nigeria was one of physical and cultural class formation. On the other hand, proletarianisation was an effectively male process, since female household members continued to be employed mainly in traditional informal sector activities. The question of the degree to which these and related processes were unique to Nigeria is one worth bearing in mind in relation to other differences between the authors that will be described.

Forms of accumulation and social structures during the adjustment period

Bangura, Gibbon, Hermele and Mustapha all examine changes in both economic and social structures during the adjustment period itself. A high degree of complementarity is shared by their conclusions. These authors share the view that despite the intention of adjustment to shift accumulation in a less predatory direction, the results have rather been the opposite. Instead of a new generation of independent private capitalists emerging, the tendency has been to accelerate both pilfering of existing state resources and the diversification of the state bureaucracy into "private" activity, as formally "grey" areas of economic life have become legitimate and as the state bureaucracy itself perceives new limits to purely state-based accumulation. In this connection, Gibbon argues that the ability of a state bureaucracy to diversify its economic base in this way will in large part be determined by the shape of the non-state (though often equally state-dependent) sections of the bourgeoisie. State bourgeoisies will encounter difficulty in entering areas of economic activity already occupied by others, and in the process may be forced to transfer the entire costs of adjustment to the subordinate classes.

Mozambique, as Hermele shows, is one country where there are no obstacles of this kind, and where what he calls "wild capitalism" has come into being, with an apparently random and uncontrolled expansion of economic activity by administrative and political leaders. The only common thread of these activities (land grabbing, construction, transport, trade) is that they are all more or less speculative and short-termist.

Bangura, Hermele and Mustapha also examine some of the parallel trends and tendencies occurring amongst subordinate classes. Both Hermele and Mustapha indicate that there has been some private accumulation in agriculture under adjustment, particularly where (as in some areas of Mozambique) capital and incentive goods have become available for the first time for many years. On the other hand, in Nigeria, a reduction in the availability of many previously widely available inputs has occurred. This is owing to a withdrawal of subsidies, privatisation of supply and devaluation. Alongside accumulation, a tendency here has been for a large proportion of peasants to abandon input-dependent crops in favour of local traditional ones. Accompanying this, the profitability of certain branches of "straddling" activity has collapsed, and a secondary social differentiation of the peasantry has developed corresponding to the lines of non-agricultural specialisation in which farmers were previously involved.

Both Hermele and Mustapha also note a dynamic of informalisation amongst the working-class and middle-class, and the partial disintegration of their social and ideological identities, as they become seriously affected by a mixture of casualisation, unemployment, falling real wages, higher taxes and subsidy removal. Mustapha notes three particularly significant processes in this respect. One is the breakdown of the sexual division of labour *between* the formal and informal sectors and its reconstitution *within* the informal sector. Male proletarians typically engage in farming or use of vehicles (including motorcycles) for small-scale business, while women continue in "traditional" informal activities such as trade. Another is that workers always *retain* wage labour involvement (wherever possible), however remunerative their "sidelines" become. A third is that class divisions are reproduced in the process of informalisation, as the professional classes respond to crisis by diversifying into small-scale manufacturing, small-scale commercial agriculture or (in the case of women) running "fashion houses". The political correlates of these developments will be indicated in the next section.

Adjustment and authoritarianism; adjustment and democracy

Before turning to the precise ways in which the different contributors see the relationship between adjustment, authoritarianism and democracy it is worthwhile pausing for a moment to look at the way in which these two concepts are understood by some of the contributors.

Bangura, Toye and Gibbon (explicitly) and Hermele (implicitly) see authoritarianism as a *structural feature* of pre-adjustment social formations in Sub-Saharan Africa—though for different reasons. For Toye, authoritarianism is a necessary condition of a system combining centralised state economic control with the parcellisation of rewards through a centrally-directed patronage system. For Bangura, it is a necessary feature of monopolistic economic accumulation, in the absence of a strong working-class. Even where formally private, such accumulation depends on a privileged relation to the state and hence on the absence of public accountability in order to guarantee specific product—and labour—market conditions. For Gibbon, authoritarianism is a necessary correlate for a form of accumulation resting, in last instance, on extra-economic coercion. For Hermele, it is a product of a rejection of a peasant-based form of economic development in favour of a "gigantist" state one.

The fullest treatment of the concept of democracy is found in Bangura's essay. This distinguishes between democratic movements, stable democracy and two forms of democracy found historically on the African continent—guided democracy during the decolonisation period and current African pluralisms. Structurally, according to Bangura, democratic movements arise from contradictions within particular modes of accumulation as a result of the contestation of dominant economic interests by more than one subordinate class. Critically, they combine struggles of workers and struggles of the middle class. However, these struggles are democratic by virtue of the fact that they take an other-than-economic form. In Africa this form has usually been struggles for organisational autonomy and/or struggles against corruption.

The conditions for stable democracy are rather different. For Bangura, these involve a major change to the form of accumulation in which two basic conditions are met: for the peasantry to be incorporated into the national economy on a new basis (inter alia, so that politics will not be confined to the towns) and for workers to achieve a basic level of economic security. This in turn, Bangura argues, implies an expansion of transnational capitalist production at the expense of rent-seeking capitalism in combination with petty commodity production. The "guided democracies" which existed in some parts of Africa at the end of the colonial period lacked these conditions and were in fact never intended to embrace the rural masses. They were rather sponsored by colonial governments as means of sharpening local differences and hence diluting the unity of the anti-colonial opposition. Meanwhile, the pluralisms currently found in Botswana, Gambia and Senegal reflect the relatively powerful role of transnational capital in these countries, in combination with petty commodity production. Because of the continuing strength of the latter they tend to be regulated from above, with strong clientilist dimensions.

A useful contrast can perhaps be drawn here between certain of the positions described above and those of Beckman. Whereas for some of the contributors a link is assumed between authoritarianism and statism at the one hand and democracy and anti-statism on the other, Beckman argues with considerable force that democratic forces in Nigeria are themselves largely statist in orientation, and despite seeking autonomy from state control for themselves see maintenance of state economic control as a necessary condition for the realisation of their sectional objectives. Beckman lists these as protection of existing business enterprises and the administrative distribution of privatised ones, custodianship of common resources and protection of popular welfare. Moreover, the subordination (or expression) of democracy to (or through) statism is only one part of the picture. According to Beckman, pressures for democratisation in Africa emerge in a form in which the dominant ideological element is *nationalist* rather than self-consciously democratic. The force enjoyed by pro-democracy sentiments is in effect a "borrowed" one, lent them by the state's failure to maintain custodianship over "national" values.

Beckman's treatment of this issue is closely related to his treatment of the relation between adjustment and authoritarianism, for here—again in contrast to most other contributors—he argues that authoritarianism is essentially a property of *adjustment* itself, rather than of states which are adjusting. While the African state was already undergoing a crisis prior to adjustment, it is adjustment's insistence on the termination of its traditionally popular and national basis which obliges it to resort to dictatorship. Hence while the state has "independently" diminished in capacity to maintain its traditional co-optive and clientilist mechanisms of political management, its principal and decisive difficulty is to overturn popular expectations of what it can provide, *in the context of its submission to external forces.* A linked argument of Beckman's is that authoritarianism, as a property of such conjunctures, is inherently unstable. Given the level of resistance to the changes adjustment entails, authoritarian solutions become self-defeating and inadequate to maintain adjustment's supporters in power.

Bangura and Toye interpret the adjustment-authoritarianism relation in a somewhat different way. In their view adjustment *intensifies* authoritarianism rather than plays the major role in creating it. However, they follow different routes to this same conclusion. Toye, tracing the political stratagems of the international financial institutions (IFIs) in the early 1980s, notes how the IFIs themselves exhibited a preference for authoritarian regimes in this period. This reflected assumptions about their greater capacity to face down the substantial resistance which, it was believed, adjustment measures would create. Hence countries targetted for adjustment programmes, at least initially, were typically authoritarian ones—who tended to use the additional funding provided by adjustment to resist democratisation. Bangura's argument is that adjustment intensifies authoritarianism because, while instituting measures that create widespread opposition, it fails to generate changes which would create or strengthen meaningful pro-adjustment constituencies. For example, while improving incentives for some groups of peasants its main effect is to promote forms of economic activity which disarticulate urban and rural sectors. Most of the other potential constituencies created for adjustment, if not also marginalised, tend to be intrinsically politically weak or fragmented. Hence, in confronting opposition the state has little choice but increasing recourse to a banning of unions and professional associations, an administrative silencing of critics, and so on.

Gibbon acknowledges that this is one very probable outcome of adjustment, but only in countries where civil societies exist which can offer a basis for resistance to structural adjustment. In many countries these are simply absent or only developed to a rudimentary extent. Here adjustment need not be associated with increased authoritarianism at all. In fact it may be associated instead with a process of "democratisation from above". The latter, in Tanzania and possibly in Mozambique, represents an attempt to legitimate a new development strategy in which developmentalist and welfarist pretensions are discarded, usually in favour of private accumulation with state resources.

Gibbon's discussion of "democratisation from above" is accompanied by one of "democratisation from below". In this, he relates adjustment to contemporary trends of popular democratisation in Africa not *directly*, through adjustment strengthening "bourgeois-democratic" groups or calling forth an intrinsically democratic opposition, but indirectly. The mechanism which he specifies is basically that of Bangura and Toye's intensification of authoritarianism. Where civil societies are present, authoritarian governments react to real or perceived opposition by attempting to restrict the autonomy of particular forces in civil society. Struggles directly over autonomy and democratic rights then arise. Gibbon argues that this is more likely to take place where the dominant element in civil society itself is represented by modern, secular organisations like trade unions— even if these enjoy relatively little economic bargaining power.

Bangura presents a case study from Nigeria which shows that "democratisation from above" (which he calls "authoritarian democratisation") may also occur under conditions in which strong and internally differentiated civil societies are present. Here the need for the ruling class to renew its political legitimacy was also present, but in the context both of a military coup and because adjustment was associated with a high degree of resistance. In this situation the military government found it necessary to seek to co-opt one ("new-breed") section of Nigeria's traditional political class in order to act as buffer between itself and the masses.

Beckman's contribution stresses the important role played in the articulation of current democratic demands by the *range* of forces who oppose adjustment. This range is important in two ways. On the one hand, the inclusion of professional groups angry about the deterioration of their own living standards and working conditions means that forces are mobilised whose interests can be identified with by *all citizens*. On the other hand, in order for these and other groups to defend their specific interests, they are obliged to build alliances. This contains within itself an impetus toward emphasising the interests of the majority. Beckman and Bangura also both share Gibbon's view of the importance of the issue of organisational autonomy.

A final important contribution on this question is made by Hermele. In examining the case of Mozambique, he contends that normative aspects of the behaviour of the ruling class have been a major factor in unleashing popular discontent (which, however, has not as yet fed into a democratic movement). By this he refers to the metamorphosis of the Frelimo leadership from self-styled guardians of the revolution into (in the case of some individuals) land-grabbers and spivs. The relaxation this illustrated in Frelimo's behavioural norms had a galvanising effect on the urban masses, who previously had been prepared to withstand quite severe levels of hardship. This relaxation was, of course, one of the major public consequences of Mozambican adjustment.

Donors, superpowers and the politics of adjustment

Successive works by Toye (e.g. 1989 and this volume) were amongst the first to turn the spotlight on the politics of adjustment to the international financial institutions and their political interplay with the developing countries. Toye's main interest has been in the early 1980s, when structural adjustment became adopted as a new aid paradigm by the international financial institutions. He points out how its adoption amounted in part to a political adjustment by the IFIs to heightened real pressures from the incoming Reagan administration. A second, related aspect of the politics of structural adjustment in the IFIs was the adoption of what Toye calls a "Gestalt" for understanding the political situation pertaining in the recipient countries. It was this "Gestalt", with its emphasis on the importance of urban coalitions in the formation of pre-existing economic policies and its acknowledgement of an inevitable time gap between the implementation of adjustment and the materialisation of its benefits, which led to the initial preference for authoritarianism described above.

Beckman and Gibbon both focus also on the new World Bank political line, as embodied in its major 1989 report *Sub-Saharan Africa: From Crisis to Sustainable Growth* (World Bank, 1989a). Beckman views this report as marking a turning point in respect of the IFIs' positions on the African state. While throughout the 1980s the IFIs had insisted on the need for a retreat in the function of the African state, this had been largely argued on "efficiency" grounds. By 1989 however, "shrinking the state" was advocated as a strategy for "liberating civil society and empowering the people". Intellectually, this strategy rests on a series of deliberate confusions by the Bank, including most importantly those between the formal economy and the state on the one hand, and the informal economy and civil society on the other hand. The politics of this intervention has two related aspects. Firstly, with the collapse of state socialism in Eastern Europe, Third World nationalism has replaced socialism as the principal obstacle to the IFIs' "global market project". Secondly, because this project cannot be implemented except in a repressive way, in order to protect itself from international criticism the Bank has to depict its intentions in a democratic light. For the Bank, democracy and good governance tend to be seen in terms of better management rather than the sovereignty of popular institutions, however.

Gibbon adopts a different interpretation of the new emphasis on governance by the Bank, seeing it more narrowly as a product of frustration with the failure of structural adjustment to live up to its promises—or even to be wholeheartedly adopted—in most of Sub-Saharan Africa. He also discusses another dimension of the international political conditions for movements toward democracy in Africa. This is the change in the international relations situation which occurred during the 1980s. In international relations terms, the decade opened with the adoption of a new doctrine (globalism) within US foreign policy circles which, because of its hostility to multilateralism, proved just as much a stimulus toward the IFIs' adoption of Reaganite economic policy doctrines as the increasing respectability of these doctrines themselves. Globalism had a subversive aspect, however in that it strengthened the position of a number of governments (including—in Africa—Liberia, Somalia, Sudan, Zaire and Kenya) designated as of US strategic interest. One obvious side effect of this was to strengthen their ability to resist adjustment.

A new international relations situation was brought about in the second half of the 1980s by the adoption of a new Soviet foreign policy of international disengagement and the related collapse (under popular pressure) of state socialism in Eastern Europe. This directly gave encouragement to popular struggles against authoritarian forms of rule in Africa. It also indirectly led to the relative international isolation of some regimes previously considered strategic to western interests. In the case of the former French and British clients, the latter tendency was speeded up by the increasing importance of internal European affairs which followed the break-up in Eastern Europe. Both these developments in turn stimulated certain African governments to initiate processes of controlled democratisation, in order to pre-empt both popular opposition and the threat of discrimination in aid.

Hermele's case study of Mozambique provides a useful reminder that the dominant donors continue to operate in a highly politicised manner in relation to national as well as international developments. Hermele argues that ever since their re-engagement with Mozambique, the World Bank and the US have had a clear strategic objective of seeking to reintegrate the country into the southern African economy as basically an extension of the service sector of the Republic of South Africa. The Bank's stances on particular questions have been calculated in terms of realising this objective. In relation to Frelimo, an initial aim was to detach it from its traditional urban constituency in order to increase its dependence on outside forces. Hence a home-grown version of structural adjustment was resisted. Later, once Frelimo had abandoned any ambitions of an independent development path, the Bank supported the introduction of a social action programme to ensure that its position vis-à-vis the urban population was not made politically untenable.

Clearly, these contributions do not represent a definitive answer to all the issues thrown up in considering the politics of adjustment, but it is the editors' conviction that they address previously neglected or misunderstood issues in a novel, intellectually serious and politically critical manner.

Authoritarian Rule and Democracy in Africa: A Theoretical Discourse

Yusuf Bangura

There is an awakening of interest in democratic theory and politics in Africa. Military and one-party regimes are faced with serious problems of legitimation, stemming from the crisis of the social contract that underpinned their post-colonial models of development. A variety of social groups are seeking protection against state repression and calling for alternatives to the structural adjustment programmes launched in the 1980s. Yet, until very recently, following the democratic uprisings in Eastern Europe, very few countries had followed the Latin American and Asian examples of establishing frameworks for transitions to democratic rule. What accounts for the dominance of authoritarian rule in Africa? Under what conditions is democracy likely to emerge and remain stable? In this contribution, I shall question received theories that ruled out democratic possibilities in Africa because of the logic of modernisation or dependence, and those that currently try to establish a positive relationship between structural adjustment and democracy.

I begin by constructing a framework for theorising the problems of authoritarianism and democracy. I shall situate the argument at the level of the organisation of economic enterprises, with particular focus on forms of accumulation. I will relate these to socio-political processes that influence the development of state-civil society relations and social contracts, giving rise to either authoritarian or democratic rule. I will argue that although underdevelopment per se should not constitute a fundamental obstacle to democratisation, the establishment of stable and sustainable democracy requires substantial changes in the forms of accumulation; the promotion of an acceptable level of welfare that will allow the majority of the people to have confidence in the capacity of democratic institutions to manage economic, social, and political conflicts; and the resolution of the contradictions between authoritarian relations that are dominant at the political sphere and nascent liberal pressures that are to be found in civil society.

In the second part of the presentation, I will examine the stages in the development of authoritarianism and democratisation, emphasising the changing strengths of the national coalitions for democracy. In the third and final part, I shall focus on the problems of democratisation in crisis economies, with a Nigerian case study. I will conclude by examining the case for linking struggles waged around questions of formal democracy with those that focus on aspirations for broader and more substantive forms of popular rule.

Accumulation, authoritarianism and democracy

Wealth creation is an integral part of class formation. It embodies relations of domination and subordination. Social and political life largely depend on how material production is organised and the methods used in reproducing/defending advantages and minimising/overturning disadvantages. The relevant question is whether dominant groups use authoritarian or democratic methods in regulating their economic practices, and whether disadvantaged groups can freely pursue their interests and improve upon their life chances through open and non-repressive forms of transactions. The way production and business activities are organised have implications for the organisation of civil society and state power.

Authoritarianism and democracy represent opposing modes of regulating conflicts thrown up by the dynamics of accumulation and development. These dynamics are strongly instrumentalist. Social groups and political authorities opt for democratic strategies if the latter can protect their advantages or minimise their losses in the economy and society (Beckman, 1988a). Struggles are waged over questions of representation and accountability, and the right to free expression and organisation. Although democracy is primarily concerned with the rules and institutions that allow for open competition and participation in government, it embodies also social and economic characteristics that are crucial in determining its capacity to survive.

Three major processes appear to be central to democratic transitions from authoritarian military and one-party regimes: the demilitarisation of social and political life; the liberalisation of civil society;

and the democratisation of the rules governing political and economic competition. The first concerns the supremacy and regulation of civilian governmental authority; the second, the democratisation of the state apparatus and the relative freedom of civil organisations; and the third, the capacity to democratically manage conflicts in civil and political society and economic practices. At this stage, the need is to approach the question of democracy from its antithesis. Why has authoritarian rule persisted in Africa?

I shall focus the discussion on the structural foundations of authoritarianism and situate the analysis within what I consider to be the three principal forms of accumulation in Africa. I identify these forms of accumulation as wage-exploitative monopolistic practices, incorporating both national and transnational enterprises; rent-seeking state capitalism; and the regulation of petty commodity production. The three encourage the growth of authoritarian values. Authoritarianism is inherent in the first two, whereas it expresses itself in petty production primarily in the way such petty production is linked with the reproduction of ruling classes that are organised around the state, local communities and markets.

Transnational firms embody the problems of economic concentration which Marxist and corporatist theories of the firm have highlighted. Dahl has argued that "with very few exceptions, the internal governments of economic enterprises are flatly undemocratic both de jure and de facto" (Dahl, 1985:55). The ownership and management structures of transnationals deepen inequalities and undermine effective participation in the governance of the enterprises.

The rise of the transnational firm led to profound changes in Western social structures and the relationship between markets and states. Habermas, for instance, contends that the quest for stable accumulation and political order required the state to supplant the market as the principal steering mechanism for the social and economic system and to effect "a partial class compromise" through welfare programmes and high wage levels that are set "quasi-politically" (Habermas, 1973).

Habermas foresees a legitimation crisis arising from the state's support for accumulation while simultaneously attempting to legitimate itself to the populace. Such a crisis threatens the democratic order of Western societies. There is little doubt, however, that the structural incorporation of the working class in the management of modern economies has helped to check the anti-democratic tendencies of transnational firms in Western societies.

The problems of transnational monopolies are, however, accentuated in developing countries by the firms' supranational authority which compromises national sovereignty and allows managers to impose authoritarian regimes of industrial relations at the work place. The limited transformations of African economies by transnational capital produced a small labour force, unable to influence the state to regulate the anti-worker practices of multinational companies. Most decisions are taken by employers with little or no input from the work force. The principles of collective bargaining are poorly developed as many unions still grapple with the problems of recognition and organisation and the right to participate in the determination of working conditions. Industrial disputes are often resolved by methods of co-optation and repression than by democratic persuasion and bargaining.[1]

The second mode of accumulation highlights the way dominant groups in the economy and society appropriate rent through the state. Transnational and local firms may combine the formal modes of surplus appropriation with the siphoning off of public resources. Neo-classical political economists associate economic distortions in developing economies with the emergence of powerful urban coalitions who use their privileged access to state resources to exploit rural communities (Bates, 1981; Lofchie, 1989). Rent-seeking activities, it is argued, cause developing economies to operate at suboptimal levels (Bhagwati, 1982; Buchanan, 1980).

Törnquist has analysed the different types of rent-seeking activities employed by various socio-political groups in India and Indonesia and their implications for authoritarian and democratic forms of rule (Törnquist, 1988). Toyo and Iyayi, examining the phenomenon in Nigeria, demonstrate that rent capitalism, which they call primitive accumulation, takes the form of contract inflation, the appropriation and valorisation of land, and the use of bureaucratic positions for corrupt enrichment (Toyo, 1985; Iyayi, 1986). Patron-

---

1. I make no distinction between local and foreign capital in terms of the organisational practices of their enterprises and their policies towards labour. In fact, several studies have shown that indigenous firms tend to be more contemptuous of the rights of workers to form labour unions. See, for instance, Olukoshi (1986).

client relations, sometimes ethnically based, but often inter-ethnic, are built into the alliances for the control and administration of state power. Ibrahim has shown how the methods described by Toyo and Iyayi were used by the leading groups in the ruling National Party of Nigeria to consolidate their grip on the political system of Nigeria's Second Republic (Ibrahim, 1988). The state became a central organ in private accumulation and class formation. It is in this sense that Ake talks about the over-politicisation of African economies (Ake, 1987). The state is subjected to non-Weberian values of irrationality, inefficiency and disorder. Constitutionalism and the rule of law, central to democratic politics, fails to take root in the body politic.

The petty commodity sector presents a contradictory picture. Its authoritarian character arises mainly in the context of its incorporation into the modern economy. I use the concept of petty commodity production in a broad sense to cover activities in which producers are basically self employed, rely on family or non-waged labour, and use rudimentary tools and skills to sustain their livelihood. These activities embody several complex social relations and straddle both urban and rural areas. They include peasant production and informal sector activities. Colonial historiography traces the constraints on African development to the traditional values embedded in the social practices of the actors in these enterprises.

A more sophisticated version of the thesis combines fragments of historical materialism with modernisation theory to highlight the resilience of the "peasant mode of production", and the need for a proper capitalist revolution to overcome the problems of underdevelopment, corruption and authoritarianism (Hydén, 1983). "Tribalism", an impediment to democracy and accumulation, is understood to be a direct attribute of the "relations of affection", rooted in "pre-capitalist" values and practices. The contemporary African state is projected as a pathetically poor moderniser as it has failed to "capture" the small-scale producers buried in these "relations of affection".

Other scholars and peasant-oriented activists contend that some of the essential values of small-scale farming societies are conducive to the growth of a democratic culture and practice (Berg-Schlosser, 1985). Nyerere based his strategy of Ujamaa, for instance, on the "democratic" and growth potentials of peasant social relations (Nyerere, 1967). Informal democratic processes are, undoubtedly, present in many peasant societies, expressed specifically in the way collective decisions are taken in the governance of common resources and the resolution of conflicts. Others with a neo-liberal outlook argue that the proliferation of non-governmental organisations and independent small-scale producers, following the crisis and market reforms, will eventually provide the foundations for the establishment of democracy (Bratton, 1989a,b).

Both perspectives ignore the way petty commodity activities have been structured historically, being subjected to various layers of authority as capitalism and the state penetrate the countryside. The limitations of Hyden's central concepts and thesis have already been exposed by a host of authors (Williams, 1987; Kasfir, 1986; Mamdani, 1985; Cliffe, 1987; Beckman, 1988b; Himmelstrand, 1989). The optimism of the neo-liberals in seeing the informal sector as the vanguard for democracy and for surviving the African crisis is also being seriously challenged (Meager, 1990a; Mustapha, this volume).

Mamdani has shown, with particular reference to Uganda, the rigidities in agrarian social relations brought about by the undemocratic character of the rural power structures (Mamdani, 1986; 1987). Similar studies for other countries show the authoritarian content of the structures that pull the peasantry into the national economies and the world market. The interests of the groups that dominate transnational monopolies and state projects hold sway in the petty commodity sector. Such interests block the development of the democratic potential of independent small-scale production. The values of communal life are manipulated by the dominant groups to sustain support for their struggles over political offices and economic resources. Hyden's "tribalists", far from being the product of "pre-capitalist relations of affection", are rather the creation of modern conditions and activities (Mamdani, 1985; Eke, 1975). Patron-client relations regulate peasant production and incomes and facilitate the administration of state power. Clientelism prevents self development and social independence, critical for the construction of democracy.

The basis for democratic struggles

The authoritarian thrust of the three forms of accumulation is, however, not uncontestable. Disadvantaged social groups challenge authoritarian rule and advance alternative, sometimes democratic, forms of politics. I shall try to capture the structural basis of such struggles in the contradictions that are inherent in the three forms of accumulation. Pressures for democratisation are not exclusively confined to the politics of subordinate groups. Business groups may also play active roles in democratisation, depending on the changing nature of the forms of accumulation and the capacity of the political system to manage conflicts between the dominant groups.

Törnquist has argued that in discussions on classes and democracy, it is more important to highlight "how capitalists... try to gain and protect their economic strength" than to emphasise, as Martinussen does in his study on India and Pakistan (Martinussen, 1980), the strength of the national bourgeoisie and its political forms of organisation (Törnquist, 1985). The dependence of Indonesian capitalists, and by extension their Pakistani counterparts, on rent-seeking activities is interpreted as the basis for the failure of democracy in both societies. But in countries such as South Korea and Taiwan where wage labour has been generalised and where vital sectors of industry are manned by skilled employees, entrepreneurs may be forced to accomodate popular pressures for democracy as a trade-off for industrial stability (Lindstrom, 1989; Cheng, 1989). Most countries of Africa share the Pakistani and Indonesian characteristics. The popular classes may become the primary force for democratisation in such societies.

But how does one conceptualise the basis for democratisation while avoiding deterministic formulations? How do pressures for authoritarianism and democracy translate themselves at the level of civil society and the state? Barrington Moore has demonstrated that a single mode of accumulation, situated within specific historical contexts, can give rise to complex patterns of societal development, and that it is the latter that is the primary determinant of the political forms of organisation (Moore, 1966). Moore's work shares some affinity with Gramsci's, whose major contribution to democratic theory is his retrieval of the concept of civil society, which Marx, following its dominant usage at the time, had equated with material relations. Gramsci situates civil society outside the realm of both material relations and state power. Yet in contradistinction to liberal thought, he sees civil society as the "soft underbelly of the capitalist system" (Pelczynski, 1988). Civil society offers the popular classes an opportunity to deny the ruling class hegemony in the realm of ideas, values and culture, as a basis for the ultimate seizure of power and the transformation of capitalist property relations and the state.

I argue that the basis for authoritarian rule should be located primarily at the level of material relations, i.e. it expresses a particular resolution of the contradictions in particular forms of accumulation. But the dynamics of authoritarian rule and struggles for democratisation develop at the level of civil society. Workers organise themselves into unions and contest the power of transnational capital at the work place and in the wider society. In an authoritarian context the defence of seemingly economic interests—wages and welfare—draw workers and their unions into the arena of democratic politics. They demand accountability, independent union organisation and the right to free expression and collective bargaining, critical for the resolution of wage and welfare disputes.

Similarly, rent-seeking activities generate their own intractable problems. Firstly, the expansion of state expenditure creates a public sector labour force which shares similar concerns with workers in transnational firms for the establishment of institutionalised frameworks to promote reasonable working conditions. Secondly, state capitalism creates a large middle class of teachers, journalists, lawyers, doctors and students, who yearn for professional competence and autonomy. Thirdly, the state itself may be caught up in a "fiscal crisis" that is structural, having to defend both the demands of accumulation and the need for public revenue (O'Connor, 1973).

Rent-seeking activities may compound the fiscal crisis of the state, and may threaten the jobs, incomes and working conditions of the groups that owe their livelihood to the public sector. Such groups are likely to be critical, in the long run, of corruption, inefficiency and mismanagement. Rent-seeking methods become illegitimate as the perpetrators of corruption, usually discredited ruling groups and private entrepreneurs, come under public censure. Probes on corruption are, in fact, very common in contemporary African politics. They open up possibilities for the democratic allocation of resources.

Finally, the politics of patronage at the sphere of petty commodity production can be undermined by the very logic of transnational and state capitalist penetration of that sector. Two tendencies may be at work here. The authoritarian structures that incorporate peasant and small-scale producers into the modern economy may be in conflict with the demands for autonomy, free transactions and secure welfare that modes of self employment usually generate. African history is replete with peasant revolts against unfair prices, arbitrary land acquisitions and authoritarian rule. Similarly, the resultant social differentiation and sharp inequalities in resource use may produce an agricultural labour class and new rural alliances, possibly linked to mass urban social movements, and pressures for democratisation.

The forces of authoritarianism and democratisation enter the arena of civil society in a complex, rather than in a deterministic manner. The dominance of the ruling classes in production and state activities does not easily translate itself into hegemony in the sphere of civil society. I use the term hegemony to mean the capacity of rulers to secure compliance from the populace through non-explicitly coercive methods. Disadvantaged groups can, and do, contest attempts to establish ruling class hegemony on the civil terrain. Their capacity to press for democratisation does not lie at the productive base, but in the wider civil arena where *national strategies* can be formulated and *broad coalitions* built. Workers' agitations for industrial democracy become effective only when they are linked to broader concerns for national democracy. For instance, workers strikes in factories become a central force in democratisation only when such strikes have meaning for broad sections of society. Specific agitations against retrenchment and declines in real wages may be linked with popular dissatisfaction with deteriorating living conditions on a national scale to generate broad public support. Problems of factory victimisation may in turn be linked to wider issues of organisational autonomy and the rule of law.

Similarly, the complaints of teachers, students and doctors for better salaries, higher grants, improved working conditions and professional autonomy enter the democratic arena only when such issues are linked to national concerns for falling educational standards and health facilities, and the general problems of state repression. Such linkages bring unionist and professional agitations into the wider civil sphere, and may give rise to issue-oriented pressure groups and national alliances for democratisation. Such alliances may encompass a variety of social groups such as fractions of the dominant power blocs, and ethnic, gender, environmental and religious social movements that feel aggrieved by the existing distribution of power and resources. Issue-oriented pressure groups may, in fact, play key roles in initiating and sustaining the demands for democracy.

The capacity of state authorities and ruling classes to establish hegemony in civil society depends on their record of political legitimation and their ability to improve the quality of life of major sections of the population. Failures exacerbate the crisis of legitimation, erode social hegemony, and strengthen the forces pressing for democratisation. Once democratisation is widely perceived as a viable mode for regulating social and political conflicts, it ceases to be an exclusive project of any one class or social group. Ruling classes can incorporate, for instance, the demands of subordinate groups and influence the democratisation process. This may be a strategy to resolve differences among the dominant power blocs and to blunt the militant demands of the popular groups.

Conversely, leaders of dominated groups may employ authoritarian practices in conducting the affairs of their organisations and in resisting the policies of business managers and the power elite. Such strategies may weaken the democratic project even though they may also force policy makers and managers to opt for democratic concessions. We end up with an articulation of a multiplicity of values and strategies, traversing the authoritarian-democratic divide, but with the dominant political values determined by the balance of social and political forces.

There is nothing in the modes of accumulation of African societies that prevents social groups from struggling for democracy. What we have instead are obstacles to the realisation of stable democratic rule. But these obstacles themselves are not fixed and uncontestable since they engender antithetical forms of political behaviour in the contestants for public resources and state power.

Structural preconditions for stable and sustainable democracy

A distinction is necessary between conditions for sustainable democracy and for struggles for democracy. The latter, as we have seen, can be located at the level of the contradictions of authoritarianism, rooted in the dynamics of accumulation and civil society. Democratic struggles do not necessarily lead to stable democratic rule. The triumph of democracy, and its consolidation, not its fleeting appearances, may require some changes in the organisation of the patterns of accumulation themselves.

I will focus the discussion on structural conditions, leaving out

standard explanations based on individualism, market industrialisation, political culture and multi-ethnic pluralism that litter the literature on preconditions for democracy in developing countries. These
provide at best partial explanations to the problem. The bulk of liberal democratic theory establishes a close relationship between the
economy—referred to as levels of development—and stable democratic rule (Lipset, 1983; Dahl, 1971; Huntington, 1984; Vanhanen,
1989). But levels of development are located outside the context of
forms of appropriation and methods of production, and restricted
primarily to questions of incomes, resource distribution and welfare.
When such scholars attempt to integrate forms of accumulation and
social classes into their analysis, as Diamond does in his study of the
collapse of Nigeria's First Republic, ruling classes are reduced to
elites and politicians, and the process of surplus appropriation is
restricted to the rent-seeking state capitalist type (Diamond, 1988b).
There is an additional normative dimension to liberal theory which
renders it less useful to the analysis of third world experiences.
Theorists tend to work their way backwards by identifying the end
values of democracy in Western societies—tolerance, moderation,
loyal opposition etc. (Powell, 1982; Pye and Verba, 1965). How such
values can be developed in societies marked by intolerance, violence
and polarisation is left largely unexplained.

A different starting point, and that favoured here, is to distinguish a number of possible conjunctures or models of change
with regard to forms of accumulation in Africa. Each conjuncture or
model has different emergent political properties. By changes in
forms of accumulation I mean either the intensification of a particular mode or its weakening. Thus we can have as an example an
intensification of transnational capitalist production (TCP) and rent-
seeking state capitalism (RSC), and a weakening of petty commodity
production (PCP). Based on this example, we end up with six possible conjunctures. These are illustrated in Figure 1.

A, B and C can be regarded as conjunctures of economic expansion;
and D, E and F as conjunctures of economic crisis. Conjunctures of
expansion do not rule out possibilities of crisis. In fact crisis is embedded in all the models, given the problems usually associated with
markets, state interventions and mixed systems of accumulation. I
do not discuss specific cyclical crisis situations. A model of expansion
in this context represents positive structural transformations, and a

Figure 1. *Illustrative models of forms of accumulation*

Model	Forms of accumulation
A	The intensification of TCP; and the weakening of RSC and PCP
B	The intensification of TCP and PCP; and the weakening of RSC
C	The intensification of TCP and RSC; and the weakening of PCP
D	The intensification of RSC and PCP; and the weakening of TCP
E	The intensification of RSC; and the weakening of TCP and PCP
F	The intensification of PCP; and the weakening of TCP and RSC

Note: Two other permutations have been ruled out in this chart, viz. the simultaneous intensification or weakening of all three forms of accumulation. It is assumed that if TCP is being intensified it may lead either to the weakening of PCP and RSC, or to an intensification of PCP and a weakening of RSC, or to an intensification of RSC and a weakening of PCP. Similarly, it is assumed that if PCP is weakening, TCP and RSC may either be intensifying, or TCP alone is intensifying, or RSC is intensifying and TCP is weakening.

model of crisis is associated with negative structural changes. The two deal with development processes that lead to qualitative changes in forms of accumulation. In this context negative structural changes can be associated with economic growth. These models are illustrated on the following scale:

+3	+2	+1	0	−1	−2	−3
A	B	C		D	E	F

The focus on forms of accumulation in constructing the models obviously downplays, some would say leaves out completely, other crucial variables like resource endowment and class structure. The theoretical focus is, of course, to establish a linkage between forms of accumulation and political systems that can be classified as either democratic or authoritarian. In any case, some of the other variables, though not explicitly treated, could be deduced from the six models which, in a way, give us some idea of different patterns and levels of development. It is necessary to relate changes in forms of accumulation to questions of rural-urban integration, the nature of system-maintainance social contracts, the provision of public welfare, and the dynamics of state-civil society relations. These represent the crucial factors in establishing whether African countries can experience authoritarian or democratic rule. I make no attempt, however, to develop quantifiable variables around these issues. I highlight the qualitative links between these issues and authoritarianism/democracy in Figure 2.

The peasant question, which is at the heart of rural-urban integration, is central to any discussion of democracy in Africa since most people live in rural areas and depend on agriculture for their main source of livelihood. Rural populations are the major source of national food supplies, export revenues and industrial development (Barraclough, 1990; Mamdani, 1986; 1987). I understand by rural-urban integration the process of sustaining the economic, social and political life of rural communities, leading to a transformation of the structures of dualism that have underpinned all facets of rural-urban relations. Low levels of national integration restrict democratisation to an urban phenomenon, relegates peasants to the fringes of civil society, and undermines their ability to develop *national strategies* and enter into broad *democratic coalitions*.

The alienation of rural societies from the mainstream of national life exposes the peasantry to continued manipulation from state authorities and rural/urban patrons, anxious to maintain authoritarian forms of rule. Solving the rural-urban dilemma may, in fact, provide the basis for coming to terms with the problems of unbalanced ethnic and regional development. The resolution of this dilemma should obviously give prominence to the transformation of the regulatory mechanisms that have undermined the independence of petty producers, and provide support for the dynamics of petty accumulation. This boils down to a question of making economic development and democracy national projects, as opposed to the current practice where they are mainly an urban phenomenon dominated by the power elites. Figure 2 shows how this issue is related to the six different models of accumulation.

A stable and sustainable democracy must also be able to create a social system that will accomodate the conflicting claims of diverse groups in society. The social groups remain committed to the fundamentals of the existing order while competing, sometimes militantly, for overall dominance. Classical liberalism relies on the depoliticising

Figure 2. *Forms of accumulation and socio-political systems*

Forms of accumulation	Rural-urban integration	Welfare	Social system	State/civil society	Potential political system
A	very high	very high	social contract (corporate)	autonomous (civil society)	liberal democracy
B	moderate	moderate/ high	patron-client	regulated civil society	clientilist democracy
C	moderate	high	social contract (controlled)/ patron-client	state/part control of civil society	authoritarian
D	low	low	collapsing social contract/ resurgence of kinship ties and self-interest	intense pressures for autonomy of civil society	authoritarian
E	low/ extreme dualism	very low	collapsed social contract	intense pressures for autonomy of civil society	authoritarian
F	collapsed modern economy	collective kinship family welfare	fragmented kinship ties	fusion of state and civil society	authoritarian/ informal democracy

functions of the market as the bedrock for the construction of such a stable social order. The hegemony of the capitalist class is presented as anonymous and the losses inflicted by the market on disadvantaged groups is interpreted as a natural fate which can befall all individuals (Lawrence, 1989). In this context, liberals see democracy as the natural political shell of capitalism.

There is, however, no natural correspondence between capitalism and democracy (Therborn, 1977). To sustain democratic rule, capitalist economies—however advanced—must devise appropriate social systems. Such systems must provide welfare/economic support, however contestable, for the deprived majority to exercise their formal democratic rights, which in turn should allow them to sustain and develop their livelihood aspirations. Western democracies were consolidated in the post-1945 period with the construction of welfare states. Social democratic parties provided political leadership to restless workers and deprived groups to usher in the so-called "historic class compromise". Social democracy has strong built-in elements of corporatism as governments try to balance the conflicting demands of unions and the organised private sector. The leading actors and their organisations bargain with the state as independent entities but their co-option into the policy apparatus entails major compromises, including the regulation of the behaviour of their members (Cawson, 1989; Carter, 1989).

The corporate type of social control is contrasted with social contracts in which the ruling authorities define the rules and regulate the participation of the other contestants. Invariably the contending social actors are denied autonomous political space to canvass for the views and interests of their members. The social contract is top-down and authoritarian. Despite its authoritarian character, its legitimacy may rest on relatively high levels of welfare. The level of this type of welfare may be lower than the corporate type because of the low level of development and the political constraints imposed on the bargaining positions of social actors. Another type of social control is patron-client arrangements which can operate in both formal democracies and authoritarian systems. Where patron-client relations sustain democratic rule, the contending groups and their organisations may enjoy formal autonomy, but the political authorities may co-opt the leadership or introduce policies that compromise the political effectiveness of the groups. Public welfare supports the patronage system even though such welfare does not need to be as high as in the other systems of social control. The relative freedom of the groups frees the ruling authorities from defending a costly social contract. The state then relies on the fragmented rural communities, through patron-client networks, to counter the political weight of the urban groups. Where patron-client relations are used to buttress authoritarianism, the social groups lose their formal independence, but they may be compensated with relatively higher expenditure on welfare to sustain compliance.

Models of accumulation and political systems

Model A creates conditions for the emergence of sustainable liberal democracy. Rent-seeking activities become less central to the business practices of the private monopolies and the local entrepreneurs.

The private capitalist sector expands and transforms the petty commodity enterprises. Some of the groups in this sector are transformed into wage workers, others join the ranks of the power elite or
remain as peasants, but with sustainable agricultural systems. The
disparities between town and country are reduced. Economic expansion encourages the establishment of integrated rural enterprises. Corruption is minimised, resources are "rationally" allocat-
ed, classes mature, and patron-clientelism is checked. The authoritarianism associated with monopolies is restrained by broadening
the social base of the firms and by making extensive economic and
political concessions to the dominated groups at the work place and
civil society and in the administration of state power. This may
necessitate the establishment of a corporate social contract. The nature of the concessions and the character of the democracy may vary
according to the specific demands of the social forces.

In model B the excesses of rent-seeking activities have either been
checked or minimised. The state tends to act more rationally, in a
developmental way, but largely in defence of private capital. Industrial monopolies and capitalist agriculture are, however, not strong
enough to transform the petty commodity sector. Although the state
is still open to manipulation from privileged groups, the political
elites insist on some rational legal order in regulating conflicts of interests in the economy. The limited nature of transnational capital
and the checks imposed on rent seeking activities forces social
groups in the modern sector to maintain an active presence in the
petty commodity sector. Patron-client relations thrive. The model
allows for some kind of clientelist democracy, such as those operating in Botswana, Senegal and the Gambia. The patronage social
order acts as a constraint on the relatively free social and political
organisations to effectively challenge governmental authority. Such
constraints limit the development of civil society.

In Botswana, for instance, the ruling Botswana Democratic Party
makes use of traditional political systems such as the *kgotla* to legitimise its rule and blunt the effectiveness of opposition parties
(Molokomme, 1989; Holm, 1988). High levels of sustained growth
have allowed the regime to raise incomes, provide public welfare
and support rural schemes that benefit peasant farmers—the backbone of its patronage network. Weak working class and professional
groups make less critical demands on the political system.

The ruling Union Progressiste Senegalaise transformed itself from an authoritarian into a "social democratic party" between 1978 and 1983. It attempted to infuse some rationality into the administration of the state and economy by insisting on public accountability and cleansing the party and state apparatus of corruption. But in order to administer its highly contested democracy it has had to depend on the old patronage system that co-opts the *marabouts*, the main social and political force in the countryside, into the policy making apparatus (Coulon, 1988). But whereas Botswana has been able to sustain its clientelist democracy without much opposition, that of Senegal is undergoing serious stress. Opposition political parties and urban-based groups have challenged the dominance of the ruling party. It would seem Senegal's economic crisis is eroding the ruling party's ability to oil its patronage machine and govern without much coercion. Botswana on the other hand has one of the fastest growing economies in Africa. Its growth rests, however, on mineral revenues, whose collapse may strain the patronage system that underpins its fledgling democracy.

Model C represents an economy in rapid transition to capitalism, where rent-seeking activities play crucial roles in supporting private capital. Most African economies were launched on this path of development at independence. Authoritarian rule accompanied such expansion. I shall analyse the details of this development and that of model D in the next section dealing with stages in the struggles for democracy. Here it is significant to point out that various authoritarian ideologies—*negritude*, authenticity, African socialism—and political regimes such as military and one-party dictatorships were devised to push forward the frontiers of accumulation and maintain a firm grip on the political process.

Model D represents an economy in crisis. There is de-industrialisation, excessive pilfering of public resources and dependence on the petty commodity sector for social reproduction. The fiscal crisis and adjustment measures introduced to cope with the recession lead to further repression as disaffected groups try to resist them. The social contract comes under considerable stress. Pressures for democratisation intensify. This may even lead to the establishment of democratic governments as in many Latin American countries that are in transition from authoritarian to democratic rule. But stable and sustainable democracy cannot be guaranteed without substantial changes in the forms of accumulation and socio-economic development.

Model E represents an economy in deep crisis. De-industrialisation is buttressed by the failure of the petty commodity sector to absorb the displaced groups in the modern sector. Rural-urban relations are marked by extreme dualism. Competition for state power intensifies. Authoritarianism is rife. Individualist solutions flourish, further weakening the collective struggles for democracy. State terror intensifies with the collapse of the social contract and the failure of patron-client relations to check the instability generated by the depression.

Model F represents the collapse of the modern economy and a return to petty commodity production. Economic activity is marked by subsistence production, low levels of exchange and barter. Fragmented kinship ties tend to regulate social relations. Collective family and kinship support systems take the place of public welfare. Civil society disappears as the public and private roles of individuals and enterprises become fused. This can lead to mixtures of authoritarian and informal, village level democracy. Recent scenarios of the withering away of the African state and general theories of state decay, in a way, fit this model of accumulation (Chazan, 1983; Sandbrook, 1985). This perspective does not ignore the progressive role that has been played by the petty commodity sector in most African societies in building modern states and supporting the activities of large-scale capital. It is also the case that in the current crisis, informal sector and peasant activities provide useful fall-back positions for many individuals and households that have been displaced by modern enterprises and the state. Some forms of petty commodity production also show some promise in providing a basis for sustained economic development. Petty commodity production cannot, however, generally be viable in the absence of a properly functioning modern sector.

Most African countries are currently operating either model D or E. The IMF and World Bank programmes seek to check the expansion of the state, which they believe is responsible for rent-seeking activities and the economic crisis, and move the economies to model B and eventually to A. But there is the danger that the adjustment programmes will lead to stagnation at D or a movement to E. The scenario of decaying states (F) should also not be ruled out. Popular forces may be interested in a strategy that pushes the economies to model B or A in order to strengthen their bargaining positions in the new democratic polity. Peasants and artisans may not be opposed to model B in order for them to continue to function as petty commodity producers; whereas workers and urban professionals may prefer model A, which is likely to give them better leverage in improving their living conditions and political rights. The construction of specific types of democratic systems is, at bottom, an empirical issue which depends on the projects social movements and ruling classes have set for themselves and the obstacles they are likely to face in implementing them.

The basis for democratisation exists in all the models but democratic rule cannot be sustained in models C, D, E and F. Stable and sustainable democracy requires some level of economic development, a viable social contract, and the capacity of both dominant and subordinate groups to weaken the monopolistic forms of transnational capital, minimise the role of rent capitalism and transform patron-client relations in the petty commodity sector into relations of self reliance and social independence.

STAGES IN THE STRUGGLES FOR DEMOCRACY

In this section a more concrete examination of the interplay of authoritarian and democratic rule will be undertaken. Of the six models outlined only B, C, D and perhaps E approximate concrete African experiences. This excludes the South African case, whose forms of accumulation are similar to those of model A, but whose apartheid system has prevented the development of a national democratic system. In discussing the stages in the struggles for democracy, I focus mainly on C and D. Only a few countries have practiced model B, the clientelist type of democracy. I am at this stage mainly concerned with general historical patterns. No attempt is made to focus on any particular country. Needless to add, such broad historical surveys tend to simplify and, in some cases, gloss over unique characteristics.

The struggle for democracy in Africa has a complex and tortuous history. Democratisation triumphed at certain historical conjunctures, but it was blocked and suppressed in other phases. I identify three stages in the contemporary struggles for democracy: the decolonisation period of guided democratisation; the post-colonial period of state capitalist expansion and authoritarian rule; and the period of economic crisis which is currently generating pressures for redemocratisation. The character of the democratic project differs in each period, being structurally related to the underlying forms of accumulation, the level of development of the corresponding civil societies, and the nature of the social contracts and public welfare.

Decolonisation and guided democratisation

Decolonisation in much of Africa occurred within the context of guided democratisation. After much prevarication, the colonial authorities were forced to embrace democracy as a strategy for maintaining core residual interests. It was envisaged that plural forms of politics would sharpen local differences and dilute the militancy of the anti-colonial opposition. Furthermore, the values of individual self-interest were expected to permeate the social milieu of the leading nationalists. The emerging elites, on the other hand, saw democracy as a strategy to end their subordinate positions in the colonial economy. Educated professionals wanted greater access to state resources and an improved standard of living that would reflect their training and perceived social status. Those in the commercial sector were anxious to break the monopolistic power of the colonial banks and trading companies.

Subordinate groups also pushed through their own demands. Workers wanted to have independent unions to negotiate freely with employers realistic wages and benefits that would reflect the post-war cost of living. Peasants and artisans were concerned about improved prices for their products; and students wanted to expand the frontiers of African education and political power. Democratisation provided an institutional framework for reconciling the conflicting interests thrown up by the authoritarian colonial economy. It checked the absolutism of colonial rule by opening up space for popular participation in government and the rise of independent organisations.

But the authoritarian character of the colonial economy prevented the growth of liberal democracy. The colonial state forcibly restructured pre-existing economies and subsequently regulated peasant production through monopolistic trading companies and marketing boards. The trading monopolies and the state failed to transform the petty commodity sector and rural society in general. There was also hardly any major form of urban industrialisation. Underdevelopment and dependency theory has adequately described the enclave dynamics and rural-urban socio-economic disarticulation that informed this type of development. What is more, public welfare occupied very low priority in the governance of those societies as very conservative fiscal and monetary policies were pursued. Public welfare did not become a major issue in state policy until the structures of decolonisation were put in place in the 1940s.[2] Colonial rule was maintained through the use of force and the clientelist structures of indirect rule.

Democratisation and decolonisation took place against the background of a poorly developed civil society. Intense struggles had to be waged over the question of making the modern elites and their political parties the vanguard and pathways to self-government, rather than the traditional structures of authority which were dominated by the state (Nordman, 1979).

The original colonial agenda was subsequently defeated. The struggle for democracy and self-rule was conducted mainly through the medium of urban-based political parties, communal associations and workers unions. Although a class structure was already discernible, those who participated in the nationalist struggles did so mainly as individuals rather than as representatives of corporate organisations. This was the case whether the actors were journalists, academics, doctors, students, farmers, artisans or market women. Their respective organisations, where they existed, were too poorly developed to advance any viable corporate strategy. Individuals tended to act almost unilaterally on behalf of their social groups. The underdevelopment of civil organisations allowed the educated elites to determine the direction of decolonisation. The elites were the only groups with the capacity to pull the disparate social forces together and articulate national development strategies.

But democratisation also strengthened the alliance between the emerging elites and the colonial authorities. This facilitated the

---

2. Riots in the West Indies, Mauritius and the Gold Coast culminated in the decision by the British government to review the Colonial Development Act of 1929. The Watson Report on the riots set the stage for the Colonial Development and Welfare Act of 1945. See Parliamentary Command Papers 6174 and 6175 (UK) 1940.

growth of a nascent local bourgeoisie. It gave the anti-colonial alliance a decidedly class character and blunted the popular orientation of the democratic project. Rather than democratise the colonial economy, the nationalist elites ruled through the state monopolies and the colonial patronage networks to consolidate and expand their economic and political power. In Nigeria, for instance, the regionalisation of the marketing boards in the run up to independence led to the transfer of accumulated peasant surpluses into the hands of competing politicians and business groups. Public probes showed how these resources were plundered by the emerging dominant power elite (Osoba, 1978). Decolonisation did not fully establish democratic rule, even though the period stands out as a major landmark in democratic experiments in Africa. Representative governments were introduced in controlled stages (Collier, 1982); the right to free expression and association was coloured with proscriptions, the banning of radical literature and the arrest of activists considered to be too militant for the transition process.

State capitalist expansion and authoritarian rule

The first decade and half of independence was remarkable for the emergence of a model of accumulation that questioned the limited advances in democratisation. Elaborate strategies were formulated by the new rulers, donor agencies and the World Bank to accelerate the pace of development. The basic model was influenced by the dominant Keynesian-oriented paradigm in development economics, which stressed the need for state intervention to correct market failures and stimulate the process of industrialisation (Taylor, in Taylor and Shapiro, 1990). The state would use the proceeds of peasant surplus and rents from extractive industries to finance regimes of import-substitution industrialisation. Where such surpluses were not enough, donor agencies and private foreign capital would provide the extra finance. The state was to offer a package of incentives to foreign enterprises, subsidise the growth of local capital and transform the petty commodity sector. Social expenditure projects were to be launched to provide basic infrastructure for development, and to sustain the loyalty of the subordinate groups of the anti-colonial alliance. The fledgling business groups would ultimately appropriate a large chunk of the resources of such projects for their own development.

The model registered some interesting rates of growth in a number of African countries, particularly Kenya, Nigeria, Côte d'Ivoire, Cameroon, Gabon and Malawi, prompting many Marxists and liberal development economists to question the static assumptions and predictions of underdevelopment theory. As Mkandawire notes, "Between 1960 and 1975 ... Africa's industry (which) grew at the annual rate of 7.5 per cent ... compared favourably with the 7.8 per cent for Latin America (and the) 7.5 per cent for South East Asia" (Mkandawire, 1988a:31). The GDP growth rates for the period 1965–1973 was 6.1 per cent (World Bank, 1989b). In most countries, the state became the major source of investment and national employment. State expenditure in schools, health, public services and food supplies grew exponentially. In 1972, just a year before the first world oil price shocks, central government expenditure for 21 sub-Saharan African countries[3] for which data are available was 21.1 per cent of their gross national products (World Bank, 1989b). Although there were attempts in a number of countries to promote integrated rural development, the overall development strategy worsened the rural-urban terms of trade and led to flights of rural populations into urban centres. Economic growth intensified class differentiation and encouraged the growth of institutional forms of social organisation with mandates from members to bargain for the expanding public resources. The era of rent-seeking forms of state capitalism had arrived.

What was the social and political basis of this model of accumulation? In his seminal work of 1973, O'Donnell challenged one of the central hypotheses of liberal democratic theory that associates rapid economic development with political democracy. In the Latin American context of the 1960s and 1970s, high rates of growth and modernisation produced, instead, what O'Donnell called "bureaucratic-authoritarianism" (O'Donnell, 1973). Indeed, Brazil's military rulers relied on their country's record of high growth rates to legitimise their authoritarian rule for much of that period (Martins, 1986).

Taking into account Africa's lower levels of industrialisation and bureaucratic development, it seems to me that O'Donnell's proposition captures some aspects of the African experience of the same

---

3. Botswana, Burkina Faso, Burundi, Chad, Ethiopia, Gabon, Ghana, Kenya, Lesotho, Madagascar, Malawi, Nigeria, Rwanda, Sierra Leone, Senegal, Somalia, Sudan, Tanzania, Uganda, Zaire, Zambia.

period. Democracy was seen by the new African rulers and emerging local entrepreneurs as obstructive of both corporate and private accumulation. It encouraged demands for large-scale redistribution of resources as opposed to production, and forced rulers and entrepreneurs to be accountable to the wider populace for the way they handled public resources; it was also felt that democracy would facilitate ethnic polarisation at the expense of national unity. Military and one-party dictatorships were defended as necessary political arrangements for nation building and economic development. (Huntington, 1968; cf. Mamdani et al, 1988; Anyang' Nyong'o, 1988b).

Several ideologies, ranging from African socialism and humanism to *negritude* and authenticity, were propagated by the new rulers to control dissent and project African societies as homogeneous. The democratic impulse of the decolonisation period had taught the emergent social groups the power of collective action in the politics of resource allocation. The logical growth of civil society that the expansion of unions, professional associations and interest group organisations created was seen by the dominant groups and state authorities as a threat to economic development and private accumulation.

Various strategies were employed to regulate the activities of the social groups. One-party regimes with "socialist orientations" simply co-opted some of the popular organisations into the party structures and floated alternative organisations at various levels of society to check the development of new autonomous organisations. Such practices were common in Guinea under Sekou Touré, Ghana under Nkrumah, Tanzania, Benin and the Congo. Other less ideological one-party states imposed restrictions on the activities of unions and associations, co-opted the leadership of popular organisations into policy-making institutions, and strengthened patron-client relations with traditional authority. Sierra Leone, Kenya, Malawi, Côte d'Ivoire, Senegal (before the democratic reforms) and Cameroon fall under this category. Military regimes such as those of Zaire, Nigeria, Togo, Niger and Mali tended to follow the practices of the latter, although some, like Nigeria, were relatively less successful in controlling dissent and co-opting popular organisations. The relative openness of political life that flourished under decolonisation was severely curtailed in most countries.

Authoritarianism did not however destroy the social contract that underpinned the nationalist struggles. Indeed, the legitimacy of authoritarian rule rested on the ability and willingness of the political authorities to promote public welfare. Such an ability depended on the sustainability of economic growth. The social contract that provided such legitimacy was unabashedly top-down. Popular struggles against these repressive arrangements were initiated and sustained in a number of countries (Anyang' Nyong'o, 1988a), but the balance was unmistakeably in favour of generalised authoritarian rule.

Economic crisis and pressures for redemocratisation

The authoritarian model based its legitimacy on continued accumulation, positive rates of growth and the provision of public welfare. But African societies entered a stage of profound crisis in the late 1970s/early 1980s as a result of the recession in the world market and the structural problems of the state capitalist model of development. Whereas only 10 out of 34 Sub-Saharan African (SSA) countries experienced negative per capita GDP growth rates between 1965 and 1980, only nine registered any positive per capita GDP growth rate between 1980 and 1987 (Helleiner, 1990; World Bank, 1989b). Average GDP growth rates for all SSA countries fell from 6.1 per cent in 1965–73 to 2.1 per cent 1980–89. Agriculture, industry and services registered marked declines in rates of growth, with industry falling from 13.5 per cent in 1965–73 to 0.7 per cent 1980–89. The same poor record is demonstrated in export volume and terms of trade. The total debt of SSA countries jumped from US $21.1 billion in 1976 to US $137.8 billion in 1987. The ratio of external debt to GDP increased from 45.2 per cent in 1981 to 66.1 per cent in 1986 (IMF, 1988; Taylor, 1989). Table 1 highlights some of the negative trends in economic performance.

The crisis narrowed urban-rural terms of trade and differentials in social livelihood (Jamal and Weeks, 1988). This did not, however, strengthen rural welfare and urban-rural integration as most economies experienced sharp declines in their major macro-economic and social indicators. It was mainly a question of lowering urban living standards without necessarily raising those of the rural communities. Available data for 11 African countries in Table 2 show the effects of the crisis on public expenditure on education and health. The percentage of total expenditure on education declined in four countries, and

Table 1a. *GDP growth rates, sector growth rates and growth of export volume (1965–1989), Sub-Saharan Africa*

	1965–73	1973–80	1980–89
GDP growth rates	6.1	3.2	2.1
Sector growth rates			
Agriculture	2.4	0.3	2.0
Industry	13.5	4.7	0.7
Services	4.1	3.6	2.3
Growth of export volume	15.1	0.2	0.6
Manufactures	7.6	5.6	3.4

Source: World Bank, *World Development Report*, 1991.

Table 1b. *Terms of trade, Sub-Saharan Africa 1965–1989*

	1965–73	1973–80	1980–85	1986	1987	1989
Terms of trade	− 8.5	5.0	− 2.3	− 23.2	3.3	4.0

Source: World Bank, *World Development Report*, 1991.

expenditure on health it declined in five. Stewart reckoned that real government expenditure per head fell in 55 per cent of African countries between 1980 and 1984 (Stewart, 1987). The situation would have deteriorated further in most countries in the mid-to-late 1980s.

Radical reform programmes, influenced or initiated by the IMF and the World Bank, have been introduced to check the unprecedented economic decline. The reforms aim to restructure economic relations in the production and consumption of commodities. The restructuring primarily affects incomes, public welfare and prices, which in turn affect the configurations of power. The aim is to eliminate distortions associated with the expansion of the post-colonial state by giving the market a relatively freer hand in the allocation of resources. These distortions are to be found in the exchange rates, tariff regimes, the organisation of parastatals, interest rates and public expenditure. It is a major challenge to the state capitalist model of macro-economic management and the values and group interests that have been nurtured around it.

Table 2. *Central government expenditure in selected countries of Sub-Saharan Africa (1972 and 1989)*

	Percentage of total expenditure				Total expenditure (percentage of GNP)		Overall surplus/deficit (percentage of GNP)	
	Education		Health					
	1972	1989	1972	1989	1972	1989	1972	1989
Botswana	10.0	20.1	6.0	5.5	33.7	50.1	−23.8	27.1
Burkina Faso	20.6	14.0	8.2	5.2	11.1	11.2	0.3	0.3
Ghana	20.1	25.7	6.3	9.0	19.5	14.0	−5.8	0.4
Kenya	21.9	22.1	7.9	5.9	21.0	28.0	−3.9	−4.4
Lesotho	22.4	n/a	7.4	6.9	14.5	n/a	3.5	n/a
Liberia	15.2	n/a	n/a	n/a	16.7	n/a	1.1	n/a
Malawi	15.8	12.3	5.5	7.3	22.1	29.5	−6.2	−6.0
Nigeria	4.5	2.8	3.6	0.8	8.3	28.1	−0.7	−10.5
Tanzania	17.3	n/a	7.2	n/a	21.8	n/a	−5.0	n/a
Uganda	15.3	n/a	5.3	n/a	21.8	n/a	−8.1	n/a
Zambia	19.0	8.6	7.4	7.4	34.0	20.0	−13.8	−4.6

Source: World Bank, *World Development Report*, 1991.

Rolling back the state does not only affect popular classes and groups, it also affects ruling class forces. Large-scale public expenditure, as we have seen, was not just a strategy for protecting the poor, it was also an avenue for dominant groups to siphon off public resources. The same applies to over-valued exchange rates, discriminatory tariffs, the establishment of parastatals and low interest rates, all of which played crucial roles in the accumulation of capital, class formation and the subsidy of the consumption habits of the rich and powerful. Structural adjustment poses, therefore, problems for all classes and groups. In fact, the economic reforms seek to purify the business groups, provide a new type of legitimacy for their class rule and consolidate their positions in the wider political economy. Such a project is to be achieved at the expense of the nationalist coalition and social contract that underpinned the state capitalist model of development.

Market reformers seek to reconstitute the relationship between foreign and local capital (liberalisation strengthens the hands of the former), restructure agrarian relations to support export agriculture and hold back the urban classes of workers, sections of middle class professionals and the urban poor. It is not surprising that the strongest opponents of the reforms are a new coalition of middle class professionals, industrial unions, students organisations and the urban dispossessed. Pressures from such coalitions have led to riots in the Sudan, Nigeria, Algeria, Ghana, Zambia, Egypt, Tunisia, Sierra Leone, Liberia and Benin. Given the benefits that are likely to accrue to rural communities because of the price reforms and devaluation, some governments have tried to mobilise the rural groups to counter the political weight of the organised urban sector (Gyimah-Boadi, 1989), but the response so far has been lukewarm. Peasants remain sceptical of crucial aspects of the reforms such as fluctuations in prices, the withdrawal of subsidies from farm inputs, escalating costs of production, and general levels of inflation that affect their consumption of traded goods.

Struggles to protect living standards in the context of crisis and adjustment tend to take on a democratic character. Organised groups demand the institutionalisation of collective bargaining, the independence of unions and associations and respect for the rule of law and civil liberties. These are considered to be critical for holding employers and state authorities accountable for their economic policies. Social movements are emboldened by the collapse of the postcolonial social contract and growth rates to press for the reconstitution of the relationship between the state and civil society. Repressive policies to support the implementation of adjustment programmes have not been effective in controlling dissent. Military and one-party forms of rule have come under increasing opposition from organised groups and individuals. Co-opted unions and associations agitate for organisational autonomy from established parties and governments to defend the declining welfare of their members (e.g. Zambia; the Congo). Current developments seem to contradict the predictions of neo-liberal theory which expects the business class to play a leading role in democratisation (Diamond, 1988b). The market reforms, it is argued, will liberate the enterprising potentials of the business groups and encourage them to opt for more democratic modes of government.

Although some business groups and organisations have sided with the popular groups in demanding the reintroduction of multiparty rule in such countries as Zambia, Benin and Kenya, most of the demonstrations for democracy have been organised by opposition groups and parties with traditional sympathies for the aspirations of the poor. Even those who have joined the pro-democracy movement from the top have done so in the context of advancing the general interests of the populace and advocating development programmes that would protect the poor and vulnerable sections of society. Contrary to neo-liberal formulations, democratisation is seen by the majority of dissident groups as an instrument for obstructing structural adjustment and protecting some of the gains in public welfare and living standards threatened by the reforms. A number of military and one-party regimes have come under considerable pressure to initiate programmes for transitions to multi-party rule. Indeed, partly encouraged by the experiences in Eastern Europe, there has been an intense debate for multi-party democracy in most African countries. The link between alternative strategies of development and democracy has featured in most of these debates. Some governments such as Benin, Côte d'Ivoire, Gabon, Zaire, Mozambique, and Zambia, have had to concede the right of opposition parties to organise. Other regimes like those of Kenya and Sierra Leone have not conceded much ground to the opposition groups. Similarly, struggles in the existing democracies of Senegal, Zimbabwe and the Gambia have focused on the question of curtailing the post-colonial dominance of the ruling parties and extending the social content of democracy (Bathily, 1989; Moyo, 1989).

The next section examines the politics of transition from authoritarian military rule to democracy. Issues relating to democratisation are different from those of sustainable democracy. Sustainability, as we have seen, deals with a complex of economic, social and political factors which may profoundly influence the orientation and character of democratisation. Democratisation is, however, explicitly political. It concerns the processes of liberalisation in the key areas of political life, viz. the demilitarisation of the state apparatus; the strengthening of civil society and its institutions; and the democratisation of the rules of economic and political competition. The nature of the links between civil and political society occupies a central position in the dynamics and regulation of democratisation. I discuss these issues against the background of the Nigerian experience.

AUTHORITARIAN DEMOCRATISATION: THE NIGERIAN EXPERIENCE

Nigeria is one of the few African countries whose leaders have tried to link democratisation with structural adjustment. Democratisation in the late 1970s produced a civilian regime that lasted only four years. But the two transitions and the circumstances that produced them are different. The democratic experiment of 1979–83 coincided with extensive state interventions in the economy. Democratisation was carried out in the context of massive oil revenues and booming economic activities. The current experiment is taking place in an environment of industrial crisis (MAN, 1987; 1989), negative rates of GDP growth, a sharp drop in formal employment and real incomes, an expansion of low value-added informal sector activities, and huge cuts in public spending on social development, particularly health and education. Table 3 highlights some of these negative trends.

The structural adjustment programme launched in 1986 emphasised the principal role of the market in correcting structural distortions and getting the economy out of the crisis. A competitive foreign exchange market was expected to eliminate import licences and the corruption associated with them; privatisation and balanced budgets were to end subventions and inflated contracts; and trade liberalisation was to allow the principles of comparative advantage to determine production activities and check state support for inefficient firms. Pro-reform theorists contend, therefore, that the state's liberalisation programme is in agreement with liberal democratic theory which identifies the market and an enterprising bourgeoisie as conditions for democratic rule (Diamond, 1988a).

But is liberal democracy the political shell of structural adjustment? Will market reforms liberate the "political class" and business groups from rent seeking activities and transform the petty commodity sector into a supportive avenue for democratisation? If, on the other hand, democracy and structural adjustment are a bad mix, as radical critics argue, what accounts for the military's keen interest in democratisation? Why doesn't the military simply implement its economic programme without recourse to democratisation? Can the military usher in a successful and stable democratic order? How strong are the popular groups in influencing the direction of the democratisation process?

Table 3 a, b, c. *Performance of GDP, education and health sectors in Nigeria 1980/81–1987*

3a.   *GDP 1981, 1985, 1986, 1987*

	1981	1985	1986	1987
GDP at 1984 value (million naira)	80 354	77 092	78 905	78 799

3b.   *Education sector indicators*

	1980/81	1985/86	1987
Number of primary schools	35 625	35 433	31 354
Number of primary school teachers	393 144	292 821	280 344
Number of primary school students (thousands)	13 760	12 915	10 817
Recurrent expenditure on education (million naira)	713	697	482
Capital expenditure on education (million naira)	217	126	391

3c.   *Health sector indicators*

	1980	1985	1986	1987
Number of hospitals	694	765	765	763
Numbers of beds	44 208	48 994	48 136	50 126
Recurrent expenditure on health (million naira)	173	164	247	65*
Capital expenditure on health (million naira)	188	59	65	59*

* Provisional figure
Source: Federal Office of Statistics (Nigeria), Lagos.

Demilitarisation and civilian governmental authority

Central to democratic theory and politics is the question of the supremacy of civil governmental authority over the armed forces. The military is expected to be insulated from politics and civil society in general. But the Nigerian military has been in power for 20 of the country's 30 years of independence. Civil authority collapsed in January 1966 after about five years of self-rule. Military rule lasted until 1979 when civil rule was reconstituted within the framework of a Second Republic. It survived four years before the military again seized power in December 1983. Factional differences led to a coup in 1985 and the launching of both a structural adjustment programme and an elaborate programme of re-democratisation, to be completed in 1992. A political bureau was established to monitor a nation-wide debate on an appropriate political system. A new constitution was drafted by a Constituent Assembly, in which a fifth of the members were appointed by the government. Local government elections were held on non-party basis, followed by the formation of two government-imposed political parties and the promise of elections at state and federal levels. What prospects does the transition programme hold for the demilitarisation of the state apparatus? Can the military preside over a democratic transition that will subordinate its role to that of civil political authority?

The military has been a central institution in the development of the state capitalist model of development (Othman, 1987; Turner, 1982; Ekuahare, 1984; Fadahunsi, 1984). It has extended its grip on the national economy through its conquest of state institutions and the award of contracts and company directorships to retired and serving officers. Despite the massive cuts in budget deficits (from 10.3 per cent as a percentage of GDP in 1986 to 2.9 per cent in 1989), the military continues to enjoy a disproportionate share of the federal budget and an array of privileges. The ratio of military expenditure to combined health and education expenditure was reckoned to be 56 per cent in 1986, and military expenditure as a percentage of GNP rose from 0.2 in 1960 to 1.0 in 1986 (UNDP, 1990). The military's share of the state's capital expenditure jumped from 0.8 per cent in 1986 to 4.6 per cent in 1988. That of internal security jumped from a mere 0.1 per cent to 3.9 per cent. These figures contrast sharply with education's share which fell from 4.3 per cent to 3.9 per cent and the health sector's share which increased from 0.7 per cent to 1.9 per cent for the same period (CBN, 1988).

A similar picture emerges for recurrent expenditure where the military's share jumped from 9.5 per cent in 1986 to 12.6 per cent in 1987, whereas that of education and health dropped from 6.3 per cent and 3.2 per cent to 2.3 per cent and 0.4 per cent respectively. Defence took a relatively hard knock in the reflationary budget of 1988, following widespread protests, enjoying 6.9 per cent of the total compared to 7.5 per cent and 2.2 per cent for education and health respectively (CBN, 1988).

Many of the corporate strategies of consolidating the military's dominance in the society and polity gained momentum after the transition programme was launched. These strategies include the establishment of the defence, airforce and naval academies, the procurement of an armoured carrier assembly plant, the formation of a research and development cell within the defence ministry, the proposal to have an army bank, and the expansion of the output capacity of the defence industry corporation (Othman, 1987). Military officers are also being posted to the diplomatic service and appointed to head parastatal organisations. They also sit on the councils and boards of educational establishments and social service institutions.

It is not surprising that several Nigerian scholars and politicians see the military as a brute fact of life—an alternative political party to the civilians.[4] Ideas of a civil-military diarchy have even been advocated by prominent politicians and business groups as a framework for political stability (Ibrahim, 1986; Bangura, 1986). Popular consciousness questions, however, the expansive presence of the military in civic life. Conflicts have erupted between civilians and military personnel, resulting, in several cases, in considerable loss of life and the violation of legal procedures and civil liberties. (*Newswatch* 19.6.89:20).

Democratisation has been coloured with strong authoritarian practices. Elected local council chairmen have either been dismissed,[5] or not sworn in by military governors even when the councillors get favourable verdicts from the courts.[6] Other acts of authoritarianism include the arbitrary dissolution of all the local government councils before their full tenure and the appointment of sole administrators to run the councils, the creation of a military consultative council to co-exist with the evolving representative civil institutions, and the anomalous situation whereby the federal military

---

4. The former president of the Second Republic, Shehu Shagari, was among the first group of politicians to argue that the only two political parties in Nigeria are the military and the civilians. Some left intellectuals see sections of the military as capable of providing a vanguard for revolutionary change. For a review see Beckman, 1986.

5. The chairman of the Enugu local government council was removed from office in September 1988 for his "actions, utterances and activities".

6. The Nigerian Bar Association ordered its members to boycott all courts in the country for a few days to protest the refusal of the Gongola state governor to respect the ruling that had upheld the petition of two candidates for posts in two local government areas in the state.

Yusuf Bangura

government will have to supervise elected state and local governments between 1990 and 1992.

Why is the military interested in democratisation if it cannot tol-
erate liberal democratic practices and the rule of law? And what are
the implications of the authoritarian conduct of the military for the
democratisation project? Finer has developed a model that seeks to
explain why the military institutionalises or abdicates power. He
constructs a matrix of several variables which are related to two
summary variables viz., "dispositions" and "societal conditions",
which in turn are related to "motivations" and "necessary conditions". The variables on dispositions include belief in civilian supremacy, threat to the cohesiveness of the military, lack of self confidence, internal consensus to withdraw from power, and adequate
protection of corporate interests. The last two are seen as necessary
conditions, while the others are strictly motivational. The societal
conditions include internal challenges, external factors, and the
availability of a civilian organisation to hand over power to. The first
two are motivational and the last is a necessary condition (Finer,
1985).

Despite the insights it offers, the model does not fit the Nigerian
case. Even though the military is highly visible in most public institutions, the leadership has not abandoned its "stratocratic" character[7] to rule through a civilian cabinet, a party and a legislature. Nor
is the programmed retreat to the barracks a result of the military's
belief in civilian supremacy, the threat to the internal coherence of
the military,[8] or its lack of self confidence. The military's contempt of
"bloody civilians" is deep-rooted. Its belief in its capacity to rule has
not been seriously dented, as it was in 1974/75. Explanations for the
military's interest in democratisation should be sought elsewhere.

It seems to me that the political traditions that govern civil-military relations, the irrepressible nature of civil society (Ibrahim,

---

7. Some of the features of institutionalisation can, however, be recognized.
   Babangida is the first military leader to declare himself President; the first to dismiss his second in command; and the first to dissolve the entire Armed Forces
   Ruling Council; he also makes use of civil patronage to co-opt and neutralize
   opponents. The press calls him the "Maradona" of Nigerian politics.
8. The decision to democratize came before the abortive military putsch of April
   1990. The putsch certainly reinforced calls for the speedy implementation of the
   transition programme.

1989), the circumstances that gave birth to the current regime and the political imperatives of the adjustment programme are crucial factors in explaining the regime's commitment to some form of democratisation. Despite the military's profound distrust of civilian rule, a tradition has developed that sees the military as an aberration. Gowon's (1966–75) attempt to postpone indefinitely the return to civil rule precipitated his overthrow in 1975. Buhari's regime (1984– 85) also became unpopular when the leadership refused to discuss the question of civil rule as part of the stabilisation programme. Babangida's regime (1985–) was forced by the circumstances of its birth and its determination to win popular support to make the issue of civil rule central to its economic programme. The most important factor, I believe, is the political imperative of the structural adjustment programme. It made strategic sense to take the initiative in the political arena in order to prevent the civil groups from emerging as a hegemonic force at the political level. This allowed the regime to co-opt sections of the "political class" to its controversial programme, and confront the more unyielding groups at the terrain of the economy and civil society.

Democratisation appears, therefore, to be a strategy to regulate the anticipated popular opposition to the economic reform programme. In this regard, the military wields considerable authority in determining the evolution of the transition plan. The contending political forces that are to form the bedrock of civil governmental authority remain extremely weak. Of the 13 political parties that applied for registration to contest for the slots of the decreed two parties, none attempted to challenge the authority of the military in any significant way. The four dominant parties—the People's Solidarity Party, the Nigerian National Congress, the People's Front of Nigeria and the Liberal Convention—were either reincarnations of old political formations or new outfits for launching new millionaires into politics. The four parties were outspoken, in varying degrees, in their support of the military's economic programme even though it was widely believed they did this for clearly opportunistic reasons. The Nigeria Labour Party which was expected to be the mouthpiece of workers and other deprived social groups remained ambivalent on the question of structural adjustment—the leadership being careful not to antagonise the government and ruin its chances of becoming one of the registered parties (Olukoshi, forthcoming). A major contradiction, therefore,

exists between the liberal pressures in civil society and the authoritarian practices at the level of political society. Democratic institutions and values are not likely to grow in such an environment.

Civil society and the state

The military, acting through the state, has found it much more difficult to impose its hegemony in civil society. There is generalised
dissatisfaction with the economic reforms. Pressures for democratisation and the protection of civil liberties are much more potent in
the realm of civil society. It will be wrong to counterpose the state
and civil society in absolute terms. Indeed, it is virtually impossible
to separate the two spheres, given their inter-penetration. The state
plays a key role in managing all modern economies and in regulating social organisations and the lives of ordinary citizens. But the
complex inter-connections between the two spheres does not reproduce the state in all facets of civil society. There are several social
organisations, covering occupational, household, community, voluntary, gender, media, religious, and ethnic activities that do not fall
under the direct control of the state in many societies. Although the
class hierarchies in civil society are conditioned by the inequalities
in property relations we should also refrain from collapsing civil
society with the economy. The state-civil society relationship presents contrasting pictures across socio-economic systems. The state,
civil society and the economy should be treated as problematic concepts but may still be used in order to be able to ask interesting
questions about how social groups perceive of the relationships and
what their programmes are in restructuring the three spheres.

Neo-liberals talk of civil society in terms of privatisation and a
market-based economy. But there is no reason why such a limited
view of the concept should hold for all theorists and social actors.
We have seen above that for Gramsci, civil society is distinct from
the economy and constitutes "the soft under-belly" of bourgeois rule
and an arena for people's power. The concept as Keane has recently
demonstrated, never in fact had a single unproblematic meaning in
classical political thought (Keane, 1988a, b).

There is a wide spectrum of positions in contemporary discources
on the relationship between the state and civil society. In Taiwan,
democratisation led to a slackening of the state's grip on the econ-

omy and the strengthening of private civil institutions (Cheng, 1989). Most of the authors of the four volume study on Latin America's transition from authoritarian rule believe that the social hegemony of capitalism and the retreat of the socialist revolutionary alternative is what will ultimately consolidate the continent's democratic experiments (O'Donnell et al, 1986). Yet a pre-1989 reform programme of the Solidarity movement in Poland emphasised the need for the transfer of the control and management of factories from the state to democratically elected workers councils, and the introduction of a system of self management for educational, cultural and media organisations (Pelczynski, 1988).

The Nigerian situation is rather complex. Both the left and the right hold statist positions, even though they also advocate the autonomy of sections of civil society. Nigerian entrepreneurs have combined their statist outlooks with passionate calls for the privatisation of public enterprises. Major sections of this group still insist on state protection and adjudication on how the enterprises should be distributed. The left, of course, sees the state as the custodian of common resources with a mandate to protect popular welfare. The convergence of left and right positions on the state should not be surprising. The state is the largest employer of labour, controls substantial resources and an array of social services. Schools, universities, hospitals and vital sections of public transportation will collapse without state support. Industries, commercial enterprises and modern agriculture will not function without the state's funding of the foreign exchange market.

Most urban social groups, such as trade unions, students' organisations and academic unions, advocate the reform of the state apparatus. But they remain extremely critical of the power of the market in effecting the required changes. In fact their alternative programmes to the current structural adjustment programme insist on an extension of the state sector, under popular control, and the introduction of a planning system (ASUU, 1984; NLC, 1985; NANS, 1984). Such a statist outlook does not prevent them from agitating for the autonomy of their organisations and the defence of the rule of law and civil liberties. Academics, for instance, operate largely within state structures, but agitate for union independence, academic freedom and university autonomy. Workers accept the union structures imposed on them by the state in 1978, but advocate union autonomy, free collective bargaining and accountability. The same can be said of the judiciary, large sections of the press and religious/ ethnic organisations which are heavily dependent on the state for funds and infrastructural support, yet struggle for autonomous civil space to conduct their respective activities. This contradiction between the acceptance of state intervention and the campaign by the disparate social forces for liberal civil relations is underpinned by a complex system of checks and balances which, Ibrahim has argued, "has prevented the rise of tyrannic or even oligarchic regimes at the national level" (Ibrahim, 1990).

How has the military related to the problematic of the state and civil society in the context of its reform programme? The neo-liberal prediction that the market reforms will promote liberalisation at the social and political levels has not been borne out by the evidence. Conditionality has certainly increased the tempo of the pressures calling for democratisation, but state authorities see such pressures as obstructive of the reforms. The state has intervened in civil society in many instances to control dissent and block the popular will for alternatives (Bangura and Beckman, 1991). Many unions and professional associations have been banned; the state security and transition to civil rule decrees (Nos. 2 and 25) have been used extensively to silence critics; academics and journalists have been dismissed from their jobs on political grounds; students, labour activists, journalists and academics have been consistently arrested and detained; organisations have been formed to undermine industrial strikes and intimidate student activists; and the formation of a special anti-strike squad is being contemplated to control national demonstrations against the adjustment measures (Mustapha, 1988; Ibrahim, 1990).

The state has not been able, however, to impose its hegemony in civil society. State repression is being resisted by several interest groups and voluntary organisations. Internal differences within the military, which at times mirror the geopolitical divisions in the country, help to strengthen the resistance of the civil forces. New organisations have emerged specifically focusing on human rights abuses and civil liberties.[9] Traditionally conservative organisations, such as

---

9. The most prominent of the new human rights organizations is the Civil Liberties Organization. Its courageous intervention in the struggles for democratic rights earned it a cover story in one of the leading national weeklies, *Newswatch* 25 Sep. 1989. Other organizations include the Committee for the Defence of Human Rights and the National Association of Democratic Lawyers.

the Nigerian Bar Association, are being pulled into the arena of democratic politics (Jega, 1989). There is a radical impulse for democratisation struggling for expression and dominance in an atmosphere of controlled political competition.

The democratisation of the rules of political competition

A central theme in democratisation is the extent to which political actors can develop democratic rules to regulate conflicts emanating from the spheres of production and political society. Existing democracies in Africa and elsewhere are still bedevilled with the problems of managing competition between legitimate political parties (Senegal, the Gambia, Zimbabwe, Jamaica, India, Sri Lanka, Mexico). A culture of "winner takes all" encourages political leaders to be distrustful of each other. The strongest dictates the rules.

Nigeria's current transition programme has not broken with this tradition. Political competition has been restricted to just two parties, appointed by the military. This is in marked contrast to the five parties registered in the Second Republic and the open party system of the First. Even the rules governing the transition programme remain fluid. Instead of choosing the two parties (itself a restriction of liberalisaton) from the National Electoral Commission's list of 13 applicants, the state decided to establish two parties whose constitutions, programmes and ideologies were developed by the government and the national electoral commission (Babangida, 1989). Several individuals have been banned from participating in the established parties, and current participants are wary about the frequent changes in the rules of political contestation. A "cat and mouse" game is being played between banned politicians who remain powerful brokers in their constituencies (and, therefore, command the loyalties of government-approved politicians) and the military, which is determined to block the ambitions of the "old politicians" and let the "new breed" run the show.

The policy of excluding old politicians from politics stems from the general belief that it was the traditional political class that is responsible for wrecking the economy. Most of the prominent politicians of the Second Republic and some business persons were detained during the brief rule of Buhari and Idiagbon, following the overthrow of the Shagari government. Although they subsequently gained their freedom under Babangida, the feeling persisted that old politicians would fundamentally review the adjustment programme and continue with the reckless spending programmes of the past, if they were allowed to get back into power. The manner in which the conflict between the military and the old politicians is being conducted makes it difficult for open democratic rules of bargaining to emerge and get consolidated. The military uses its executive authority to impose new rules; and the politicians use their informal networks and concealed political power to undermine the objectives of the rules.

The problems of establishing democratic frameworks to regulate social conflicts are brought out in bold relief in the area of industrial relations. To be sure, there are several institutions that have been created to regulate industrial disputes. These include the Industrial Arbitration Panel, ad hoc worker-management committees and consultative meetings, and the courts (Yesufu, 1982). But such institutions have either been manipulated by the state and employers or have failed to take into account the current problems of the recession for workers' welfare. Collective bargaining has been suspended; employers arbitrarily dismiss workers, slash take home pay, and impose levies on dwindling wages (Bangura, 1989). The state has also intervened in industrial relations to weaken workers' organisations and in some cases to arrest unionists.

Some unions have opted for militant methods of protest because of the intransigence of employers and the limitations of the existing institutions for managing disputes. The state has tried to exploit the internal divisions among unionists as a basis to either tilt the internal balance of power in favour of its preferred candidates or to suspend the organisation and blunt what it perceives to be a radical union orientation towards the reforms. The rules governing the election of officials to the executive of the Nigeria Labour Congress were set aside in February 1988, in an attempt by the government to impose its will on the leadership of the organisation. The transition programme has failed to provide a democratic framework for handling industrial, political and systemic disputes.

CONCLUSION

What are the general conclusions to be drawn from the Nigerian experience? The first is the close relation between economic liberalisation and political authoritarianism. Economic liberalisation imposes tremendous hardships on disadvantaged groups and undermines the social contract of the post-colonial development model.[10] Experiences elsewhere, such as in Latin America and Eastern Europe, show that democratic regimes come under considerable pressure as they try to manage complex transition programmes in the context of economic crisis and restructuring. Attempts to impose a sense of "realism" on the population, i.e. getting people to accept the macro-economic policies of stabilisation, is often accompanied by calls for welfare support, which would entail some relaxation of budgetary discipline. The need to make concessions to vulnerable groups has been recognised by most governments. The international financial institutions have also been trying to link adjustment policies with poverty alleviation programmes in many African countries.

It is apparent that economic reforms of the type formulated in most African countries in the 1980s will be difficult to implement in a liberal democratic framework. And yet the reforms themselves require a new political legitimacy for their success. Democratisation is supposed to provide the basis for a new social contract predicated on new social and political alliances. But the forces in support of the reforms (or those likely to benefit from them) remain fragmented and politically weak. Given the state's continued control of huge oil revenues, most of the dominant social groups still perceive of politics as a struggle for the control and appropriation of public resources. Difficulties in forging a sustainable social alliance[11] have contributed to the intensification of authoritarian practices. The adverse conditions created by both economic liberalisation and authoritarian rule

---

10. The civil war of 1966–70 seriously weakened the social contract of the early post-colonial model of development. The social contract was relaunched in Gowon's "Dawn of National Reconstruction" speech of January 1970 (*New Nigerian*, 1970).
11. Programmes such as MAMSER (mass mobilization for self reliance) and DFRRI (directorate for food, roads and rural infrastructure) have not achieved their objectives of creating a new social order despite the huge resources they command and their co-optation of many professionals.

provide an "enabling environment" for civil groups to press for democratisation. Democratisation in this context is an antidote to structural adjustment. This distinguishes the democracy movement in Africa from that of Eastern Europe and explains the ambivalence of Western powers and international financial institutions towards the struggles for democracy in Africa.[12] While in support of democracy, they remain opposed to any attempts to change the direction of the economic reforms.

The second conclusion is that a contradiction exists between the dynamic pressures for democratisation at the civil arena and the conformist thrust of the political actors at the state level. Democratisation requires the liberalisation of both civil and political society. Most of the active groups in civil society have not been able to make much impact at the wider political arena. The military and the principal political parties continue to dominate this sphere. The decision by the civil political class to accept the military-decreed parties is an indication of its reluctance to open up the political system to democratic challenges and establish effective links between the pressures in civil society and the democratisation of state practices. On the other hand, the strength of the civil groups is compromised by the virtual lack of participation of the peasant communities in the pro-democracy movement. Both the military and the politicians rely on the disarticulations in rural-urban relations, and the patronage networks that arise therefrom, to maintain the status quo at the political level.

Underlying the authoritarian character of democratisation is the crisis of state power and capitalist hegemony in civil society. The debate on capitalism in Africa has been concerned more with the dominance of capitalist property relations than with the social context in which they operate.[13] Radical political economists tend to assume that the hegemony of the business class and the power elite will naturally follow from the development of capitalism. But the recession and the market reforms seem to have generated an intense

---

12. French troops were sent to oil-rich Gabon in 1990 to defend Omar Bongo's regime against the mass demonstrations for democratisation.
13. The debates on capitalism in Kenya in the *Review of African Political Economy* (Nos. 8, 17, 19) and on classes and imperialism in Africa, in Dar es Salaam (Tandon ed., 1982), did not address the social dimensions of capitalism.

ideological and cultural opposition to capitalist rule. The rate of popular rebellions and withdrawals from formal state and transnational projects is a function of weak ruling class hegemony (Rudebeck, 1989; 1990a). This weakness has undermined the capacity of the ruling authorities (both civil and military) and business groups to opt for democratic forms of government. Beckman's advocacy of "bourgeois democracy" in Africa, with strong pressures from popular forces, is difficult to sustain in this context (Beckman, 1990). As Gutto puts it, African ruling classes "fear free and fair elections" (Gutto, 1988). Elections, conducted fairly, will impose some accountability on state practices and check the excesses of rent-seeking activities. The dilemmas of the ruling groups have meant that in most countries in the continent, popular social movements have come to play a major role in the struggles for democracy. This has not excluded sections of the dominant power groups from joining these forces in the pro-democracy movement.

The central role of the poor and disadvantaged in the democracy project underlines the need to link formal democracy with more substantive forms of popular rule. I shall highlight two arguments for this linkage. The first, primarily theoretical, is derived from my original formulation of the problem, in which authoritarianism is linked with particular forms of accumulation and social structures. Stable democratisation logically assumes significant changes in the structure and forms of accumulation, rather than an exclusive focus on rules and institution building. Such changes, as we have argued, involve the integration of rural-urban relations, and democratic participation of popular groups in the governance of economic enterprises. This calls for the empowerment of the socially deprived, the provision of popular welfare and the reduction of inequalities.

The second argument is political or normative. Social movements have themselves linked the struggles for democracy with questions of alternative development strategies (Mamdani et al., 1988). Indeed, it is primarily the debate on how to overcome the economic and political problems of the crisis and economic reforms that has brought to the fore questions of political rights and accountable government. For instance, the original decision of the Nigeria Labour Congress to launch a Labour Party was to provide a platform to strengthen workers' struggles against repression and the economic hardship of structural adjustment (Olukoshi, 1990). A Labour Party in government was expected to implement the union's alternative programme to the economic reforms (NLC, 1985).

This linkage between democracy and alternative development questions an aspect of the current African debate that emphasises the struggle for "democracy in its own right" (Nyong'o, 1988(b, c); Mkandawire, 1988(b); Gutto, 1988; Shivji, 1990; Ibrahim, 1990). Pressures for democratisation do not present themselves in such idealist and abstract terms. While it is an ideal to be cherished, democracy must make sense to the interests of the contending social groups. These interests do not have to be narrowly defined as economic; they can also be social and political. Linking democracy to the restructuring of the economy allows individuals and organisations to pose the question of democratic governance of public resources much more sharply. It is a more realistic way of surmounting the colossal tasks of launching underdeveloped crisis economies along the paths of stable and sustainable democratisation.

Empowerment or Repression? The World Bank and the Politics of African Adjustment

Björn Beckman

This is a discussion of the political theory and practice of the market-oriented economic reforms, commonly known as "structural adjustment programmes" (SAPs), which are currently implemented by a wide range of African states, mostly with World Bank and IMF sponsorship.[1]

The focus is on an authoritative report from the World Bank, *Sub-Saharan Africa: From Crisis to Sustainable Growth* (World Bank, 1989a). It contains the first major effort by tl ... theory of adjustment. The new focus ... restructuring the African state in ord ... long-term strategy for the liberation (... preneurial potentials of African society. The report explains the failure of the state and the need to cut it down to size, thereby releasing the creative forces that have suffered under its oppressive deadweight. Civil society and especially the grassroots are to be empowered. The report is an intervention in ongoing ideological struggles between nationalism and neo-liberalism. It seeks to delegitimise nationalist and popular resistance to SAP and to construct an alternative basis for political legitimacy. It seeks to discredit the opposition, partly by pretending that it does not exist, partly by projecting it as

---

1. This paper contributes to a research programme on "Structural Adjustment and Democracy" pursued by the AKUT Group (AKUT, 1990). For an outline of my part in that programme, see my project proposal, "Structural Adjustment and Democracy: Interest Group Resistance to Structural Adjustment and the Development of the Democracy Movement in Africa" (Beckman, 1990). The study develops, empirically and theoretically, propositions that were first raised in a joint paper with Yusuf Bangura on working class resistance to structural adjustment for the April 1989 conference of the United Nations Research Institute for Social Development on "Economic Crisis and Third World Countries: Impact and Responses", Kingston, Jamaica (Bangura and Beckman, 1991).

narrow and selfish. The World Bank message needs to be situated in the context of the repressive political practices of SAP. I argue that SAP accelerates erosion of the political capacity of the state. SAP faces critical problems of political legitimacy that threaten to block the reforms. The organised interest groups that oppose SAP, while representing "narrow interests" also articulate wider popular aspirations. The reforming capacity of the state depends on its ability to accomodate them. The legitimacy crisis of SAP is reinforced by its dependence on foreign support. In conclusion, this essay disputes the democratic claims made on behalf of SAP and argues that it is resistance to SAP rather than SAP itself that offers a source for democratisation. This may have wider implications for an understanding of where democracy and good governance come from.

"Underlying the litany of Africa's development problems", says the report, is a crisis of "governance". The failure of public institutions is "a root cause" of Africa's weak economic performance. The quality of government has deteriorated with "bureaucratic obstruction, pervasive rent seeking, weak judicial systems, and arbitrary decision-making". Red tape and corruption impose heavy costs on the private sector, undercutting its international competitiveness. The breakdown of the judicial system scares off foreign investors who fear that contracts cannot be enforced. Such an environment cannot readily support a "dynamic economy". "A deep political malaise stymies action in most countries" (1989a:xii, 3, 22, 30, 60–62, 192). SAP, says the Bank, cannot work without a well-functioning state. The economic reforms are frustrated by lack of effective implementation. "The fundamental weakness in these programs is the lack of local capacity, both private and public, in their design and execution" (1989a:62). The political environment must inspire the confidence of the private investors, local and foreign.

What went wrong? The World Bank suggests that Africa inherited at independence "simple but functioning administrations". But these were not geared to the development role assigned to them by African leaders. The state was enormously expanded, while its staff was inexperienced, politicised and inefficient. It was unable to cope with the "political stresses of rapid modernisation and the unstable external environment of the 1970s and 1980s" (1989a:30, 38). Much must be blamed, says the Bank, on the ideologies of the first generation of African political leaders who believed that the government had to play the dominant role and who distrusted foreign business and the market mechanisms. The new states were poorly rooted in African society. Moreover, these leaders believed that development meant achieving Northern standards of living. They had a vision "couched in the idiom of modernisation—meaning the transfer of Northern values, institutions, and technology to the South". As a result they opted for "poorly adapted foreign models". Governments drew up "comprehensive five-year plans" and invested in "large, state-run core industries". Thinking was dominated by "the dichotomy between capitalist and socialist development models". Non-Africans played an "overly dominant role" in elaborating these inappropriate strategies (1989a:16, 37–38).

What needs to be done? The state must be made to retreat, the deadweight removed. It should no longer be an entrepreneur but promote private producers, including foreign investors. Africa must abide by "the world wide trend towards privatisation" (1989a:4–5, 55). Africa needs "not just less but better government". Private sector initiative and market mechanisms must go hand-in-hand with good governance. It requires "a public service that is efficient, a judicial system that is reliable, and an administration that is accountable to its public". "Capacity building" needs to be pursued at every level of government, including reforming the civil service, installing effective economic management in the public sector, and strengthening local government (1989a:xii, 5, 15, 54–59).

Good governance requires a concerted attack on corruption and the elimination of unnecessary controls, reducing the scope for "rent seeking". Intermediary, non-governmental organisations can exert pressure on public officials for better performance and greater accountability. Public debate should be encouraged (1989a:6, 15, 61, 55, 192). The failure of the judicial system to "protect property and enforce contracts" has discouraged investment, foreign and local. The lack of a reliable legal framework has exacerbated uncertainty and unpredictability. "The rule of law needs to be established", including the independence of the judiciary and the "respect for the law and human rights at every level of government" (1989a:9, 30, 192).

The retreat of the state, however, is more than a question of accountability and efficiency. It is a strategy, according to the Bank, for liberating civil society and "empowering the people". The retreat should go hand in hand with the fostering of grassroot organisations capable of promoting entrepreneurship. The objective should be to "release private energies and encourage initiatives at every level" (1989a:xii, 1, 4, 55, 59).

CONSTRUCTING POLITICAL LEGITIMACY FOR SAP

The World Bank claims that its proposed strategy represents a growing consensus: "Fortunately disagreements in practice are few". It suggests that whatever differences existed in the past (they are not specified) have greatly narrowed during the 1980s. "Whatever the political vantage point, there is a broad understanding". The remaining problems are essentially "technical" which "professionals will continue to debate" without in any way diminishing the "broad consensus on objectives" (1989a:185).

Who is included in this consensus? The focus of the argument shifts between the "development community" and the affected societies. There is a particular concern to mobilise a united front of donors behind SAP, ensuring that countries which show good behaviour are rewarded and those who don't are punished. To achieve this united front, particular effort is devoted to prevent the desertion from the hard-line by such donors that have a past record of being soft on the state/market divide. The surprising propagation of the "Nordic development model" (1989a:186–87) may therefore be taken as an ideological bate, not so much for impoverished, non-industrial African nations, as for such soft-hearted donors, being thus reassured that they trail behind the Bank on a respectable track.

Who on the African side is covered by this consensus? The controversies surrounding SAP are neither acknowledged nor addressed. The report avoids entering into any direct argument with opposing views such as those expressed in the Lagos Plan of Action (OAU, 1980) and the Abuja and Khartoum Declarations (ECA, 1987,1988). With little justification, the report even claims that it tries to "reflect the evolution" of the views embodied in these documents. It appropriates for its own purposes some of the ideological planks of the opposition, such as "respect for African values" and "self-reliance" (1989a:2).

The consensus that the World Bank seeks to conjure is fictitious. It dodges the core conflict between its own neo-liberalism and the nationalist and structuralist concerns of the critics, especially at the African end. The assertion of a growing consensus serves to isolate and belittle the opposition to SAP. Far from being insignificant, opposition to SAP is widespread and keeps on causing obstruction. It is responsible for much of the "hesitation and procrastination" over which the report complains (1989a:189). Indirectly, this is also recognised when the report speaks of the failure to "internalise" SAP, the failure to overcome "political malaise", and the difficulties of achieving a consensus locally because of "vested interests" and hostile "intellectual and ideological positions" (1989a:62, 192–3).

The World Bank report is an ideological intervention. The Bank is the principal protagonist, challenging on a neo-liberal platform the state-led, nationalist development ideology which, in the view of the Bank, has distorted development thinking in Africa since Independence. It intervenes in conflicts between social groups with different stakes in the reforms and the changing structure of incentives and class relations that they generate. It seeks to shift the balance of forces in favour of political coalitions, nationally and internationally, that are capable of sustaining SAP.

By extending the time-perspective, looking beyond SAP, the Bank sidelines the controversies surrounding the current practice and impact of SAP. It paints an attractive future scenario of "growth with equity", including a vision of increases in public welfare expenditure, in stark contrast to the social inequities and cuts currently protested by the opposition. The picture of a consensus, where disagreements are minor and technical, and where the real challenges lies "beyond", is a confidence trick. It conceals the ideological role of the report in enforcing SAP in the face of intellectual and popular resistance. The political crisis of the African state is also the crisis of SAP. This explains why the World Bank sees itself obliged to enter the deep waters of political theory. The poor capacity of the African state to handle resistance to SAP casts serious doubts on the political feasibility of the reforms. The Bank seeks to boost this capacity, not by addressing the objections of the opposition, but by seeking to undercut its political and ideological legitimacy.

Nationalism is the potentially most dangerous ideological and social force confronting SAP. It draws on the history of resistance to foreign political domination, cultural humiliation, and economic exploitation. Anti-colonialism and anti-imperialism have demonstrated their capacity in the past to generate cross-class alliances, uniting members of an aspiring bourgeoisie, patriotic professionals, technocrats, intellectuals and workers committed to radical strategies for national emancipation. Such alliances have been capable of arousing broad popular support. From a nationalist perspective, SAP is a foreign imposition. The "conditionalities" linked to the foreign finance that goes with SAP are the hallmark of rising neo-colonial domination. The liberalisation of foreign trade and foreign exchange regimes deprives the state of the means of directing scarce resources to areas of priority for national development. It is seen as a capitulation to a world market that works in favour of the strong and at the expense of the weak. There is little trust in nationalist quarters in the notion of "comparative advantage". The withdrawal of state support for a fledgling industrial sector, state or private, means abandoning the effort to lay a foundation for an alternative to the colonial and neo-colonial division of labour.

The World Bank tries to turn the table on the nationalists by questioning their national credentials, suggesting that they are merely the mouthpiece of foreign and inappropriate ideas of modernisation and socialism, uncritically borrowed from outside and often implanted by foreigners. They portray the post-colonial state project as poorly rooted in African society, its indigenous culture and traditional leadership (1989a:37–38, 60–61).

In its attempt to discredit economic nationalism, the Bank brandishes a stereotype of post-colonial development that exaggerates the foreign and "socialist" features. It claims that governments drew up "comprehensive five-year plans" and invested in "large, state-run core industries" (1989a:16). This is misleading. Most industrial investments were in simple import-substitution, often in crude assembling, very little in "core industries". Few plans were "comprehensive" and few had any major role as steering instruments. The Bank tries to discredit the large state sector by depicting it as the child of socialist ideology, hostile to private capital and foreign capital in particular. This again is misleading. The state sector has also been large in the majority of African countries that have had a predominantly capitalist orientation. Foreign capital, having other reasons for avoiding risks in small African countries, has often favoured joint ventures and other forms of collaboration with the state. State companies have played a strategic role as patrons for an aspiring indigenous bourgeoisie. In West Africa, for instance, marketing boards have been a valuable source of finance and monopolistic protection for a local merchant class.

In projecting a stereotyped image of the ideological illegitimacy of the post-colonial state, while also confessing to a collective guilt on the side of the "development community" for having been uncritically supportive of the developments leading to failure, the Bank obscures the long-standing involvement of that "community" in struggles over ideology and strategy in Africa and the third world in general. The Bank, for instance, has been deeply engaged in projecting the success story of Ivorian capitalism, with its strong state involvement in promoting world market oriented expansion. It has sponsored a wide range of state development finance companies, acting as "trustees" for an emerging capitalist class.

With the world wide and local shift in the balance of forces in favour of capitalism, nationalism and not socialism is the principal enemy to the global market project of the World Bank. The "failure of socialism", however, is useful as a means of delegitimising nationalism.

While nationalism is the principal ideological force confronting SAP, wage earners make up the most coherent and potentially disruptive social group in the opposition bloc. They are acutely affected by the "restructuring of incentives" enforced by SAP, including cuts in public sector employment, the fall in domestic industrial production, removal of price and rent controls and subsidies, and the rise in the cost of imports. While the fall in real wages predated SAP, the reforms have offered more of the same, along with accelerated retrenchment. Wage earners are those most affected by public service cuts and increases in fees as they are those who depend most on access to public transport, education, health, electricity and water supply, in the reproduction of their everyday existence.

The deflation of the wage-earning economy reinforced by SAP has also hit hard at sectors of the economy directly or indirectly dependent on wage-earners' income, including a large petty commodity and petty service producing sector. The urban informal sector is particularly badly hit because of its greater dependence on imports, both for consumption and trade. But also rural producers, both agricultural and non-agricultural, have faced a drop in the demand for their goods and services, except in some pockets where export production has faced favourable world market conjunctures. Again, it may be argued that much of this deflation of purchasing power and markets predated SAP and that further deflation was inevitable because societies were "living beyond their means". While this may be true, the hardships experienced by those affected are bound to have serious political repercussions, threatening the implementation of SAP. The need for reform does not settle the issue of its direction and design. Nor is it obvious who was actually living beyond whose means.

The World Bank report offers future relief from current hardship. But the report also attempts to undercut the significance and legitimacy of the resistance to SAP. It conveys a picture where, on the one hand every one (almost) stands to gain from SAP, while on the other hand those who don't, apart from being few, are portrayed as having illegitimate claims. In the world view of the World Bank, "the individual" is pitted against "the system" (1989a:22). The individual is bound to gain from the reforming of an oppressive, inefficient, and corrupt system.

Resistance is portrayed as emanating from narrow, self-seeking elements, "the vested interests that profit from the present distorted incentives and controls" (1989a:192). "The vast majority" of the population working in agriculture and the informal sector will enjoy "a significant increase in income and consumption". The squeeze would mainly affect the consumption of "the top 5 percent belonging to the formal modern sector" and the recipients of "rents", that is, those with illicit earnings from public office (1989a:46). The report lumps together corrupt officials and the mass of wage earners as the illicit beneficiaries of the old, distorted order. It is not clear what is "top" about the employees in the formal sector, especially after decades of decline in real earnings and with a majority unable to provide basic sustenance for their families from their wages. The reference is clearly not to the *top earners* within the formal sector. On the contrary, the Bank argues that incomes at the top must be raised in order to secure adequate incentives, while at the bottom wages should be allowed to find their true market level.

Mass redundancies and a continued decline in real wages are the principal grievances allowing the opposition to SAP to rally on a platform of social justice and equity. Even here the Bank tries to turn the table on the opposition, drawing on standard neo-liberal arguments. The most equitable policies, according to the Bank, are those that foster enterprise development because this will spur job creation which is in the interest of all. Minimum wage legislation and "other restrictive labor regulations" that prop up wage levels therefore stand in the way of equitable development because they discourage the expansion of employment (1989a:191).

Central to the World Bank argument is the linking of two perceived divisions, that between state and civil society, on the one hand, and that between wage and non-wage economies on the other. The wage economy is treated largely as an adjunct to a parasitic state sector, while true civil society seems to flourish primarily in the non-wage economy. Pitting the one against the other is problematic because of the actual integration of the wage and non-wage economies, at the level of the individual producer, the household, the extended family, and the community.

From the point of view of securing political legitimacy of SAP, it becomes particularly problematic that the best organised and most articulate elements of actual civil society tend to be found in the wage sector, in the trade unions and professional associations and in urban based community organisations with a strong wage-earner component. Moreover, wage earners and professionals, such as teachers, midwifes, and students, although a tiny minority, also play an important role in community politics in rural areas.

In the face of nationalist and popular resistance, the theoreticians of SAP—alongside their attempt to delegitimise resistance—seek to establish an alternative basis of popular legitimacy. The notion of "grassroots empowerment" seems central to this exercise. On the one hand, empowerment is seen as the liberation from an excessively interventionist state: The creative force of the grassroots will be set free. On the other hand, it stands for participation and mobilisation; the active involvement of local communities in development projects. The two aspects shade off into each other. It is not clear when "empowering ordinary people to take charge of their own lives" merely stands for the freedom of local entrepreneurs and when it involves participation in some institutionalised collective decision-making.

Concepts like participation and mobilisation are ambiguous. They have a political-democratic side and a managerial one. The latter dominates the World Bank report. The emphasis is on "releasing" and "tapping" local energies and capacities. The concern is less with popular power, in a political sense, than with ensuring that development programmes are better attuned to local demands. Agricultural extension officers, for instance, should be responsive to the farmers' needs; they should listen, not command (1989a:4–5).

The primary concern is with development, not with democracy. Empowerment is encouraged because it is good for development. It is revealing that when the report counters allegations that local (traditional) leaders are exploitative, it ends up claiming that they are efficient to work with (1989a:31)! Empowerment is for the prospective beneficiaries of development in order to ensure that projects are well rooted in local society (1989a:191). This has been a long-standing managerial concern within the donor community. Such empowerment does not address the scope for resisting state policies by those who see themselves as losers rather than beneficiaries.

Without addressing the link to state power, empowerment is primarily a means of securing local support and cooperation. In the face of popular resistance, however, empowerment also becomes a means of claiming popular legitimacy. But empowerment is for those who implement SAP, not for those who oppose it. It is a managerial populism that fits well with the populist political practices of the regimes implementing SAP. World Bank-style empowerment is poor compensation for the lack of popular political support for SAP. It may even help in justifying repression—in the name of the empowered grassroots—against the "vested interests" that resist SAP.

"Empowerment" may be a poor substitute for democracy. But the World Bank also claims to be in favour of open debate, human rights, the rule of law, and accountability. Does this not suggest that it takes democracy seriously? Does this herald the coming of a new stage of SAP—"Adjustment With a Democratic Face"? Just as it did in the case of the "Human Face" debate, the Bank is now responding to criticisms of SAP for being associated with repressive political practices, the suppression of opposition and public argument (see e.g. Bangura, 1986; Bangura and Beckman, 1991; Campbell, 1989; Hutchful, 1987; Ibrahim, 1989, 1990; Mkandawire, 1991a; Mustapha, 1988). The need to maintain the consensus of international support for adjustment increasingly requires the Bank to emphasise issues like democracy and human rights. The more responsibility the Bank appropriates for overall state policies, the more exposed it becomes to criticisms of the repressive political framework within which these policies are pursued.

Even so, the World Bank's venture into political liberalism is steeped in a managerial and developmentalist mould. It criticises policy makers for being "reluctant to allow open discussion of economic policy issues". It argues that a "broad and vigorous debate" is vital if options are to be understood and consensus achieved (1989a:193). The context is that of enlightened management rather than democratic politics. It suggests consultation, not contestation.

Allowing policy to be publicly debated does not change an authoritarian regime into a democratic one. In its account of Nigeria's "lessons of adjustment", the World Bank report claims that "after intensive public debate" the government adopted a programme to liberalise the economy (1989a:48). What it does not mention is that the debate was predominantly hostile to the programme that was adopted. A proposed loan from the IMF was rejected because it was, correctly, believed to be tied to such a programme. But "public opinion" was crudely cheated. The government, while abstaining from the IMF loan, went ahead with the substance of the programme, now with World Bank funding (Olukoshi, 1989)! The Bank's commitment to the virtue of "vigorous public debate" is not convincing. The tactics displayed in the report shows little evidence of such a commitment, with its fictitious consensus-mongering, dodging of divisive issues, reduction of major political divisions to technical ones, and ignoring or delegitimising opposition to its policies.

Are other aspects of the Bank's political liberalism more credible? "Scrupulous respect" for human rights is mentioned as something to be desired but without consequence for the argument. The report is more substantial when it comes to the rule of law. The perspective that dominates, however, is that of the private investor, especially the foreign one. Without the rule of law, business confidence in general and the sanctity of contract in particular cannot be upheld.

Is not the plea for accountability a plea for democracy? The suggestion that "leaders must become more accountable to their peoples" (1989a:15) is sufficiently modest to be acceptable by any president-for-life. On one occasion the report links accountability with representative government: public auditors should be responsible to a representative legislature (1989a:192). This is the closest the report comes to a democratic argument, one however modest enough

to accomodate one-party assemblies and representation by appointment. Generally, accountability is treated more as a managerial problem, not a democratic one.

Good governance, says the Bank, requires enlightened leadership
that makes a "systematic effort to build a pluralistic institutional
structure", that is determined to respect the rule of law and to protect the freedom of the press and human rights (1989a:61). But where
does good governance and democracy come from, and why is it that
the politics of SAP is so repressive?

RESISTANCE AND REPRESSION

The World Bank's effort to construct political legitimacy for SAP
needs to be seen in relation to the weakness of the political arrangements meant to secure its implementation and the political practices
by which it is accompanied. Those practices, say the critics, are authoritarian and repressive not liberal.

In Ghana, a show-case of adjustment, early openings in democratic directions were stifled in the interest of authoritarian control as
SAP gathered momentum (Hansen, 1987; Kraus, 1989; Akwetey,
1990). In Senegal, the authoritarian features of one-party dominance
were reasserted in the face of the political tensions precipitated by
economic reform (Bathilly, 1987; Diouf and Diop, 1989). Zambia
illustrates the vacillations and repressive reflexes of a regime under
cross-pressure from domestic opposition to SAP and international
financial and aid agencies (Akwetey, 1990). In Nigeria, adjustment is
accompanied by widespread opposition. Regime strategies show a
mix of repression and concessions, including efforts to co-opt oppositional forces into the ruling block. Public debate on SAP has been
discouraged. Only those groups who have declared their support for
SAP have been allowed to participate in the process of transition to
civilian rule (Bangura, 1986, 1989b; Ibrahim, 1990; Mustapha, 1988).

These are scattered pieces of evidence that need further empirical
investigation (Beckman, 1990). A prima-facie case, however, can be
made that SAP breeds repression. It seems as if adjusting states lack
the political capacity to implement SAP in the face of heavy opposition without recourse to repression. The deepening economic crisis
has undermined steering ability. The "restructuring of incentives"

brought about by SAP makes it difficult to sustain the political coalitions underpinning the state, SAP drives wedges into pre-existing alliances, it undercuts the structures of interest mediation previously managed by the state and it obstructs ideological legitimation. External conditionalities contribute to the accelerated erosion of political capacity. Repression compensates for the capacity gap.

By political capacity I mean the ability to construct and maintain a working political coalition capable of sustaining the implementation of state policy. It includes capacity to exercise control over the state apparatuses (not just presiding over them); to maintain an upperhand at the level of ideological contestation ("legitimacy"); to secure the necessary minimum of cooperation (non-obstruction) from autonomous centres of power in society; and, in particular, to contain opposition within bounds compatible with state policy.

The erosion of political capacity did not begin with SAP. It has a long history, specific to each country (Sandbrook, 1985; Dutkiewicz and Williams, 1987; Beckman, 1988a). It is closely related to the ability of the state to deliver goods, services, and other values to constituencies of relevance to its power base. It is affected by shifting world market conjunctures for primary exports. Inability to reduce state expenditure in the face of declining earnings compounds the crisis of the export base, loading it with overheads which it is unable to support. Even in cases where export earnings are maintained, public economies run into crises of reproduction, with a declining ability to meet demands placed on the state. Foreign and domestic borrowing sustain state spending temporarily, but inflationary deficit financing creates new demands and tensions.

The pattern of cumulative fiscal crisis is well known. For our purposes, it suffices to point to the outcome: a general decline in the ability of the state to sustain a pattern of public spending that historically had provided the backbone of its identity and political capacity. The decline accelerated during the late 1970s and 1980s. It opened up a space for foreign intervention on an unprecedented scale, with indebtedness and aid as stick and carrot. The World Bank speaks of a "free fall", a process out of control (Jaycox, 1990). The choice of metaphor seeks to justify the drastic intervention. It delegitimises the domestic policy process and rules out alternatives. Either you grab the life line thrown to you or you stand condemned for having allowed the nation to continue the free fall into the abyss.

The economic crisis that precedes SAP is accompanied by sharp political tensions. Inflation eats into real wages, shortages multiply, employment opportunities dry up, public services decay. The political demands that dominate public agitation before the introduction of SAP focus on the restoration of real incomes, the expansion of employment, the resuscitation of public services and better access at reasonable prices to imported consumer goods. Consumers agitate for price controls and producers, including farmers, manufacturers and transport owners press for special allocations and state subsidies for imported inputs. Very little of this is offered by SAP. On the contrary, the logic of SAP is to deflate the wage and public service economy which is to be reduced to levels considered compatible with existing resources. It seeks to remove the inflationary impact of public sector deficits. But even more importantly, it seeks to bring about a "systemic change", a shift in incentives away from a presumably inefficient and low productive wage and public sector to the benefit of a more efficient and productive private sector.

Trade liberalisation and devaluation brings back imported goods on the shelves but at even less affordable prices. This too is deliberate. The aim is to improve the competitiveness of the local economy in the world market. Devaluation makes imports more expensive and exports more competitive. The deflation of the wage and public service sectors helps by cutting social overheads and allowing wages to find their "true market levels". If it works, SAP is supposed to bring expanded exports and employment, especially in agriculture and the private sector, and in the long run both an improved fiscal basis for the state and higher income for everybody. In the meantime, however, it has little to offer to the constituencies that have historically developed in relation to the post-colonial state.

It is pointless to just speak of "vested interests", suggesting that those constituencies are primarily made up of former beneficiaries. It is not merely a question of who got what out of the state in the past, but of a whole pattern of expectations focused on the state. This pattern is shaped by those who feel discriminated against and hope to benefit as much as by those who actually do. Expectations of the state as a source of income, employment, and welfare is not specific to wage-earners and urban dwellers. Rural communities may feel that they have got less out of the state in the past but this does not turn them into a constituency for "rolling back the state". They want more of the state, not less. More roads, schools, health stations, pumps, jobs, contracts, cheap seeds, fertilisers etc. "Modernisation" to them is not a fanciful "western" idea, inappropriately "borrowed" by misguided nationalists. It represents deeply entrenched popular expectations.

Such expectations are concretised in specific demands and community agendas. However misplaced some of the priorities may seem, there is no doubt about the popular commitment that goes into the modernisation of a "home area", as defined within the shifting parameters of communal competition. Communities value "representatives" as far as they voice such demands and "deliver" when in office. This is the stuff that politics is made of. Ruling groups reproduce themselves in power through complex coalitions and alliances in response to such community agendas, more or less manipulative and divisive, more or less committed to popular welfare. In their turn, contenders mobilise alternative coalitions and seek to disrupt existing ones.

SAP affects the capacity of ruling groups to sustain existing patronage relations and respond to and manipulate sectional claims. This may be partly compensated for by special programmes "to sweeten the bitter pill". Such "alleviation" measures, however, do not remove the conflict between neo-liberal strategy and popular conceptions of what the state is for. The logic of SAP is to further weaken the motivation of the state to respond to the popular demands that have been built into the process of post-colonial state formation. SAP accelerates the erosion of the political coalitions and alliances which have been constructed in the course of that process. This is not primarily a question of urban based/biased coalitions losing out in favour a rural/agrarian ones. While SAP in some cases shifts income differentials between certain urban and rural producers in favour of the latter, *all* popular expectations of the state, urban and rural, are frustrated by SAP. Although the purchasing power of some urban groups may fall more rapidly than that of some rural ones, both are upset by the declining ability of the state to deliver what is expected from it.

The problem is compounded by the break up of the structures of domination erected by the post-colonial state in relation to organised interest groups in society. Trade unions and professional associations cause particular problems to SAP in this respect (Beckman,

1990; Bangura and Beckman, 1991). They have the "vested interests" in the public sector economy, both as producers and consumers. But they also have an organised base from which to challenge SAP. African governments have in the past shown varying degrees of success in their efforts to subdue and control such organised interest, by restrictive legislation and by co-opting, buying-off or imposing leaders. Such statist-corporatist arrangements come under severe strain under SAP. The capacity of co-opted leaders to mediate the relation between the state and their member constituencies deteriorates. They face a dilemma of either distancing themselves from SAP or losing whatever may remain of credibility in the eyes of the members. They are increasingly unable to constrain the rising forces of unrest from below.

Professional groups, like lawyers, doctors, and university lecturers, have traditionally steered cautiously close to state power. They, too, face a combination of external and internal pressures pushing them into resisting SAP. The crises in their domains of operation, for instance the disintegration of hospitals and schools, combine with the impoverishment and declassing of their members (cf. Nigeria's "lumpen lawyers") in precipitating confrontation with the state (Jega, 1989).

Interest group opposition is regarded as particularly illegitimate by the advocates of SAP. It is seen as coming from a small, privileged minority, pursuing narrow self-interests at the expense of the mass of the people, the poor, the underprivileged, the unorganised, the "silent majority". Interest groups are accused of taking undue advantage of being better placed, more organised, more articulate. Governments therefore feel justified in applying repressive policies against such organisations. In doing so, they draw support from neo-liberal theories as well as from populist arguments about "labour aristocracies" (Waterman, 1983) and "urban bias" (Bates, 1981; Bienefeld, 1986; Bangura and Beckman, 1991).

Interest groups may indeed be "self-seeking", but in defending their interests they also actually tend to see themselves as guardians of the public institutions and the national developmental and welfarist aspirations of the post-colonial state. In that sense, they become a mouthpiece not just for their own corporate interests but for broad popular concerns about the state and the future of social services and public development projects. This is what happened, for instance, when Nigerian doctors went on strike in protest against the terrible conditions in the nation's hospitals which had been starved of essential inputs. They received wide public sympathy, even if they also had their own "conditions of service" in mind (Jega, 1989). Moreover, interest groups are obliged to enter into wider alliances in order to fend off attempts by the state to isolate, control and repress them. Governments and their backers underestimate the capacity of interest groups to offer both leadership and backbone to wider popular movements against the state. It is because of this capacity, not merely because they defend the interests of an entrenched and privileged minority, that interest groups are in a position to obstruct SAP.

The crisis of political capacity is also a crisis of ideological hegemony, of legitimacy. SAP hits at those social forces who have developed the most advanced national consciousness and identity and whose fate is most closely linked to the nationalist project. The national and welfare values that are central to the ideological legitimation of the post-colonial state are now most credibly defended by the anti-SAP forces. The crisis of legitimacy is exacerbated by externally determined conditionalities and foreign funding (Mkandawire, 1991a). Foreign intervention is open, explicit, and humiliating. The general mood of the "development community" is brazenly interventionist. There is "disappointment" and "loss of confidence" in African political leadership, contributing to a decline in respect for national autonomy. Donors and bankers feel free to justify intervention with reference to their own notions of desirable development, rather than the development objectives of national governments (Beckman, 1988c). They see themselves as trustees for the "common man", the "silent majority". Foreign paternalism reinforces the authoritarian logic of SAP. Regimes are urged to show courage and commitment in face of local obstruction. An illustration: In 1986, while deliberating over a loan to Nigeria, the World Bank Board was cautioned by the Nordic Executive Director that quick disbursement would reduce the Bank's "leverage" vis-à-vis the Nigerian government. However, Senior Vice President Ernest Stern urged the Board not to hesitate because experience had shown that many governments were "put out of action" if "radical and political sensitive reforms" were not swiftly supported (Nordic Office 1986).[3]

---

3. Cf. also on this point Toye (this volume) p. 106. (The editors).

The changing mood of the development community mirrors the erosion of state legitimacy that has taken place within African countries. But its encouragement is also a deliberate strategy to intensify this process of delegitimisation in order to weaken resistance to SAP. The post-colonial state is declared redundant or irrelevant (Hydén, 1988; Beckman, 1988b). Moreover, there is in addition the unintended delegitimisation that comes with foreign intervention. The state institutions on which the international reformers depend for access and implementation are undermined. The political crisis of the post-colonial state is simultaneously the political crisis of SAP.

DEMOCRACY AND SOCIAL CONTRACT

African leaders are advised by the World Bank to be tolerant and strive towards consensus and free debate. They should be accountable to their peoples and respect the rule of law and human rights. The liberal political message contrasts with the illiberal political practices of SAP. The imposition of SAP enhances political repression. The interventions of the development community reinforce rather than alleviate that tendency.

How can the liberal message of the Bank be situated in relation to these illiberal practices? First, the political liberalism of the message should not be exaggerated. A managerial perspective dominates. Empowerment has more to do with releasing the presumed dormant and repressed entrepreneurial talents and energies of "civil society" than with democratisation. Similarly, accountability and the rule of law are related more to the development of an enabling environment for private investment than to the establishment of a democratic political order. Yet while the managerial perspective dominates, the Bank simultaneously attempts to construct political legitimacy for SAP on a pluralist platform. In this, the Bank responds to the erosion of the political capacity of the state which obstructs the implementation of SAP but which SAP reinforces by further alienating the welfarist and nationalist aspirations that are attached to the post-colonial state. Its support for pluralism is thus in the context of an ongoing conflict within African society over strategy and state power. This is partly a struggle of ideology, with neo-liberalism and nationalism as the main contenders. It is also a conflict of concrete social forces on the basis of their positions in the political economy and how they are affected by crisis and adjustment.

The empowerment of the new order is juxtaposed to the "vested interests" of the old. The Bank seeks to undermine the legitimacy of the opposition by belittling, discrediting, and ignoring it. The "vested interests" are pitted against the "common man", urban privilege against rural poverty. The dichotomies distort and obscure the nature of the social and political conflicts precipitated by SAP. In the new order of legitimacy, chambers of commerce and industry figure prominently while trade unions are conspicuously absent. Empowerment is for those who support, not for those who oppose SAP.

Central to the legitimation exercise is the construction of a fictitious consensus encompassing the international "development community" and all except a small illegitimate minority within Africa itself. There is no recognition of contending forces. The liberalism of the Bank has no place for politics and contestation. It comes close only when it speaks of the importance of "countervailing power", the absence of which explains, according to the Bank, why "state officials in many countries have served their own interests without fear of being called to account" (1989a:60–1). The "countervailing powers" envisaged by the Bank, however, are all part of its managerial world of consensus and policy-making. It recognises "intermediary organisations" because they create links "upward and downward" and bring "a broader spectrum of ideas and values to bear on policy-making". Professional associations of bankers, doctors, lawyers, accountants are useful because they are means of releasing "private energies and encourage initiative at every level" (1989a:59, 61). It advises the state to engage in "systematic consultation with organised interest groups such as chambers of commerce and industry" in order to enhance accountability and responsiveness (1989a:5). The non-recognition of divisions and contestation serves to conceal the partisanship of the Bank. The effort to assert ideological hegemony is part of the repressive political logic of SAP.

The pluralism of empowerment stops short of democracy and is compatible with the current repressive political practices of SAP. The democratic claims on behalf of SAP, however, just as the claim to promote welfare, lie primarily in the future, beyond the current phase. A four volume study on democracy in the Third World sponsored by the US National Endowment for Democracy argues that "statism must be rolled back" if democracy is to have a chance: "The increasing movement away from statist economic policies and structures is among the most significant boosts to the democratic prospect in Africa" (Diamond, 1988a:27). The vision is of a civil society that, once liberated from an oppressive state, gives life gradually to the actors and institutions that ultimately will make the state accountable to the people. An enabling environment for entrepreneurs and markets forces is therefore simultaneously enabling for the future agents of democracy (Hydén, 1988; Beckman, 1988b).

It is an attractive vision, especially if one is convinced of the virtue of the liberal economic reforms. In this case, democracy comes in the bargain as a bonus. It is also attractive for those who are all in favour of democracy, in principle, but who may feel that Africa is not yet quite ripe for it, and that some reasonably efficient authoritarian management is the best bet for the meantime (Sandbrook, 1985; Himmelstrand, 1989; Beckman, 1988a, 1989). The vision is more disturbing when such promotion of an "enabling environment" goes hand in hand, as suggested above, with the suppression of those organisations of "civil society" that can make claim to give voice to public grievances and that seek to defend some measure of autonomy vis-à-vis the state, such as trade unions and professional associations. Are today's democrats to be suppressed in the interest of those of tomorrow?

Where do democrats come from? What will make states more democratic, accountable, and respectful of law and human rights? In concluding this essay, I will argue that it is resistance to SAP, not SAP itself, that breeds democratic forces. SAP can be credited with having contributed to this development, not because of its liberalism but because of its authoritarianism (Beckman, 1990). The democratic forces grow from the confrontation between the state and organised social groups in society. The impetus comes from groups that feel threatened by the state and seek to resist repression. Organised groups, such as trade unions and professional associations play a particularly important role. The policies of SAP reinforce authoritarian and repressive tendencies in the state's mode of dealing with organised interests in society. In resisting SAP, interest groups seek to secure greater autonomy from the state. The confrontation enhances their stake in a pluralist political order. While in pursuit of the material interests of their members, interest groups enter into alliances in defence of autonomy and rights of organisation. Demands for democratic reforms at the level of the state, including the reform of legal institutions and procedures, become tied to the defence of such organisational rights. They serve as a bridge between the material grievances of members and the question of the democratic constitution of the state. Interest group contestation of the legal and political regulation of their mode of operation is central to the process of democratisation.

The emergence of democratic forces in opposition to SAP can be placed in a wider context of economic crisis and political reform. Recent developments, not only in Africa but even more prominently in Latin America and Eastern Europe, suggest that authoritarian regimes of both capitalist and socialist orientation are undermined politically by their incapacity to protect citizens against material decline. The political crisis is exacerbated by popular resistance to economic reforms, e.g. the removal of subsidies, retrenchments, cuts in public services etc., reforms that all tend to bring additional suffering.

Faced with resistance, regimes vacillate between economic concessions and political repression. The scope for either is constrained and the net effect may be long periods of political stalemate, as for instance in Poland, Ghana, Argentina and Zambia. The stalemate blocks economic reform and accelerates economic and political disintegration. As a result, regimes may be obliged to consider a trade-off between economic and political reform. Limited political concessions are offered in exchange for the acceptance of unpopular economic measures. The political capacity of the regimes, however, has been further eroded as a result of the stalemate. Their bargaining position is weak. Factional divisions within the ruling power group, prompted by disagreements over the direction of the reforms, heighten the pressure for more far-reaching political concessions. The divisions undermine the repressive capacity of regimes and strengthen the autonomy of non-regime political forces. Repressive solutions become more costly and impracticable.

The dynamics of democratisation in this scenario lies in the declining political capacity of authoritarian regimes in the face of growing resistance to its policies. The current move towards multiparty rule in Africa may illustrate this cycle of decline, repression, and concessions in the context of economic crisis and reform. Rather than being encouraged by the "successes" of SAP this process has been hastened by its failure to deliver material improvements to constituencies significant to the reproduction of existing authoritarian regimes.

This may, for instance, explain why the repressive arrangements which have so far have sustained SAP in Ghana have come under increasing pressure. The populist institutions under which SAP was imposed are cracking, as evidenced by the current democracy debate which is breaking out from the tight reins imposed by the regime (West Africa, 1990). The rise of the Zambian democracy movement, spearheaded by trade unions and defiant of SAP, may point in a similar direction (Akwetey, 1990). In Mozambique, the political openings in pluralist direction of early 1990 were preceded by a strike wave, precipitated by workers' grievances against SAP (Hermele, this volume). It may also fit such a pattern.

The argument may be extended to the process of state formation. Where does "good governance", rule of law and accountability come from? The World Bank advises leaders to set good examples. They should distance themselves of corrupt habits. From its managerial perspective, rule of law and accountability are primarily about enforceable contracts, predictability, and cutting the costs of corruption. The "empowerment" of the business communities and their organisations may be helpful in this respect. What about the wider relation between ordinary people and the state? Who, for instance, is accountable for SAP?

Different aspects of the state and the legal system have different constituencies. The protection of contracts and the protection of trade union rights are demanded by different social forces. The pressures for accountability and the rule of law need to be situated in the context of conflicting interests and antagonistic social processes. Resistance to bad laws and corrupt and arbitrary officials is a motor for the disciplining of the state. As in the case of democratisation, the state is moulded by interacting processes of resistance, repression, and concessions. The outcome may be a "social contract", recognising the limits imposed by the balance of social forces on the scope for either repression or resistance.

Can a social contract be worked out between the state and the organised interests opposed to SAP? Attempts by governments to override, sideline, or ignore interest group opposition are self-defeating.

The failure of the state to recognise the limits of its own power is a major reason for the stalemate that characterises so much crisis management in Africa (and elsewhere!). Foreign intervention tends to reinforce the impasse by propping up and shielding regimes from local political pressures. While succeeding temporarily in shifting the balance of forces in favour of ruling coalitions, such interventions simultaneously undermine the process of accommodation that may be required for more lasting solutions.

The World Bank report is part of this intervention, obstructing a new social contract. Its own contribution is the effort to *de*-recognise, *de*-legitimate the forces opposing SAP. It is as unhelpful to the process of state formation as to that of democratisation. The Bank may operate on the seemingly comfortable assumption that the post-colonial state project has effectively discredited itself and therefore cannot provide a platform for a viable alternative to SAP. It fails to distinguish between the performance of post-colonial regimes and the aspirations of social forces that continue to be attached to the project of national development. The failure of the state does not make those aspirations less potent. On the contrary, for many the failure is a basis for a reassertion of betrayed objectives.

The nationalist, developmental and welfarist visions of the independence movement continue to be a major ideological force in Africa. The reconstruction of a national project on the basis of that ideological tradition is the principal alternative to SAP. Due to the experience of repression and resistance, there is a chance that such a reconstituted national project may be a good deal more democratic in its orientation than either the original post-colonial project, or that of SAP.

Interest Group Politics and the Implementation of Adjustment Policies in Sub-Saharan Africa

John Toye

When at the very beginning of the 1980s international agencies like the IMF and the World Bank suddenly started to advocate policies of structural adjustment to the governments of developing countries, discussions of the political aspects of structural adjustment were very much *sub rosa*. They were not on the formal agenda of debate. To the extent that politics was discussed clandestinely, however, a clear conventional wisdom existed about how the politics of adjustment would work—what the political problems would be, what challenges these would pose to politicians who sought structural adjustment and how donor agencies could assist the successful meeting of those challenges.

In this paper, a sketch of this conventional wisdom is given in the following section. In the third section a summary is given of the findings of the recent study by Mosley, Harrigan and Toye (1991) as they relate to the politics of implementing adjustment policies in three developing countries in Sub-Saharan Africa (SSA)—Ghana, Malawi and Kenya. Finally, the implications of these findings are examined in the fourth and final section in the context of current calls for greater democratisation of political life in developing countries.[1]

THE POLITICS OF STRUCTURAL ADJUSTMENT: A SKETCH

The most powerful and comprehensive analysis of the political economy of development available to influence thinking about structural adjustment at the end of the 1970s was *Why Poor People Stay*

---

1. I would like to express my thanks to Mike Faber, Joan Nelson and Robert Wade for their helpful comments on earlier versions of this paper. Useful comments were also given by participants in conferences where early versions were discussed, at Manchester (September 1990), Bergen (October, 1990) and Leicester (April, 1991).

Poor by Michael Lipton, which was published in 1977. This influential book codified and rationalised the concept of urban bias, and eloquently denounced its malign effects on the policies designed to promote development. Many others had, from the 1960s, onwards, examined parts of the urban bias story—excessive industrialisation, distorting trade regimes, the failure of redistributive taxation strategies, the neglect of agricultural investment or the virtues of primary health care compared with modern curative medicine. Lipton's book tied all these things (and more) together and created a powerful polemic against the "urban coalition" which was undermining development and efforts to alleviate poverty. After structural adjustment policies had been launched, Bates (1981) made an even sharper statement of this polemic and the "Berg Report" identified persistent anti-agriculture bias as African governments' chief policy error (World Bank, 1981).

Not surprisingly, the politics of structural adjustment were interpreted with the concept of urban bias in mind. The need for structural adjustment had arisen because governments in developing countries had been "captured" by workers and industrialists to form an urban coalition, it was believed (Bates, 1986: 6–8). Captive governments had legislated their economic policies to advance urban interests at the expense of rural interests. The whole dirigistic apparatus of trade and exchange control, state-owned banks and industries, trading corporations with monopolies of agricultural export crops, food procurement agencies and so on was seen as a single great scheme to exploit the rural hinterland and grow rich on a variety of artificially created rents in the cities and towns. A new *Gestalt* had arrived. Instead of a series of isolated "policy mistakes", developing countries were seen to be in the grip of a syndrome, in which dirigisme and rent-seeking were mutually reinforcing, and of which the perpetrators and the beneficiaries were the urban coalition. The academic public choice theorists expressed this more clearly than officials of the World Bank, but the latter were also strongly influenced by this idea all the same.

From this new Gestalt, the problems and paradoxes of the politics of structural adjustment proceeded. Taken together, they can be described as the politics of the knife-edge. This starts from the *distributional* proposition that stabilisation and structural adjustment reduce the rents accruing to urban interest groups and benefit rural interest groups whom dirigisme has systematically disadvantaged. To this is added a proposition about *timing*—that the negative effects on urban interests will be felt almost immediately, as the prices of imported consumer goods rise and subsidies on food, transport and other utilities are withdrawn, while the positive effects on rural interests will not accrue until new crops are planted, harvested and sold at the new, more favourable prices. A third proposition concerned *expectations*. The benefits of stabilisation and structural adjustment would not accrue at all unless people believed that the government would persist with the policies of reform. Yet it was difficult for people to believe in government persistence because of the paradox of reform, first enunciated by Niccolo Machiavelli. In *Il Principe*, Machiavelli noted that the innovator "has for enemies all who done well under the old order of things, and lukewarm defenders in those who may do well under the new" (Machiavelli, 1968: 29). Thus during the first year or two of an adjustment programme, the situation was expected to be highly unstable. To push ahead strongly might be the path to success as the government's resolve persuades people to adjust their behaviour to the new economic environment. But it also might not, if opposition proved stronger than the government expected and was capable of surmounting. If the government were to lose confidence in its ability to persist, the programme of adjustment would quickly collapse. Hence the metaphor of the knife-edge.

This kind of political analysis informed the international financial institutions' understanding of their own role in the adjustment process. It was to provide much-needed foreign credits to ease the difficult first year or two by re-filling the shops and rehabilitating essential infrastructure which had been allowed to deteriorate. This would help to bridge the gap between the arrival of the bad news (rising prices, heavier taxes, loss of subsidies) and the good news of higher producer prices and the relaxation of the underlying import strangulation. The ability to deploy resources for the purposes of bridging the bad news/good news gap was seen as the source of the IFI's political leverage. Where opinion was divided evenly between pro- and anti-reform camps within a government, the Fund and Bank could throw its weight behind the pro-reform group and carry the day for stabilisation and structural adjustment.

Such in sketch form were the political ideas which underpinned the move to adjustment lending in the 1980s. I have not laboured to document precise instances. Many were in confidential documents. But in any case the aim here is not to convict particular individuals or institutions of error. It is merely to remind ourselves of lines of thinking that were popular at the time, as a background to presenting the results of case studies of the implementation of adjustment reforms.

Before doing so, however, some further observations may be helpful in elaborating aspects of the basic political understanding of the time.

1. The urban bias theme itself, though capturing something important about the exploitation of rural exporters, especially in Africa, ran into much criticism. Two problems relevant here are the loose and fluctuating definition that is given to the "urban coalition", and the absence of clear evidence of the ways in which urban people operate politically as an interest group (Moore, 1984; Toye, 1987:127–130). This was unsatisfactory in itself, but especially worrying for those intending to intervene to counterbalance the urban coalition's influence.

2. The concept of an interest group (apart from rural interest groups which were supposed to be a distant gleam in the eye of the external actors) came in the new Gestalt to bear an unambiguously *negative* connotation. They were divisive and parasitic; if successful they caused social rigidities or were otherwise socially destructive. This was a considerable reversal of the earlier view that their activities were analogous to a competitive process within the political arena, blunting the extremism of each other's political demands and ultimately promoting compromises and social consensus (see Toye, 1991).

3. The negative connotation given to interest groups combined with the dilemma of the bad news/good news gap to create a strong presumption in favour of the effectiveness of authoritarian governments in carrying through adjustment programmes, even if they were not regarded as desirable in any wider sense. "A courageous, ruthless and perhaps undemocratic government is required to ride roughshod over these newly-created special interest groups", wrote Deepak Lal (1983: 33) in a pamphlet that was widely acclaimed at the time. Lal was no mere academic scribbler, but an influential figure in the Research Department of the World Bank.

4. Machiavelli's paradox of reform helped to answer an important question about structural adjustment, namely why should fresh foreign credits be released to the reforming government *before* reform takes place rather than *after*? It provided a political argument for a course of action that was not, on the face of it, congruent with economic prudence. The arrival of fresh credits could, after all, reduce rather than increase the urgency of economic policy reform in the government's mind. And there was considerable scope for defaulting on promises of reform, once the credits had arrived. "Facilitating the transition" with IFI finance could just as easily result in delaying it, or even aborting it. But it made sense once given a firm belief in the story of defeating the urban coalition.

5. Finally, the presumption in favour of authoritarian regimes as managers of adjustment, and the IFI's support of such regimes with concessional finance, had to be justified. Justification was provided by a three step argument. First, a distinction was drawn between the interests of an authoritarian government and the interests of the people which it governs. Second, that the interests of the people should be defined by the Rawlsian principles of distributive justice, including the proscription of changes which further disadvantage the least advantaged groups in a society (Rawls, 1972). Finally, if stabilisation and structural adjustment programmes do redistribute income from the urban rich to the rural poor, they *are* in the interests of the people because they do not violate this Rawlsian principle. Therefore, it is legitimate for the IFIs to support the adjustment programmes of authoritarian regimes—of whom they may or may not approve on other grounds (Donaldson, 1990).

IMPLEMENTATION OF STRUCTURAL ADJUSTMENT IN THREE SSA CASES

The Mosley, Harrigan and Toye study of structural adjustment (henceforth MHT) is based in part on case-studies of nine developing countries which borrowed from the World Bank to finance adjustment programmes in the 1980s. In Africa they were Kenya, Malawi and Ghana; in Asia, Turkey, Thailand and the Philippines; in the

Caribbean and Latin America, Jamaica, Guyana and Ecuador. The general results obtained reflect obviously the initial selection of countries. The choice was aimed at a wide spread, both geographically and in terms of *ex ante* perceived performance—both Turkey and Guyana are here. One important result, however, does not seem to be particularly sensitive to choice of cases. It is that all countries do not achieve a middling or average performance in implementing the policy conditions of structural adjustment loans—an impression which the Bank fosters by quoting an *aggregate* number for condition fulfilment of 60 per cent while not being willing to provide individual country estimates. Country performances divide quite sharply between the excellent and the very poor. The evidence suggests that countries either seriously commit themselves to the adjustment process, or they do not. There are various ways of manipulating the indicators of compliance which the World Bank studies, but this is only a way of masking the underlying reality of either strong commitment, or rather little serious interest in pursuing adjustment.

The question then arises: how is the strong commitment which produces excellent implementation generated? The MHT study looks at four distinct (but not mutually exclusive) hypotheses.[2]

(i)   that authoritarian regimes are more likely to be strongly committed to adjustment and thus to be better performers at it than are democratic regimes;

(ii)   that (regardless of regime type) newly formed governments are likely to be better adjusters than governments of long standing, i.e. that "new brooms sweep cleanest";

(iii) that a sudden sharp worsening of economic conditions—an economic crisis—triggers a social learning experience (in any regime, in new or old governments) to the effect that adjustment must be undertaken as a conscious policy rather than

---

2 A fifth hypothesis was also examined, that implementation succcess was determined primarily by the economic factor of the size of the available IFI credit, relative to that available without conditions from alternative sources. As we are concerned with politics here, the findings on this are not reported (see MHT, Vol. 1, Chapter 5 for details).

allowed to happen as the inevitable outcome of inaction and policy paralysis[3];

(iv)   that commitment results from a struggle between pro- and anti-reform interest groups, in which pro-reform groups (with Bank/Fund help) become politically dominant.

Table 1.   *Type of government and level of implementation of structural adjustment loan conditions*

Country	Authoritarian?	New government?	Standard of living 1980–82 more than 25 % below average level of 1970s?	Level of implementation of structural adjustment loan conditions
Turkey	Yes*	Yes	No	95
Thailand	Yes*	No	No	70
Ghana	Yes	Yes	Yes	58
Philippines	No (post 1986)	No (yes post 1986)	No	62
Jamaica	No	Yes	Yes	63
Malawi	Yes	No	No	55
Kenya	Yes*	No	No	38
Ecuador	No	Yes	Yes	28
Guyana	No	No	Yes	15

Notes and sources: A regime is defined as "authoritarian" if any of the following do not hold: regular elections for representative assembly and head of state; freedom of press and personal expression. In countries marked * there is an elective representative assembly. "New government" denotes a change in political leadership during the two years preceding the grant of the first World Bank adjustment loan. "Standard of living" is GNP per capita as set out in successive issues of World Bank *World Development Report* (Appendix Table 1).

---

3. Miles Kahler, in a very interesting paper (Kahler, 1991) makes a much stronger contrast than is presented here between external influence over Less Developed Countries' domestic policies exercised by conditionality and bargaining, and external influence exercised by social learning and the growth of consensual knowledge. The latter, "developed primarily as an explanation for international cooperation and the evolution of international institutions ... focuses ... on the tacit and explicit alliances across the negotiating table that are created by policy dialogue, technical assistance and other avenues of influence in the policy process" apart from the leverage of conditionality.

At a superficial level, it appears that "authoritarian regimes" are better adjusters than "democratic" regimes, when the latter are defined as those with regular elections for both the head of state and a representative assembly plus freedom of the press and personal expression. Turkey, Thailand and Ghana are authoritarian on this criterion and they were among the four best performers on adjustment (see Table 1). The two worst performers were Ecuador and Guyana, who come out as non-authoritarian.

If, however, we confine our focus to the three sub-Saharan African cases of Ghana, Kenya and Malawi, the authoritarian regime hypothesis does not discriminate between the better performers in the implementation of structural adjustment loan conditions (Ghana, Malawi) and the less good (Kenya). This is because, like so many other countries in SSA, all the three case study countries fall into the category of dictatorships. The observed variations in their adjustment performances must be the result of something other than the basic nature of their political regimes.

The regime of the Provisional National Defence Council (PNDC) in Ghana, under its Chairman, Flt.Lt. Jerry Rawlings, is best described as bonapartist. Founded by a coup at the end of 1981, the new regime presented itself as a revolutionary one and instigated various measures of popular mobilisation. But in its first years it lost legitimacy through its episodic espousal of violence and summary executions, and then split on the issue of whether to call in the Bank and the IMF. After 1983, a small PNDC rump ruled without permitted opposition or press freedom, and without any representative institutions until elections for district assemblies were held in 1988.

The Malawian polity has been described as "a centralised efficient, personal dictatorship" of Dr. Hastings Banda, President—now Life President—since 1964. Coercion and patronage were the original basis of Banda's personal power, which permitted the subversion of the checks and balance in the original Independence constitution. In more recent years, a range of populist and patrimonialist strategies have been used for the ideological and material consolidation of Banda's position (MHT II: 204–5).

The regime presided over by Daniel arap Moi in Kenya is the chosen successor to Kenyatta's original Independence government, and in much the same authoritarian mode. Although Kenya has an elected assembly, dissent is not tolerated and opponents who become too outspoken have met a variety of violent ends. The bureaucracy is manipulated as a direct instrument of presidential power. Little divides Kenya from Malawi and Ghana in the degree of its authoritarianism. If the authoritarian explanation of success in structural adjustment alone were valid, little should separate the performance of the three countries. Since in fact performance was significantly different, we must turn to other hypotheses next for enlightenment.

How relevant is the newness of the government as cause of successful adjustment? Do new leaders enjoy a specially advantageous opportunity for reform when they first come to power—a political honeymoon period? The political honeymoon can be important in some situations, but it is less relevant for authoritarian than for non-authoritarian regimes. The advantages of a new leadership derive from its renewal of popular legitimacy and the willingness of those inclined towards opposition temporarily to hold their political fire. Where the new leadership is authoritarian, such considerations do not so obviously apply. Indeed, as previously noted, the PNDC in Ghana, acting with few constraints, quickly dissipated much of the popular legitimacy which it may have had and provoked internal opposition which produced numerous attempted countercoups in the first few years of its existence. The fact that Rawlings repudiated all the governments in Ghana, at least since the time of Nkrumah, was not a source of strength. One of these, that of Dr. Busia (1969 to 1972) had marked out the path of liberalising economic reform down which Rawlings himself quickly had to walk in 1983.

The three cases of Ghana, Malawi and Kenya provide examples of governments of widely ranging degrees of newness. Banda had been in power for 17 years already in 1981, when structural adjustment began in Malawi. Moi's tenure of power had been only two years when Kenya received its first SAL in 1980. In Ghana, Rawlings initiated Bank-funded adjustment after only eighteen months in power. But Malawi's record of implementation of reforms was only marginally worse than Ghana's. If an elderly government retains (as Banda's did) a high degree of authority and an efficient adminstration, it can reform the economy as successfully as a new government which sets itself up as a "new broom"—or so the MHT statistics appear to show. However, some caution is called for here. The Ghana administrative capacity was probably less than that in Malawi. Ghana's record might well have exceeded Malawi's by more than it did, had both countries had equally competent administrations. If that is so, the hypothesis that recent accession to power assists reformers may still contain an element of truth. We return to this question when we discuss the fourth hypothesis, on interest groups.

What is the role of economic crisis in stimulating successful adjustment? The depth of economic distress does seem to play some catalytic role. As Table 1 shows, only in one of the three SSA countries, Ghana, had the standard of living in the early 1980s fallen below the average level of the 1970s by more than 25 per cent. Ghana also had the greatest success in implementing its economic reforms. This association between crisis and the thoroughness of reform may not be causal, but it does not allow us to dismiss the hypothesis out of hand.

The origin of Kenya's economic difficulties was ironically a boom during 1976 to 1977 in coffee and tea prices, which the government allowed to feed through into the private sector, and followed by heavy international borrowing (including variable interest rate recycled petro-dollars) and expansion of public recurrent expenditure and investment in parastatals. When the coffee price fell sharply in 1979, a balance of payments deficit quickly emerged, which drove Kenya first to the IMF and then in 1980 to the Bank for external finance (MHT II: 271–4). Sudden falls in primary commodity prices (in this case, tobacco and tea) also triggered a substantial balance of payments deficit in Malawi in 1979 to 1980, which was exacerbated (as in Kenya) by rises in international interest rates. In Malawi the crisis was further worsened by drought and the disruption of Malawi's traditional trade route to the sea through Mozambique. Again, like Kenya, Malawi resorted to the IMF in 1979 and when this proved insufficient, to the Bank in 1981 (MHT II: 210–3).

Serious as these difficulties were, the crisis in Ghana was much more deep-seated, and brought the country to virtual economic collapse in the early 1980s. Whereas both Kenya and Malawi had been regarded as relatively well-managed economies until the second half of the 1970s, Ghana's development strategy had developed fundamental flaws in the 1960s, and Busia's hesitant attempt at correction never got very far before he was ousted by the military. Ghana then suffered during the rest of the 1970s from military rulers who not only failed to pursue *any* economic policy but who ruthlessly exploited public resources for private gain. Finally, strong exogenous shocks in the form of drought, rising oil prices and the repatriation of almost one million Ghanaians working in Nigeria completed the debacle. Although their crisis had begun much earlier than Kenya's or Malawi's and done much more economic damage, the Ghanaians took longer to apply for help to the Fund and the Bank. All of this may help to explain why, when they did finally do so, they pursued the required reforms with a more thorough commitment—virtually placing the whole task of economic reconstruction under the supervision of the Fund and Bank.

But even if we acknowledge some explanatory power in the relative depth of the economic crisis, this should not be to the exclusion of our fourth hypothesis—the struggle between competing interest groups leading to the emergence of a dominant pro-reform coalition. On this question, the MHT study provides interesting evidence that vested interests do exist, which have the power to frustrate certain types of economic reform. But the way in which those vested interests operate is quite different from the way their operation is conceptualised in the conventional view of the politics of structural adjustment with which we began.

In both Kenya and Malawi, the most central failures of the structural adjustment programmes concerned the liberalisation of agricultural marketing. In Malawi, parastatals and large holding companies were used to create a distortion *within* the agricultural sector, favouring the large estates at the expense of the smallholders. In Kenya, a National Cereals and Produce Board had a monopoly on the buying and selling of maize which had originated in the colonial period. This monopoly allowed oligopoly rents to be earned by granting licences for the movement of maize from surplus to deficit areas of the country. Despite the dominance of agriculture in Malawian exports and the economy more generally, the Bank did not set out to tackle the intra-sectoral distortions of agriculture head-on. Instead it prescribed a series of ad hoc reforms which disrupted the working of the existing system and which led to the *status quo ante* being partially restored in 1986/7. More focused pressure was applied by the Bank on the Kenyan government to review arrangements for maize marketing and allow the private sector greater scope therein. Despite agreeing to the decontrol of the maize trade when the second Kenyan SAL was signed, this measure was never implemented by the government.

Both of these failures of Bank-designed reforms have to be understood by reference to the vested interests within the agricultural sector in each of the countries. In Malawi, the President personally owned Press Holdings, a large private company holding equity in most sectors of the economy, including the commercial banks. Press Holdings borrowed heavily at home and abroad, debt that was frequently guaranteed by the government and used to finance the acquisition of tobacco estates by Dr. Banda. Press Holdings also encouraged the commercial banks to lend to leading Malawian politicians and bureaucrats so that they too could acquire tobacco estates and benefit from the incentives granted to "pioneer" tobacco farmers. These incentives for the tobacco estates were paid for by setting the prices of smallholders' export crops (including tobacco) well below export parity prices. The Malawian estate tobacco farmers, with the President at their head, had a substantial vested interest to defend. While it is not clear whether the Bank diagnosed accurately the full ramifications of the intra-sectoral bias in agriculture, it is clear that the adjustment measures required under the SALs in the mid-1980s did not succeed in removing it.

The arrangements for maize marketing in Kenya also constituted a well-established vested interest of large maize farmers, including the President. The maize marketing board's monopoly powers of purchase from farmers and sales to millers has substantially raised the price of maize to the consumer for many years. Farmers licensed to sell maize in deficit regions make inflated profits thereby, and the allocation of licences for inter-regional maize movements is therefore an important source of political patronage. In these circumstances, it is not surprising that, while those who were negotiating directly with the Bank led it to believe that the major trade would be soon de-controlled, the measure was blocked by the President's Office throughout 1983, until the 1984 drought removed it from the political agenda on the specious pretext of food security (MHT II: 290).

A striking similarity characterises the political circumstances of these failures. The general political and ideological climate of both countries at the time was not hostile to liberalisation efforts. Within both governments, a small group of enthusiastic technocrats was making a genuine effort to pursue liberalisation in the areas agreed with the Bank to be desirable. Ultimately, the Bank's good rapport with the Kenyan and Malawian technocrats proved insufficient to procure the agricultural marketing reforms. In both cases, the President of the country had a personal stake in agribusiness, and the "distortions" objected to by the Bank formed an important part of the mechanism for ensuring political support for the President's party. It is, therefore, an important finding of MHT that some of the most recalcitrant vested interests in the path of economic liberalisation were in the agricultural rather than the industrial sector, whereas the conventional justification for policy reform was the need to remove the urban biases which disadvantage rural producers.

Apart from the two cases from SSA which are discussed in this paper, the MHT study also identified a very similar failure of adjustment in Ecuador. There the *latifundistas* in the sierra and the agro-exporting oligarchy held the key economic position, and economic strength had been converted into political influence. The Bank aimed at eliminating subsidies on agricultural credit and permitting free trade in food crops. Neither objective was achieved, despite the enthusiastic cooperation of the talented economic technocrats who appeared to have policy-making in their control, and who themselves strongly favoured liberalisation (MHT II: 431–2).

Let us now review the original four hypotheses on the causes of successful implementation of adjustment loan conditions. The question of whether authoritarian regimes are helpful to adjustment cannot be addressed without going beyond the three SSA cases, because all qualify as authoritarian. All that can be said is that other factors are necessary to explain the variation in success between our three SSA dictatorships.

The comparison between reform in Malawi and in Ghana appears to show that some success in adjustment is possible for old and new governments alike—because both showed approximately average success in their performance of loan conditions. But, again, other factors seem to be relevant in this comparison. Ghana, one suspects, would have done better if it had possessed Malawi's level of administrative capacity. Malawi, on the other hand, suffered from one very powerful vested interest—the agricultural estates sector—for which there was no equivalent in Ghana. It would therefore be wrong to dismiss the "new broom" hypothesis entirely.

The hypothesis that economic crisis promotes social learning is not refuted if only SSA cases are compared. Ghana seems a strong example. But Table 1 indicates that, among all nine of the MHT countries, the hypothesis does not stand up. Leaving Ghana aside, the success rates were higher in countries which did not have an especially severe shock to living standards at the start of the 1980s.

Our fourth explanation, at its simplest, looks suspiciously like a tautology: that the strength of the impulse towards reform depends on the outcome of the competitive struggle between pro- and anti-reform interest groups. If "interest groups" includes interest groups *within* government, the hypothesis is true by definition: obviously the relative progress of reform between countries depends on the relative power of pro- and anti-reform elements. The meaningful questions evidently lie one step back from here. What caused the relative influence of different groups to diverge as between countries? Are there institutional differences which influence the way in which interest group conflicts are played out?

The MHT study suggests four main propositions:

1. Reform efforts work better *ceteris paribus* if the gainers are organised in support of the proposed reform. But typically farmers as a whole in developing countries do not constitute an organised, let alone powerful interest group. So far this goes along with the conventional wisdom sketched in Section II. But big landowners find it much easier to make common cause than farmers in general, and in Kenya (as in Ecuador) they organised themselves as a "national farmers' union", whose members were also well represented in parliament. While supporting *price-based* reforms which keep prices above export-parity levels, they frustrated *market-based* reforms which tried to remove the element of rent in the price paid by the government marketing board.
2. Industrialists do *not* constitute a unified interest group in matters of trade policy. Each industry has its own proposals and its own special pleading for protection. Thus only where a measure will benefit a majority of industrialists will it gain the backing of an industrialists' lobbying organisation. Most industrialists will benefit from a quick relaxation of restrictions on importing key inputs. Measures to liberalise imports have been among the more successfully implemented parts of structural adjustment packages.
3. The degree to which groups can mobilise themselves is only part of the explanation of the effectiveness of an interest group in

influencing structural adjustment. Countries differ in their formal
political institutions and their informal ideological apparatus.
The "thickness" or "thinness" of such institutions also determines
the extent to which a group with an organised common interest
can influence policy. A country without a free legislature, a free
press or normal liberal civil rights is much less open to interest
group influence than one with "thicker" or "denser" institutions
of civil society. In Ghana, the sphere of action available to interest
groups was highly circumscribed by the thinness or absence of
civil society. To say this does not imply that authoritarian regimes
will be more effective as economic reformers, however. It may
simply imply that the power to subvert economic reform will be
monopolised at the highest levels of the state.

4. With only rare exceptions, structural adjustment programmes
were not designed to compensate those who were losers in the
policy changes. This was so even when a compensation change
could be made without introducing any fresh distortions with the
policy mix. Explicit political calculation seemed to be largely
absent from the IFI's programmes, except insofar as loan credit
permitted a generally welcomed easing of import compression.
Perhaps lack of economic sophistication in local bureaucracies
partly accounts for this, too. Certainly, the administrative skills of
the bureaucracy emerged as a visible factor which determined
differences in implementation as between governments who
were equally committed in principle to the philosophy of adjustment. While there was little to choose in level of commitment between Turkey and Ghana, the latter, with a weaker administration, achieved only 58 per cent implementation, compared with
Turkey's 95 per cent.

SHOULD THE INTERNATIONAL FINANCE INSTITUTIONS SUPPORT DEMOCRATISATION?

If one now looks back on the initial beliefs which were in vogue at
the time when structural adjustment programmes were first devised, it is clear that the MHT study suggests some rather far-reaching revisions.

The rural–urban divide and dirigisme

MHT neither sees rural nor urban interests operating through well-functioning unified interest groups. In the rural areas large farmers can organise and do, but to help themselves rather than small family farms, let alone the landless wage workers who constitute the poor and the very poor.[4]

Sometimes, as in Malawi, they help themselves directly at the expense of the poor smallholders. In the urban areas, supporters of industry are too divided to agree on how and where to create rents and can unite mainly to support import liberalisation. It therefore seems implausible that the syndrome of dirigisme could have been the outcome of a struggle between rural and urban unified interest groups, with the urban coalition winning. Rather, it would appear to be the product of a centrally-directed patronage politics. That is to say that dirigisme results from the active search by government leaders for support—which may be built up either in the urban or in the rural sectors. It is a "top-down" rather than a "bottom-up" phenomenon (Sandbrook, 1986). This has strong negative implications for any defence of authoritarianism as a catalyst of economic reform.

Knife-edge politics and authoritarianism

The political analysis of structural adjustment has focused too much on the early period of a programme. Perhaps this was inevitable before the process had got well underway. The knife-edge problem was visible clearly only in the Ghanaian case, where a difficult first year was accompanied by some attempted coups. Even here, external factors such as drought were a major cause of the difficulties, and when they reversed themselves started the recovery *before* the adjustment policies had much chance to bite. There was an over-estimation of the importance of policy-induced changes in the economic

---

4. The Ghana Living Standards Survey of 1987 gives a snapshot of the distribution of annual per capita expenditure in Ghana. Over 80 per cent of the lowest quintile of this distribution live in rural areas. However, 41 per cent of the highest quintile of this distribution *also* lives in the rural areas. This suggests a rural sector that is highly heterogeneous in its economic and social make-up, and casts serious doubt on the notion of the rural sector as a unified interest group (Loxley, 1991:41).

situation, compared with exogenous factors like drought in Ghana and Kenya. Although J.J. Rawlings did face a knife-edge and did not lose his nerve, this seems insufficient evidence from which to conclude that authoritarian governments *ipso facto* make a better job of economic adjustment, as Lal had argued in the statement quoted in Section II above.

Political institutions and the role of interest groups

The MHT study also puts the conventional negative connotation of interest groups in developing countries in a new light. As sketched in Section II, interest groups are now generally condemned as socially destructive (e.g. Olson, 1982: 36–73). This condemnation provides the basic justification for authoritarian regimes—i.e. they are socially desirable because they ride roughshod over such groups. But one can look at the matter the other way round. In such regimes, political institutions are "thin", particularly in developing countries. Nothing much stands between the ruler, his security services and his ministers and their officials and the people who are governed. There may be very few independently organised interest groups at all—no free trade unions, a politically quiescent church, a muzzled press, no producers associations. But additionally, there may be no representative political institutions, and thus no forum where competition could discipline sectional demands and force them to advance themselves by articulating a conception of the public interest (Rawls, 1972: 224–7). The only politics may be sporadic acts of popular resistance, and it is easy to romanticise the extent to which these embody "the general will". Thus where a negative view of the behaviour of interest groups is justified, it may well be (although not necessarily, as the U.S. case indicates) a pointer to the grossly truncated political institutions of authoritarian rule. To plead for more authoritarianism in such circumstances is likely to be self-defeating. This is especially so if the existing interest groups are the creatures of government patronage, rather than autonomous and self-propelled.

The distributional argument

An important part of the case for structural adjustment was its claim to improve income distribution. Although some advocates were prepared to say that adjustment was necessary whatever the distributional consequences, many believed that arguments from equity strengthened the case for adjustment. Even with hindsight, it is hard to validate this. The size of the changes were probably exaggerated in advance on both sides of the argument. Factors like the interdependence of formal and parallel markets make it hard to quantify what the distributional effects have been—except in very dramatic cases, such as that of some of the heavily indebted Latin American countries. But in qualitative terms, we are now more aware of the rural groups who will *not* benefit—small food crop farmers, often women, and many agricultural labourers who work for wages. We are also aware that the urban losers who are affected by government lay-offs and rising consumer goods prices will be the urban poor, who will often move back silently to join the rural poor rather than benefit from the few public works projects laid on to soften the effects of adjustment.[5]

IFI credits and the timing of reforms

It looks increasingly as if IFI credit may have delayed reform in some countries. The Bank's move away from providing immediate credit in exchange for promises of action later and towards prior performance conditions and ever finer tranching of credit suggests that it learned by experience that the facilitation argument had flaws. Some countries seem to have used the credits to buy more time and postpone action, despite the fact that reform measures (when implemented) seem to have improved exports and the foreign balance, though without doing much for economic growth or increased private foreign investment.

Just as the MHT study was being completed, dramatic changes were occurring in the political scene worldwide. In the autumn of 1989, a veritable liberal revolution occurred in Eastern Europe (Toye, 1990). The restoration of human and civil rights and political representation there preceded the search for strategies of economic liberalisation.

---

5. Commenting on the GLSS results quoted in Note 4, Loxley remarks that "when combined with other information from the survey, these data caution one against generalising simplistically about the urban/rural distributional impacts of adjustment programs" (Loxley, 1991).

It was out of the question to propose that the move from dirigisme to a market-based economy could be undertaken successfully only with an authoritarian government. There, too, the delicate moral considerations for giving credits to such regimes have been simply swept aside. The charter of the new European Bank for Reconstruction and Development enshrines its commitment to "the fundamental principles of multi-party democracy, the rule of law, respect for human rights and market economics" (*Financial Times*, 21.8.90).

In Africa, disillusion with the one-party states of African socialism had already set in. The unhappy state of affairs in Tanzania had led to criticisms of the African socialism concept of which it was a model, especially the monopoly of power by the ruling party and the absence of free trade unions (Sender and Smith, 1990: 129–139). More generally in Africa, various signs have appeared of a pro-democracy movement—the increasing abandonment of one-party rule, the appearance of African efforts to promote political pluralism and the spread of human rights movements organised by Africans (Legum, 1990: 134). The Organisation of African Unity has, after many years, adopted a Charter of Human and People's Rights, with a Commission headquartered in Banjul, the Gambia, whose purpose is to make these rights more effective. These developments are likely to be further encouraged as the ending of the Cold War puts an end to superpower rivalries played out by unpleasant puppet regimes such as Doe's Liberia and Mengistu's Ethiopia.

The great post-1989 question, which has already been raised in political speeches, is whether foreign aid can be used to promote both economic liberalisation *and political liberalisation at the same time*. In answering this question it is important to begin by remembering the limitation on aid conditionality as an instrument to bring about economic liberalisation. It has not been very successful in *inducing* change in economic policy. But when policies had been changed, it often lent valuable support in maintaining or extending the new directions. The same is likely to apply to the inducement of political change. The mechanisms of aid conditionality are likely to be too creaky to exert much leverage over the recalcitrants and procrastinators of political liberalisation.

One of the interesting findings of the MHT study in the economic policy field was the phenomenon of "countervailing action". In other words, a government could comply with a loan condition, but at the same time take other actions not specifically prohibited which had the effect of neutralising that compliance. Obviously the same sort of possibilities for countervailing action exist in the political arena as have been demonstrated in the arena of economic reform. That is why it is rather arbitrary to do as is done in Table 1, for example, to specify a few simple criteria to distinguish authoritarian from democratic regimes. This can be unreliable, because it is possible to have apparently democratic institutions with representative government, election of representatives and even fairly extensive human rights and still have a single party maintaining an unchallengeable monopoly of power. Devices such as giving sitting representatives the right directly to disburse public expenditure in their constituencies, plus occasional round-ups of opponents on unspecified security grounds—followed by eventual release without charge—can ensure that democratic institutions remain nothing more than a facade for authoritarian rule.

The problem of countervailing action not only bedevils the task of using aid to induce political liberalisation, it also affects the weaker strategy of rewarding such changes once they have taken place. Even responding *ex post facto* by allocating aid only to democratic regimes requires some reliable means of discriminating them from their opposite. It would require much research to prevent such judgement being arbitrary, and therefore potentially destructive of international goodwill when the intention of aid is precisely the opposite.

Even if the judgement could be made simply and reliably, an ethical dilemma remains. If it was morally acceptable to channel aid to authoritarian governments in order to benefit their people during the 1980s, why is it not acceptable to do so today? Are those who have the misfortune to live under such a regime to be doubly punished, by being also denied the economic benefits which foreign aid projects can bring? To do so might be acceptable if the refusal of aid were likely to bring down the existing regime and allow a quick move both to democracy and to the resumption of aid. But the implication of all that has been said above is that this is most unlikely to happen.

Thus the process of democratisation will not be much assisted by aid policy. We are therefore likely to see an increasing differentiation in the mode of operation of interest groups in the process of adjustment. In authoritarian regimes, they are likely to remain creatures of the ruler and obstacles to adjustment in selected areas of economic reform. In democratic regimes, political institutions and civil society should both develop, become both more independent of the state and (unparadoxically) more effective in promoting the public interest. That is the challenge which faces the new democracies of the 1990s.

Structural Adjustment and Pressures toward Multipartyism in Sub-Saharan Africa

Peter Gibbon

Two of the major developments in the political economy of Sub-Saharan Africa in the last decade have been the adoption of economic structural adjustment reforms and the emergence of pressures toward multi-party democracy.

The period of the growth of structural adjustment reform was mainly in 1982–87. In these years at least two thirds of Sub-Saharan African countries implemented varieties of structural adjustment programmes supported by the international financial institutions (IFIs). Even amongst those which did not there were significant examples of "home-grown" programmes being adopted (Nigeria, South Africa, etc.). Of the IMF-supported reformers 21 Sub-Saharan African countries raised agricultural producer prices, 16 devalued and/or realigned their exchange rates, 14 undertook some form of privatisation of state enterprises, 14 eliminated or reduced subsidies for agricultural inputs, 13 eliminated parastatal marketing agencies or encouraged private sector competition, 10 deregulated country-wide producer prices, 8 reduced or eliminated food subsidies, 7 adopted floating market rates for foreign exchange and 7 privatised the import of agricultural inputs (ODC,1987).

The emergence of pressures for multiparty democracy is a much more recent but no less widespread trend. According to one British journalist:

> When the Berlin Wall fell (in autumn 1989) 38 of the 45 states in Sub-Saharan Africa were ruled by military junta or one-party or one-man governments.

The author wis hes to thank Y. Adam, Y. Bangura and J. Toye for comments on an earlier version of this paper. The main source of inspiration for revisions to earlier drafts is a critique by Mkandawire (1991). The argument in the second part of the paper is developed at greater length in Gibbon (1991a). The argument in the third part employs certain concepts discussed at greater lengt in Mamdani (1989) and Neocosmos (1991).

> By autumn 1990 well over half of them have promised to have had—or will
> be well on the way to—multiparty elections (*Guardian*, 11 September, 1990).

The same article went unto list eight states which had already
adopted multi-party systems, two "moving toward" them, five in
which "discussions were taking place" and one (Kenya) in which
"discussions were banned". A large majority of these 16 states were
also structural adjusters.

Multipartyist trends in the context of structural adjustment were
a largely unanticipated development for most commentators, who
for the most part had predicted that structural adjustment would be
associated with growing political authoritarianism. An apparently
prescient exception to this consensus was a study by a group of
American political scientists, funded by the U.S. National Endowment for Democracy, which argued that the "continuing and deepening
economic liberalisation" associated with adjustment should develop
"a more authentic and autonomous bourgeoisie" who would in turn
provide a force for internal democratisation in Africa. (Diamond,
1988:29)

This paper seeks to establish whether such a relation, or indeed
any direct relation exists between structural adjustment and multipartyism, and in the process will attempt to elaborate some of the
conditions under which multipartyism has recently developed in
Africa.

The procedure adopted will be to examine three separate but
interrelated dimensions of the possible relation between structural
adjustment and the development of political pluralism. The first of
these is their respective backgrounds as *regional* phenomena. i.e. as
trends emerging relatively systematically across Sub-Saharan Africa
as a whole. The changing international political scene will be addressed in this context partly as a counterweight to viewing structural adjustment simply against the background of economic crisis.
Secondly, the relation between economic and political conditionality
will be explored. Structural adjustment has been introduced to Sub-
Saharan Africa largely as a result of pressure by the IFIs in the form
of conditional lending. Proposals now abound to make lending in
the region in the 1990s conditional on pluralistic political reform.
Structural adjustment conditionality will not disappear as a result,
but may at least be relegated to one form of conditionality amongst

others. A question this raises is that of the extent to which such a change reflects problems with structural adjustment conditionality, as opposed to building on conditionality's "success" by adding an additional layer to it. Lastly, the thesis of Diamond described above will be directly addressed through an evaluation of the extent to which structural adjustment creates constituencies for multiparty democracy within adjusting countries themselves. This question will be examined on the basis of a series of case studies looking at the process of adjustment and the emergence of multipartyist trends in four Sub-Saharan African countries.

While the paper focuses on a fairly narrow question, addressing this adequately involves covering a wide range of issues and data. It is therefore worthwhile confessing from the outset that the objective of the paper is only to sketch out a general interpretive framework and to suggest a number of very preliminary conclusions which will require both further critical evaluation and elaboration. Many of the observations and arguments which will follow will probably therefore strike the reader as somewhat bald and thinly supported. At least this should not detract from their main purpose, which is to stimulate further discussion.

STRUCTURAL ADJUSTMENT AND MULTIPARTYISM AS PHENOMENA OF INTERNATIONAL RELATIONS

A first aspect of the relation between structural adjustment and pressures toward multiparty democracy refers to the international relations contexts of the phenomena and specifically to how conditions favourable to the development of structural adjustment have been modified and transformed into conditions favourable also to the development of multiparty democracy.

It is not being asserted in what follows that international relations changes were the principal factors responsible for the adoption of adjustment by the IFIs, or that they have been the main factor behind the western push in Africa for political democracy. Other factors behind the latter will be explored below. On the former, it is clear that the changing disposition of the commercial banks to less developed country economies, mainly as a result of the debt crisis, has been fundamental. Notwithstanding this, it is still worthwhile to identify the international relations background against which adjustment arose. Within this, the following characteristics can be noted.

1. A contraction of U.S. economic power relative to that of Japan and the main European powers (excepting Britain). This relative economic weakening was not accompanied by a diminution in American political hegemony, however. While a European economic bloc was emerging with the growing weight of West German capital and the overthrow of authoritarian and protectionist dictatorships in southern Europe, this was as yet reflected in only a weak form of European political union. France for example continued to maintain an extensive political-economic sphere of influence in Africa.
2. An albeit uneven assertion by the USSR of a degree of parity with the U.S. in the overall corelation of international political forces. In Africa in the 1970s the Soviet Union sought to influence the outcome of events both in the Horn (support for Ethiopia in the Ogaden dispute) and in Angola (support for MPLA). Unlike the U.S., the Soviet Union proved normally able to provide only military support. While this gave the governments it supported a high degree of flexibility in economic policy it also rendered them highly susceptible to economic destabilisation.
3. Within the advanced western countries whose economic influence was waning most (U.S. and Britain), the rise of "new right" governments. The principal elements of the new right agenda were a popularised version of supply-side economics particularly emphasising the improvement of financial incentives and deregulation; a popularised version of Hayekian political philosophy emphasising individual as against collective rights and the "rule of law" as opposed to the customary procedures of collective institutions, and a revised foreign policy emphasising the paramount character of national self-interest, national security and anti-communism.
4. Within the U.S., the consequent reinforcement of "globalism" as opposed to "regionalism" as the dominant perspective governing foreign policy (Coleman and Sklar, 1985). While regionalism viewed international conflicts as arising from sources indigenous to specific regions, later "complicated" by superpower involve-

ment, globalism viewed all international conflicts as direct expressions of superpower rivalry. While a movement toward globalism was already evident at the close of the Carter period, its dominance became complete under Reagan. Globalism's rise had a direct bearing on structural adjustment. It led to the relegation of most of U.S.'s traditionally sacrosanct multilateral involvements on the grounds that these offered insufficient leverage for expressing national self-interest. Pertinent here was the withdrawal from UNESCO, clearly intended as "a lesson to the others" (Zwingina, 1987). Globalism led also to a relative reduction of bilateral development grants and credits in favour of military and security grants and credits, themselves concentrated on a narrow range of partners. On the other hand, globalism was constrained to some extent by post-Vietnam public hostility to direct intervention, and refined by a conception of a hierarchy of international strategic priorities where Africa was on virtually the lowest rung (Zwingina, 1987).

The international relations context of the early 1980s did not independently determine the existence of structural adjustment or its development but it contributed to it in a variety of ways. The economic policy content of adjustment was similar in emphasis to the agenda being advanced by the new right in the English-speaking countries. The foreign policy changes associated with the rise of globalism in the U.S. created a perceived need on the part of multilateral agencies, especially multilateral aid agencies, to take on board the new agenda if they were to maintain their existing levels of influence (not to mention subscriptions) (cf. Toye, 1989). Hence these agencies voluntarily ceded a degree of autonomy to governments and sought ways, like conditionality, of more clearly demonstrating their "effectiveness" vis-à-vis recipients. In some respects though, the international relations context also contributed to the longer-term *inability* of the IFIs to successfully carry through their own new agenda. The primacy enjoyed by security considerations in U.S. foreign policy, and the ongoing post-imperial international ambitions of countries like France conspired to reduce the leverage of the IFIs in a variety of nations—including in Africa, among others, Liberia, Somalia, Sudan, Zaire, Kenya, Ivory Coast.

The late 1980s saw a series of fundamental changes in this international relations conjuncture which in the Third World were to

exercise pressures toward multipartyist democratic change alongside ongoing adjustment. The most important of these changes was
the rise of popular "anti-communist" movements in China and Eastern
Europe. Unlike previous movements of opposition in these countries, their political content emphasized multipartyism rather than
nationalism. More surprisingly, with the exception of China, existing state forms collapsed before them.

In global political terms the collapse of state socialism in Eastern
Europe represented a historic victory for the U.S. However, its immediate economic effects have been probably to strengthen the importance of an enlarged European Community as a political and
economic bloc, now under virtually undisputed German leadership,
and in partial rivalry with the U.S. Such trends seem to have created
increased centripetal tendencies within Europe, which in turn appear to underline France's current review of its African commitments (*Financial Times*, June 18, 1990).

The dynamics of events in eastern Europe was itself largely set in
train by the programme of perestroika launched by Gorbachov after
his accession to power in the USSR in 1985. Furthermore it was allowed to play itself out autonomously as a result of a corresponding
new foreign policy under Shevardnadze. Implicit in this new policy's
agenda was a critique of foreign policy in the Brezhnev era as em-
bodying an "overextension" of Soviet interests and capacities. In
Africa its main expressions have been a winding down of military
commitments entered into under Brezhnev accompanied by the promotion of "regional" (i.e. diplomatic) solutions to the conflicts it was
directly and indirectly engaged in. By implication, it has been accepted that the bargaining power of forces hitherto supported by the
Soviet Union will be weakened in any subsequent negotiations.

There is little sign that these major changes in the international scene
have led to any dilution of globalism in U.S. foreign policy. The U.S.
appears to be no more accommodating toward "regionalist" solutions
and no more likely to give up support for low intensity operations like
UNITA in Angola than a decade ago. If a change of emphasis does exist,
it is in relation to multilateral bodies. Except where these are seen as
irredeemably neutralist, the U.S. has signalled an intention to work
through them in order to provide an internationalist mantle for the
expression of its interests. In the words of James Baker's statement to
the Senate Foreign Relations Committee on 5 September 1990:

> The U.S. plans to design, defend and lead a new global security system under the principles of the UN Charter. Only American engagement can shape the peaceful world that our people so deeply desire. We remain the one nation that has the necessary political, military and economic instruments at our disposal to catalyse successful collective responses by the international community. (*Guardian*, 6 September, 1990)

This new disposition was firmly underlined in the Gulf War at the beginning of 1991.

One further critical new development of the late 1980s, at least in regard to Sub-Saharan Africa, was the political and military retreat of the South African government. Overextended by its efforts to simultaneously repress domestic opposition, create a constellation of satellite states and launch conventional military operations over a wide area of south western Africa, South Africa suffered a decisive military defeat at Cuito Cuanavale in Angola in early 1988 (Wright, 1989). While UNITA survived this defeat and while the subsequent resolution of the Namibian issue was on terms the South Africans themselves favoured, the latter emerged seriously weakened. A chain of events was set in motion within white politics in the country which by mid-1990 had led to an apparent revision of white supremacist objectives toward a new political dispensation where they would share power with black organisations, possibly including the ANC.

As in the case of structural adjustment, there is no direct causal link between changes in the international political conjuncture and the emergence of "multipartyist" trends in Africa. Yet multipartyism's rise has undoubtedly been facilitated by some of them. In the first place, the international political legitimacy conferred on multipartyism by its role in the overthrow of state socialism appears to have influenced both some opposition forces and some governments in Sub-Saharan Africa to undertake conversions to democratic pluralism which they might otherwise have not. In the second place, it has lent encouragement and further legitimacy to those organisations and movements in the region who were already genuinely struggling for these objectives. In the third place, it has reinforced both tendencies through the pro-multiparty stance adopted by many multilateral agencies, including (unofficially) the IFIs, in response to the convergence of U.S. support for multipartyism with its new interest in multilateralism. This tendency has itself been reinforced by a widespread perception of the possibility that events in Eastern

Europe may lead to the diversion of assistance by donors from Africa to the "new democracies" in Europe. Fourthly, the indigenous movements for democratisation in countries previously within the French and South African constellations have been strengthened by the withdrawal or partial withdrawal of these powers' support for traditional clients and/or the withdrawal of their mitigation for these clients of the full rigours of structural adjustment. Fifthly, South African withdrawal has also widened the scope of legitimate dissent in countries previously subject to South African destabilisation like Zimbabwe and Zambia.

By way of a footnote it should be underlined that the new conditions in international politics which have favoured the development of multipartyism in Sub-Saharan Africa are not ones which are likely to reverse the importance of structural adjustment. Just as globalism appears to have survived the disappearance of its *raison d'être*, so neo-liberal economic policy prescriptions have maintained their influence independently of the political fortunes of the new right. Probably the major long-term achievement of the latter has been to drag the centre (and large parts of the left) of the political spectrum in Europe and North America towards their position on economic questions, to an extent making any thoroughgoing reversal highly problematic.

Structural adjustment conditionality and political conditionality

A second aspect of the relation of structural adjustment to multiparty democracy is that of the development of "political conditionality" by donor institutions, and the relation of this form of conditionality to earlier forms of economic conditionality. It will be argued that political conditionality in the sense of demands for democratic reform as a precondition of lending or grant assistance occupies a complex relationship to structural adjustment in which there are both strong continuities and important departures, and that the particular stage at which structural adjustment lending had arrived by the end of the 1980s was itself an important, independent variable in promoting a "wager" on pressure for multipartyist reform by the main donor countries.

Two points will serve as the assumptions of the discussion which follows. The first is that, contrary to the public insistence of the IFIs on their "non-political" character, not only has their lending always been political in the sense of being linked to the promotion of specific kinds of economic policy but also that political considerations have always been present in decisions about who to lend to, how much they should receive, and on what terms. Given the dominant role played by American banks and American governments within the IFIs this could hardly have been otherwise. Governments defined as of strategic importance to the U.S. have received various forms of preferential treatment, those defined as thorns in its side have either received treatment on less preferential terms or have been leveraged into compliance by threats of no assistance at all (Portugal 1974, Italy 1976).

Hence what is involved in "political conditionality" is less the introduction of politics to lending, but the proposed tying of lending to meeting a different set of political conditions to those traditionally applying. Also new is the transparency of the link.

A second assumption is that the history of the IFIs is one of a succession of paradigm crises and paradigm shifts with respect to policy content and lending practice. This point is made throughout Please's work on the World Bank, *The Hobbled Giant* (1984) and also by John Toye in relation to the origins of structural adjustment lending itself (Toye, 1989). Hence "political conditionality" should not be viewed as a once-and-for-all break with an otherwise continuous and consistent history on the part of the IFIs, but as both the latest fashion and also a response to specific difficulties inherent in the preceding fashion, i.e. structural adjustment lending.

Adjustment lending was developed by the Bank against a background of pressure from the commercial banks to "do something" about the debt crisis at no cost to themselves, from the Reagan administration for it to fall in with its new preferences, and as a result of problems with the project form of lending arising from a collapse in recipients' aid absorption capacities. As a result, the Bank turned to policy-related lending, on the basis of policies which played to the wider audience described above. These viewed most Third World governments (especially African ones) as more or less voluntarily poor, due to certain fundamental policy deficiencies or "distortions".

The well-known Berg report of 1981 set out to list these:

...Three are critical: first, trade and exchange rate policies have over-protected industry, held back agriculture and absorbed much administrative capacity. Second, too little attention has been paid to administrative constraints in mobilising and managing resources for development; given the widespread weakness of planning, decisionmaking and management capacities, public sectors frequently become overextended. Thirdly, there has been a consistent bias against agriculture in price, tax and exchange-rate policies ... (World Bank, 1981:4)

As Toye points out in this volume, this critique was tied in with a particular sociological view of the origins of these policy deficiencies as well as of the political conditions under which they could be renewed.

The origins of the deficiencies were analysed on the basis of the concept of "urban coalitions" developed in Michael Lipton's neo-populist essay *Why Poor People Stay Poor*. Governments dominated by urban coalitions followed policies designed to transfer resources from rural to urban areas. These policies were designed to, or at any rate resulted in "the politicisation of (economic) objectives to include increasing employment, delivery of output at low prices to key groups and non-economic shaping of investment decisions" (World Bank, 1981:38), and were made possible by the extraction of "rent" from peasant producers by state-controlled marketing monopolies.

The political conditions under which such policies would be removed and free market policies introduced were analysed in terms of requisite short-term and long-term changes. In the short-term, it was probable that only the introduction of an authoritarian state form would enable governments to attain sufficient autonomy from their traditional social bases to implement policies designed to roll back the state and promote production of "tradeables". Toye quotes the leading World Bank researcher Deepak Lal's argument that a "courageous, ruthless and perhaps undemocratic government is required to ride roughshod over these newly-created special interest groups" (Lal, 1983:33 quoted in Toye, this volume). Of course, structural adjustment loans were also useful in providing a temporary cushion to contain the reaction. In the longer term, it was necessary for the IFIs to engage in developing "technocratic" institutions and cadres in the recipient countries themselves. Berg depicted this process as essentially involving the strengthening of "the control of planning agencies and endow(ing) them as quickly as possible with the evaluation (and policy analysis) capacities they need" (World Bank, 1981:33). Of these agencies, Finance Ministries were central since these "represent the general interest in the bureaucratic struggle for resources" (ibid.). Furthermore, where sympathetic authoritarian governments inconveniently failed to emerge and while technocratic capacity was "maturing" the IFIs should flex their muscles and strong-arm recipients into policy change by an intensified use of conditionality. For a time this weapon of conditionality was played to the hilt. For example, the Bank's own review of its relations with Tanzania in the 1980s refers to "an effort to force the pace of agreement on measures" and goes on to observe

> ... the Bank ... moved from a position of reluctance to initiate discussion of the country's strategy to one where policy conditionality attached to lending operations (was) the norm. The rush in the eighties to create a policy environment that the Bank believed (would) foster development (was) an uncomfortable parallel of the rush to lend for projects in the seventies ... (World Bank, 1990a: pp. xvi, xxvii)

In some respects this "heroic" or macho phase of structural adjustment lending based on conditionality is still in progress; yet what is increasingly evident is that its various components have all come under critical evaluation in the last few years, not only from opponents of the IFIs, but more importantly from sources rather closer to them. It is these sources which will be discussed here, as they alone appear to have any influence over the directions being taken by both the IFIs and donor countries.

Returning to Toye's analysis of 1989, structural adjustment-related lending has experienced three major sets of problems from the viewpoint of the IFIs themselves. The first of these is that at least in the case of the World Bank, the increasing emphasis on conditionality has been in inverse relation to the magnitude of available assistance. Hence the Bank has faced the problem of demanding more while offering less. Naturally, the overall diminution of available external financial assistance may mean that even lower levels of World Bank funding will still command a high "rent" from recipients, but this has to be set against the fact that even the most committed recipient may not receive a level of funding adequate to finance the range of changes it has agreed to meet.

Another problem for the IFIs with structural adjustment conditionality-based lending has been the breadth of the changes it has sought to induce. Consider the list as of 1987 presented in the introduction, for example. Even with the will and the financial resources to undertake change on this scale, it is doubtful whether many governments *anywhere* in the world have the capacity to carry them out. It is worthwhile referring to Britain in this connection: despite a government firmly committed to a broad structural adjustment-type programme, with relatively sizable resources, without the pressure of conditionality and with a considerable degree of public support, "sectoral" reforms have proceeded only at a highly uneven pace, and were only beginning to reach the health sector, for example, a decade after Thatcher's first election victory.

Besides "policy overload" there are plainly further "design" problems of structural adjustment reforms which impede them working their own terms. Probably the most serious of these is that raised by Bernstein (1990) of current World Bank agricultural policies, namely their extreme inflexibility and narrowness relative to the breadth and variety of conditions under which agriculture is carried out in Africa and which constrain its responses to "reform". According to Bernstein wide variations in environmental conditions, social relations of production and labour processes, forms of integration into markets and social divisions of labour are simply unamenable to a set of policy changes which are all variations of a single "pricist" theme.

A final, and for the IFIs particularly sensitive issue, is that of deliberate conditionality default. One aspect of this question is that the main objective of recipients agreeing to reforms will usually be to obtain funds. Commitment to reforms which clash with policy preferences and/or vested interests is therefore bound to be low.

There are several well-known cases of systematic "reform-default" in Africa in the 1980s. Zambia is probably the best-known since it was made a lesson of on these grounds; Zaire and Kenya, for whom US security considerations prevail, are equally guilty despite actually being presented as "successes" by the Bank. The latter examples illustrate one aspect of what has been called "reverse leverage": the IFIs are obliged to permit non-observance since there are reasons other than policy reform alone for their involvement with recipients. In addition, the IFIs themselves recognise that deliberate default is more likely to occur, and may even be domestically politically popular, if reforms are perceived as having been externally imposed. Again, the IFIs may have an interest in allowing partial default in order to avoid complete confrontation with recipients and hence the threat of total loss of influence.

By the late 1980s there were clear direct and indirect reflections of many of these problems within the donor community, together with a diverse series of views and suggestions about how they might be resolved. An interesting document in this connection is the 1989 World Bank Report *Sub-Saharan Africa: From Crisis to Sustainable Growth*, which performs an intellectual balancing act between acknowledging that economic conditions in Sub-Saharan Africa have deteriorated sharply in the 1980s, and claiming that structural adjustment has been a success. As such it has to address, at least indirectly, the question of why the structural adjustment framework has proved an inadequate instrument of stabilisation in some countries at least. This question is itself approached in two quite different ways within the Report. On the one hand the document contains an analysis of the "resistance" of African countries to economic reform in terms of the nature of the typical African state form. On the other hand it embodies a revised reform agenda which indirectly suggests a location of the problem in the nature of the typical donor-recipient relation of the 1980s.

The first of these perspectives is articulated through a line of argument on the African state developed by the same group of American political scientists as mentioned in the introduction of this paper. Thomas Callaghy, Richard Sklar and Larry Diamond have in the past half decade postulated that the problem of the African state is not its external "capture" by interest groups existing independently of it *à la* Lipton but the fact that it has itself become the main source of group- and class-formation in African societies. Further, this process occurs less through direct "over-provision" of state services and more through the normative institutionalisation within the state of criminally corrupt forms of recycling revenue: " in the majority of African states political corruption is manifestly the primary mechanism of dominant class formation" (Diamond, 1987). As a result classes are defined not by their economic location but their relation to the state, "power replaces effort as a basis of social reward" (ibid.) and "apolitical" economic activity becomes in effect irrational. As has been already seen, in Diamond's own view this need not entirely impede economic development, especially under structural adjustment, where the legitimisation of parallel activities could lead to "normal" bourgeois class formation. In turn, this same process should lead to political change. The 1989 World Bank report reverses these conclusions. Parallel activities seem to be seen as reinforcing the "crony" state rather than undermining it, and political change in the state form itself is viewed as a precondition of economic development.

> Underlying the litany of Africa's development problems is a crisis of governance. Because countervailing power has been lacking, state officials in many countries have served their own interests without fear of being called to account. In self-defence individuals have built up personal networks of influence rather than hold the all-powerful state accountable for its systematic failures. In this way politics becomes personalised and patronage becomes essential to maintain power. The leadership assumes broad discretionary authority and loses its legitimacy. Information is controlled and voluntary associations are co-opted or disbanded. *This environment cannot ... support a dynamic economy ...*
> ... The rule of law needs to be established ... this implies rehabilitation of the judicial system, independence for the judiciary, scrupulous respect for the law and human rights ... transparent accounting of public monies ... Independent institutions are necessary to ensure public accountability. (World Bank, 1989a:60–61, 192 emphasis added)

What is not explained is where such a political transformation might come from, given that for anyone "inside" the system it would be non-rational.

The second line of reasoning evident in the 1989 report is of a considerably more upbeat character. This sets out from the assumption that a key role has been played in both African economic failure and the breakdown on conditionality lending by inappropriate relations developing between donors and African states. In particular, problems have emanated from the fact that the main links in this relationship comprised only conditionality-based muscle-flexing by donors.

This strand of the 1989 Report asserts the continuing validity of the specific economic policy recommendations of Berg (devaluation, wage restraint, fiscal discipline and "rolling back the state" from productive activity (ibid., 186) plus an agenda for reconstructing the donor-recipient relation via a complex process involving "policy dialogue", political concessions on the part of the IFIs and "consensus forming" behind a programme which combines the main IFI objectives with one or two espoused by African states themselves.

This in turn is supposed to give rise to these states "owning" (taking real as well as formal responsibility for) the theory and practice of structural adjustment. "Policy dialogue" in this context is seen as an alternative to "unhelpful distancing"; the political concessions in question, or at least those described in the 1989 Report, are "social programmes" and are clearly meant to serve as tokens of IFI good faith in "genuine dialogue". "Consensus forming" involves the formation of a pro-IFI cadre by *in situ* "education" in the process of policy dialogue, rather than by external training alone. "Ownership" serves as an alternative to the one-sided imposition of conditionality.

Merely implicit in the 1989 Report, this agenda is explicit in the study of its relations with the Tanzanian government which the World Bank published in 1990, which observes *inter alia*

> The failure of the Bank to get Tanzania to undertake prompt reforms, even when the Bank's ability to use leverage must have been at its maximum, was due partly to the absence of a political consensus in favour of reform within Tanzania and partly to the fact that Tanzania was lacking in the ability to design and undertake policy reform. The Bank's appreciation of the delicacy of the political situation and its effort to help Tanzania improve its policy reform capability have been the hallmarks of the phase of maturity in recent relations. (World Bank, 1990a: ix)

As well as the two distinct emphases in the interpretation of the history of adjustment/conditionality-based lending evident in the 1989 Report, a third current position within the donor community may also be detected. This represents a kind of half way house, arguing that the problem of recalcitrance or slippage by African states is amenable to the frameworks already developed by the IFIs, but that these require the addition of stronger conditionality, greater selectivity, greater employment of "track records" in evaluating requests for assistance and greater consistency and coordination between donors (e.g. Lankester,1990).

Problems which donors have experienced in ensuring that adjustment works have been accompanied by an implicit vote of no confidence both in African governments *and* attempts to reform them, on the part of transnational capital. While the IFIs were claiming that the 1980s had been a period of at least stabilisation in a majority of Sub-Saharan African countries, with supposed correspondingly improved conditions for private investment, British companies at least exhibited a significant trend toward disinvestment. The study by Bennell (1990) which established this trait furthermore argued that British investors in Africa had actually come to view structural adjustment negatively, as devaluation reduced the hard currency value of their profit remittances and of their investments, while trade liberalisation sometimes threatened the entire viability of their companies, particularly in the industrial sector. Arguably any such loss of credibility on the part of structural adjustment creates a space for the consideration of other means of differentiating countries as sites for potential investment. In fact, one could even say "any" other means. Given the general tendency of investors to view existing political systems in Africa as serious impediments to business, it is predictable that strong signals of determination to install western-style state forms should be attractive both to investors and some potential recipients of investment. It is in this context (although not only in this context) that "political conditionality" has become seriously entertained as an alternative or at least additional criterion for lending and investment.

The remainder of this section of the discussion will be devoted to a couple of brief observations about "political conditionality" as a new paradigm for lending and investment. One is that political conditionality at least potentially implies a further reduction in autonomy for the IFIs relative to donor governments. The "agenda" of political conditionality, although it fills a vacuum partly of the IFIs' own making, derives almost entirely from politicians. In the EC it appears to have emanated from the Council of Ministers in the autumn of 1989. From here it found its way into the Lomé 4 Treaty (which also enshrined structural adjustment as a feature of EC lending, see Parfitt and Bullock, 1990), before resurfacing in a statement by François Mitterand in May 1990 as the main principle henceforth governing bilateral relations between France and its former African colonies (*Financial Times*, 13 August, 1990). The same month and in June 1990, key speeches by the (then) British Chancellor (John Major) and Foreign Secretary (Douglas Hurd) suggested that the IMF link future lending to the Third World to recipients' "cuts in military spending, movement to democratic political systems and tackling problems like health, education and birth control" (*Guardian*, 11 May, 1990). Hurd stated "political pluralism, respect for the rule of law, human rights and market principles would bring donor support" (*Guardian*, 7 June, 1990). A similar pattern is evident in the U.S. and other donors. On the other hand, the donors retain the unilateral right to determine which undemocratic practices are acceptable and which are unacceptable. The British view, for example, has been that the absence of democracy is unacceptable in Somalia and Sudan but perfectly fine in Kenya.

The IFIs have little option but to take on board these concerns, although undoubtedly they have reservations about them. These are firstly theoretical, in that "multipartyist" political conditionality clashes with traditional and revised IFI-sponsored wisdom on the appropriate political conditions under which economic policy reforms work best (in this wisdom the most positive thing that is said about democracy is that it "slows things down" (cf. Griffith-Jones, 1990, Nelson, 1990a). A second set of reservations is technical, in that the drift of IFI thinking on conditionality design has been toward favouring easily monitorable performance indicators to which political conditionality presents severe problems. A third set of reservations is pragmatic, in the sense that political conditionality is perceived as a probable source of "conditionality overloading" for recipients, endangering the economic policy reform agenda (Nelson, 1990b). It remains to be seen how the IFIs themselves "adjust" to the new agenda and to what extent these reservations are translated into "slippage" by them.

A final general observation is that while political conditionality is in most respects a new paradigm for lending relative to structural adjustment, it also embodies considerable continuities with at least elements of what preceded it. As the quotation from Douglas Hurd cited above indicates, there is no intention to *abandon* structural adjustment. Rather, its status has become redefined as one object of conditionality amongst others. In addition, "political conditionality" directly takes up the pessimistic strand of argument deriving from Callaghy, Sklar and Diamond, adopted by some "structural adjusters" themselves and present within the Bank's 1989 Report. Both this report and Mitterand, Hurd, Major, etc. share a preoccupation with eliminating "bad government". This suggests in turn some broader continuities. "Political conditionality" after all "only" insists on the imposition of an *additional* tier of political forms and institutions alongside current western economic policies and "rational legal" technocratic administrative apparatuses. As such, it is only an *additional* tier of conditionality, a third stage following macroeconomic policy conditionality and sectoral policy conditionality. Adapting the "hardheaded" IFI position, it would seem that not only is aid "addictive", this may actually be equally true of conditionality.

STRUCTURAL ADJUSTMENT AND INTERNAL CONSTITUENCIES FOR MULTIPARTYISM

The last aspect of the structural adjustment–multipartyism relation to be considered is the most obvious and the most concrete, namely that of the extent to which structural adjustment may have created domestic political conditions favouring multipartyism within Sub-Saharan African countries. Discussion of this issue should involve more than a test of the hypothesis advanced by the group of American political scientists which was described in the introduction. Pressures for multipartyism may come from sources other than "liberated" bourgeoisies—indeed, if European experience is anything to go by, bourgeoisies are one of the less likely social forces to lead bourgeois revolutions. More fundamentally, Diamond's hypothesis begs a preliminary question whose answer must be sought before further progress can be made. What precise social changes have actually been associated with structural adjustment? This question relates in turn to the issues of the forms taken by structural adjustment in specific countries and thereby to the circumstances under which structural adjustment was adopted.

This section will seek to derive some general answers to these questions through a review of case studies of the politics of structural adjustment and the subsequent politics of multipartyism in four Sub-Saharan countries: Mozambique, Tanzania, Zambia and Ghana. They have been chosen on the subjective and arbitrary grounds that the information available on them to the author was more up-to-date than for other countries in the region. This is not to say that this information is necessarily comprehensive or even reliable, nor is it based on personal field work. It is acknowledged that the generalisability of the conclusions offered will be clearly limited by these conditions. The case studies take the form of brief narratives of events in the countries concerned during the phase of structural adjustment and in the process of current political change.

Mozambique

After an unsuccessful attempt to join COMECON, Mozambique became a member of the IMF in 1984. This represented a response to the overwhelming financial problems which had arisen from the breakdown of national commercial and transport networks between 1981 and 1984, and was coupled with a peace agreement with South Africa intended to remove a major source of this breakdown. Following membership Mozambique initiated a series of deregulatory reforms, receiving in exchange a US\$ 45 m import reconstruction credit (Loxley, 1987). In 1987 these reforms were extended and consolidated into a fully-fledged structural adjustment programme (PRE). The content of the PRE appears to have emanated directly from the IFIs, although it has been publicly "owned" by Frelimo. Although Frelimo had expressed a deepening self-criticism of state productive sector-led development since 1983, PRE would clearly not have been undertaken if the Mozambican government had not been deprived of alternative sources of domestic and external sources of revenue, and had it not required continued debt relief.

PRE has involved replacing administrative controls with price incentives, restructuring agriculture, industry, banking and other public enterprises and reviving the use of fiscal and monetary policy to curb inflation and stabilise the balance of payments. About 20,000 workers were retrenched in the public sector (*Mozambique File*, Dec. 1990). Interest rates were raised sharply, public expenditure cut and the metical has been devalued from US\$ 1:39 to US\$ 1:1300. A Ugandan-style complete deregulation of forex has also been adopted.

The programme has been a limited success in narrow economic terms. The economy has grown at about 1 per cent per capita per annum for the period 1987–89, largely due to increased food production and improved capacity utilisation in manufacturing. Even so, industrial output remained at only 50 per cent of its 1980 level, 90 per cent of food grains were imported and since 1988 exports have failed to respond—actually falling 10 per cent in 1989 (*FT*, 26 April, 1990) and further since. Furthermore, the reforms have been enormously inflationary; according to Hermele (1990) the urban price/wage index grew between 150 and 300 per cent between January 1987 and January 1989. The urban food rationing was effectively withdrawn in April 1988, while massive rent increases were introduced in the state housing sector early in 1991.

Hermele (ibid.) describes the most visible aspects of PRE's social impact as being the legitimisation of unofficial and parallel economic activity, a severe deterioration of conditions amongst urban workers, salaried employees and—worst of all—rural refugees in urban areas, strikes in the formal sector and "overcrowding" in the informal sector, and an intensified struggle for land for food production in peri-urban areas. Less hard information is available on "winners" although it seems probable that these are confined to a small group of traders, larger farmers, private entrepreneurs and corrupt officials.

In the view of both Hermele and Marshall (1990), the main political effects of PRE have been to relocate Frelimo's principal base outside the country to the donor community. This is said to be reflected both in the transparently external control of economic policy and the increasing displacement of state institutions by bilateral agency-funded NGOs. Until the slowdown in military operations of 1990 the military situation reflected a similar process, with increased dependence on foreign (principally Zimbabwean) troops in the war against Renamo.

The initiative for democratisation in Mozambique comes from the dominant tendency within Frelimo, which also appears to be its main constituency. This initiative, announced in 1990, represents a sharp break with Frelimo's tradition—which from 1977 until 1989 was as a self-proclaimed vanguard party within a one-party state. However, since its 1989 Fifth Congress Frelimo has described itself as a "party of the whole people" whose immediate aim is not socialism but the development of a broad national consensus (Hermele, ibid.:30–31).

The content of Frelimo's democratisation initiative involves a formal renunciation of its claim to a monopoly of power, a commitment to a multiparty system (provided that parties could demonstrate that they are democratic, non-regional, non-ethnic and non-religious), a statement of preference for a multiparty coalition government and a change in the country's name from "People's Republic" to "Republic" (*Guardian*, 2 August and 17 August, 1990). This platform of democratisation is distinguishable from, and explicable mainly in relationship to the programme of free elections, shared state power and restoration of the powers of local chiefs which Renamo developed as a bargaining position during the spring of 1989 in preparation for the first round of Frelimo–Renamo peace negotiations (*Africa Confidential*, Vol. 30, No. 13, 1989). While formally proposing free elections, the Renamo platform in essence envisaged a "consultative" movement toward a power-sharing arrangement involving Frelimo and Renamo alone, in which elections "were not an indispensable element" (*Africa Confidential*, Vol. 30, No 23, 1989). This qualification is partly connected with Renamo's refusal to recognize the claims of other exile groups to party status.

Once announced, however, the shift toward multipartyism in Mozambique achieved a rapidity and apparent irreversibility from other sources. One has been the emancipated Mozambican media, which has not only vigourously proclaimed its own freedom from Frelimo control but has focused attention on every other instance of democratic development. The other has been an apparent decision by the Mozambican government to make a virtue of necessity by pursuing democratisation at a pace and with a seriousness designed to give it a comparative advantage with donors. Mozambique has been relatively unique in eastern and southern Africa in proclaiming a new constitution (in November 1990) enshrining multipartyism, press freedom, trade union freedom and abolition of all internal controls on physical movement. However, similarly to Eastern Europe, a major feature of the emerging democratic order has been the appearance of openly regionalist and racist political forces—both within Frelimo itself and in the new opposition parties like Palmo.

During 1990 Mozambique experienced a major strike wave, which together with the changes just described, led to a separation of the trade union movement OTM from the state. Between the spring of 1990 and November that year, strikes involving 42,000 workers occurred in 59 work-places (*Mozambique File*, Dec 1990). In almost all cases the issues raised were those of wages and managerial corruption. Strikes continued during early 1991 in the media, manufacturing, transport, construction and also the state farm sector, with an undiminishingly militant character. Few if any explicitly political demands seem to have been raised by the strikers, and in general the strike movement appears to be more a response to the increasingly acute situation for wage earners and loosening state control than an attempt to intervene in the democratisation process. Neither workers as such, nor any other identifiable social group have been associated with Frelimo's democratisation initiative.

Tanzania

After largely supportive relations with the IFIs from independence until the mid-1970s, resistance by the Tanzanian government to key economic stabilisation measures suggested by the IMF and the World Bank led to a virtual severance of ties between 1979 and 1982 (World Bank, 1990 (a):vi–vii; Wangwe, 1987:151). While from 1982 to August 1986 Tanzania had no agreement with either of the IFIs, it gradually moved toward their positions as it became evident that further assistance from other sources would be denied it. In 1983–84 a home grown structural adjustment package emerged, followed in 1985 by the retirement of Julius Nyerere from the Presidency and in 1986 by a devaluation of the shilling from US\$ 1:17 to US\$ 1:32. Agreement with the IFIs was then reached and a Bank-sponsored "Economic Recovery Plan" (ERP) launched. This had a content much the same as Mozambique's PRE, and has resulted in a further devaluation of the shilling to US\$ 1:225 (1991).

The results of ERP in Tanzania also bear a broad resemblance to those of PRE. Per capita GDP is said to have grown at about 1 per cent per annum between 1987 and 1989 and the World Bank claims that industrial capacity utilisation has risen from around 25 per cent to 38 per cent (World Bank, 1990 (b):29, 6). In the same period this claim refers to, recorded production fell of all major manufactured goods except cement and soap. In the export crop sector, cotton production rose but production of other crops has stagnated or fallen. There have been substantial increases in official purchases of the main food crops (EIU Quarterly Reports on Tanzania, various). Overall, exports grew by 16.7 per cent in 1987, 6.2 per cent in 1988 and 9.2 per cent in 1989 (World Bank, 1990 (b):29). Aggregate export earnings still remain only about half of those in good years before the crisis of the late 1970s, however and imports have grown rather more rapidly. Meanwhile, financial performance has continued to deteriorate, resulting in a further weakening of the external position. The current account deficit grew from US\$ 397 m (1986) to US\$ 841 m (1989) (World Bank, 1990 (b), ibid.). Domestic inflation has continued to climb by about 30 per cent per annum during the programme (ibid.).

While reliable figures are not available for urban real wage levels, most estimates indicate a real fall of over 60 per cent over the last decade, which has not been reversed under adjustment. Knock-on effects on the informal sector have been strong (Rugumisa speaks of a "mushrooming of moonlighting", 1990:11.). The picture with regard to the social sector is at best one of a stabilization of expenditure at post-independence lows, alongside "user charges" and/or increased "voluntary" contributions. Little published work is available on rural areas, but what there is (Rugumisa, 1990; Booth, 1990) appears to suggest that improved levels of marketed output are more the result of a response to the greater availability of imported incentive goods than to improved producer prices.

Turning to the beneficiaries of structural adjustment, evidence is once again thin. What there is of it nonetheless suggests that aside from a small group of predominantly Asian "own forex" traders in Dar es Salaam, there is little sign of clear visible benefits. Describing small and medium sized capitalists engaged in agriculture, trade and manufacturing in the provincial centre of Iringa, Booth argues (ibid.) that the effects of ERP have been blunted by a combination of the rapid implementation of subsidy withdrawals with "slippage" in the implementation of higher producer prices, marketing reforms and price decontrol. Consequently provincial capital at least has found it difficult to maintain the levels of profit in the "competitive economy" which they obtained in the "rent-seeking" one.

With the commonly made link made between the retirement of Nyerere from the Presidency to Party chairmanship and the adoption of peace with the IFIs and ERP by the government under Mwinyi, some commentators (e.g. Maghimbe, 1990) have interpreted domestic politics between 1985 and 1990 in terms of a deepening conflict between the party and the government supported by pro-adjustment academic intellectuals (cf. Rugumisa, ibid.). Certainly, the party continues to maintain an unreconstructed Arusha Declaration-style economic policy in direct contradiction to ERP, and Nyerere has continued to denounce the IMF. As late as 1989 differences continued to be publicly expressed over ERP by heavy-weight politicians in a manner "surprising in a one-party state where major decisions have traditionally been reached by consensus" (Rugumisa, ibid.).

While in the early stages of public discussion on domestic forerunners of adjustment proper some contributors raised issues about political liberalisation, this strand of discussion was not pursued at any length (Shivji, 1986:12). When debate on multipartyism was eventually revived in February 1990 this occurred as a result of a surprising intervention by Nyerere himself, following an internal discussion within the ruling party, CCM. The erstwhile theorist of single-partyism now raised two main arguments for reviewing the necessity of the one-party system. Firstly CCM was "right now not close to the people ... (leaders) are closer to their offices and desks ... (they) seek leadership positions because of money involved.". A competitive party system would oblige the party and its leaders to be less complacent and renew itself by reviving its original relationship with the people. Secondly, the original reason for single partyism, namely the need to establish a common national identity, had now been largely attained and could anyway be safeguarded under multipartyism by outlawing regionalist or ethnic parties (*Sunday News*, 25 February, 1990, *Daily News*, 26 February, 1990).

Nyerere's observations stimulated a new public debate, which has been accompanied by other important developments in Tanzanian politics. During 1990 the main feature of this debate was an increasing alienation of CCM *and* government from intellectuals. While both party and government tended to defend "single-partyist" positions during this first phase of discussion, intellectuals solidly identified with democratisation and frequently linked opposition to democratisation with demands for the elimination of corruption. At this stage however, debate was still conducted almost wholly through official channels.

Since the beginning of 1991 a number of new features have emerged in the debate. The most important of these has been the eventually successful effort of some pro-multiparty forces to establish platforms for discussion outside of official channels. A variously-titled independent committee including figures from various previous phases and sources of opposition to CCM, succeeded in organizing public gatherings in favour of multipartyism before starting to fragment in mid-1991. A second trend has been for the government to appoint an official committee to make recommendations on the future of the country's political system, after having gathered evidence between April 1991 and 1992. A third trend has been for party and government to undertake some broader political "adjustments". These include dropping important parts of the leadership code, creating conditions for the partial separation of party from other mass organisations and the stimulation of an official "anti-corruption" crusade led by the Minister of Home Affairs, A. Mrema.

The amendments made to the leadership code at the Zanzibar NEC early in 1991 centered around breaking the (official) separation between party and government membership and private capitalist activity. While party and government "leaders" (level unspecified) remained unable to enjoy a second salary from business activities, those at lower levels of authority would henceforth be able to own shares, build houses for renting and take up private employment in addition to party functions. This was defended in terms of enabling the full participation of party members in economic life, but has been widely interpreted as a precondition for attracting large-scale private capital to support CCM.

Coupled with the "Zanzibar Declaration" has been an effort by CCM to effect a controlled separation between itself and the official Trade Union movement, Juwata. Juwata, Mwinyi announced in May 1991, would in the future "be given freedom to ... write (its) own constitution, conduct (its) own affairs and even (sic) chose (its) own leaders without be cleared by CCM" (BBC Summary of World Broadcasts, 6 May 1991).

Finally, a consistent trend since the middle of 1990 has been for economic liberalisation to be accompanied by an officially sponsored anti-corruption drive. This has been energetically led by the government itself and has mainly comprised "crackdowns" on illegal parallel market activity, such as unofficial artisanal mining, smuggling and selling the few consumer goods still subject to price control at higher than approved prices. It has largely steered clear of government and party targets, although some parastatals have been investigated.

Zambia

Repeated attempts at IFI-assisted stabilisation of the Zambian economy have occurred since the world price of copper began to fall in the 1970s, with no less than seven stabilisation and/or adjustment programmes being introduced between 1975 and 1986 alone (Ncube et al., 1987). These earlier programmes were normally aborted by government failure to meet basic financial targets, all resulted in increased debt and all were followed by stronger conditionality. Until

1983 most of the programmes were of a mainly demand-management character; subsequently they have included measures of devaluation, removal of domestic price controls, as well as the proposed privatisation of segments of the parastatal sector and more recently civil service retrenchments and a revised investment code. A significant layer of leading Zambian opinion, particularly within UNIP, government and the parastatals, has been opposed to these programmes throughout (Kydd, 1989:135). But "rising debt (has) meant that pressure to pay attention to critics in the IMF, World Bank and the more right-wing governments became progressively more difficult to resist" (ibid., 129).

Two measures within post-1983 programmes have provoked particular conflict, both between the Zambian government and the IFIs, and between the Zambian government and sections of its own domestic constituency. The first of these was the abolition of administrative control of foreign exchange in favour of an auction system, coupled with import liberalisation. First attempted in 1985, this led within a year to a devaluation of the kwacha from US\$ 1:5 to US\$ 1:15 and an associated shake out in the previously highly protected manufacturing sector (Ncube, ibid.: Appendix VIII). The second has been the proposal to withdraw maize meal subsidies. In December 1986, this proposal led to riots in the Copperbelt and Lusaka in which more than 20 people were killed. Even prior to this it was clear that the programme was failing to meet its own targets. The period 1983–87 was one in which GDP per capita actually fell by 2 per cent per annum (Loxley, 1990). (Other estimates put the fall greater than this.)

The government responded to the December 1986 riots by restoring the subsidy and terminating the structural adjustment programme. A "home-grown" programme of a considerably less stringent kind was substituted. By 1988–89 this was itself in disarray, largely because of the escalating burden of maize meal subsidies on government expenditure. Dialogue with the Bank was resumed, the "anti-devaluation" head of the Bank of Zambia whom Kaunda had appointed in 1986 was removed and the general maize meal subsidy phased out in favour of a targeted subsidy-ration system for the urban poor.

A new arrangement with the IMF was eventually arrived at midway through 1990. Although broadly resembling earlier IMF-WB programmes, the new "Economic Recovery Programme" (ERP) generated no new additional resources from the IMF. Instead, Zambia received a share of the IMF's new "Rights Accumulation Programme", linking progressive debt forgiveness for "successful" adjustment implementations. Eventually the country will again become eligible for an Enhanced Structural Adjustment Facility loan. In the meantime, the adoption of ERP led to the Paris Club helping Zambia to clear its US\$ 200 mn arrears with the Bank, roll over US\$ 2 bn worth of its own debts, and promise US\$ 500 mn in balance of payments support (*Africa Report*, March–April 1991). By September 1991 this arrangement also had broken down, apparently as a result of a continued government failure to remove remaining maize subsidies.

In Zambia structural adjustment of both IFI-led and home-grown varieties has borne down most heavily on smaller rural maize producers (who were also net beneficiaries of the maize subsidy) and on the urban poor. Formal sector employment fell by 10 per cent from 1975–88 (Reinikka-Soininen, 1990:57) and real wages fell over the same period by 50–66 per cent (ibid.). With the proportion of urban households under the Poverty Datum Line rising from 35 per cent in 1985 to 55 per cent in 1987 (ibid.: 61) and with an official inflation rate 1987–89 the second highest in Africa at 55 per cent per annum (UNECA, 1990:A1) Zambia's economic situation is particularly acute. Some dispute exists as to whether any sections of the urban population have benefitted from the structural adjustment which has occurred, except perhaps importers.

The most important political feature of the Zambian situation over the last decade has been the manner in which adjustment has created the conditions for a powerful opposition movement to arise, despite the fact that this movement has been more consistently pro-adjustment than UNIP. UNIP, on the other hand, became increasingly unpopular whether it supported adjustment or not.

The corner-stone of the Zambian opposition movement has been the trade union federation, ZCTU. This has from the 1970s articulated a position that could be regarded as "business unionist" (cf. Getzel, 1984:90–95). Throughout it has called for relaxation of restrictions on foreign investment and private capital generally and for privatisation of state enterprises. But alongside this it has defended the principle of independent trade unionism and called for higher wages and the maintenance of consumer subsidies. Thus in

1986–87, ZCTU opposed the removal of the maize subsidy while supporting certain other aspects of the adjustment package (see Kydd, 1989:135).

ZCTU actually first publicly raised the demand for a return to multiparty democracy in Zambia following an unsuccessful attempt by UNIP to bring the organisation to heel by promoting a faction within ZCTU who would have agreed to its incorporation with UNIP (*AC*, Vol. 31, No. 9, 1990). Simultaneously UNIP also failed in a parallel attempt to tighten single party control, when in Parliament a new Constitution Bill which would have given the UNIP party conference the right to select a sole presidential candidate and a UNIP Control Commission the right to oversee applications, promotions and dismissals in the Civil Service, failed to obtain the requisite two-thirds majority. In response to these events Kaunda called a UNIP National Council late in March 1990 (*Africa Confidential*, No. 11, 1990). Reportedly shaken by the negative reaction from the floor, and in an apparent effort to regain the initiative, he proposed a referendum on multiparty democracy. The decision was finally announced in May.

Public opposition to UNIP and support for multipartyism widened during and after the urban riots of June 1990, which followed further attempts to withdraw of the maize meal subsidy. The riots coincided with a coup attempt and provided the occasion for a broad section of public opinion including "students, trade unions, the church, private businessmen (most of whom were once in the government ...) ... and many professionals ... to (challenge) the ... status quo" (*Financial Times*, 27 June, 1990).

A turning point in the developing conflict was the unexpected decision of the commission which Kaunda had set up to organize the referendum to recommend that supporters of multipartyism should have the freedom to organize and campaign through the media (*FT*, 18 July, 1990). This lifted the de facto ban on political opposition in force since 1973. The following week a National Interim Committee for Multiparty Democracy, later renamed Movement for Multiparty Democracy (MMD) was launched. MMD's leadership was composed of ZCTU leaders including Frederick Chiluba as well as ex-cabinet ministers and former notables of the pre-1973 parties (*Guardian*, 24 July, 1990). Kaunda subsequently unveiled a number of measures designed to weaken support for MMD, including an amnesty for those involved in the coup attempts of 1980, 1988 and 1990, a postponement (later cancellation) of the referendum, and the internal democratisation of UNIP. None succeeded in breaking the momentum of MMD's development which also easily overcame sporadic attempts at repression and was expressed in huge popular rallies, large numbers of defections from UNIP and (in the spring of 1991) a transition to a party form of organisation.

By the middle of 1991 the Zambian political situation was characterised by a number of relatively serious strikes (including one on the Tazara railways) as workers gained confidence to take on the government, and increasingly wide oscillations by Kaunda on adjustment issues. On 24 April 1991, for example, the President was reported to have declared that MMD's support for the privatisation and break-up of the copper parastatal ZCCM would lead to redundancies. UNIP on the other hand "would keep all mines open if returned". Six days later he was reported as stating that the government would not bail out parastatals failing to meet competition under economic liberalisation (*BBC Summary of World Broadcasts*, April 24, April 30 1991). Chiluba, on the other hand, maintained his own ambiguity by supporting the strikes while observing that "Zambia's current economic problems were a result of measures being postponed, delayed and manipulated for short-term political gain ..." (*Africa Economic Digest*, 11 March 1991). No political forces could any longer be identified which systematically opposed adjustment, any more than any could be found which supported every aspect of it.

Ghana

Like Zambia, Ghana suffered a severe economic crisis dating from the early 1970s involving declining export earnings, serious budgetary problems and rapidly falling per capita incomes. From the overthrow of Nkrumah onwards it also suffered a high degree of political instability, with a succession of military coups culminating in the "second coming" of Jerry Rawlings in December 1981.

At first the Rawlings regime leaned distinctively to the left. His People's National Defence Council (PNDC) government contained a number of Marxist intellectuals and sought to mobilize the support of the working-class and urban poor through support for a series of "popular democratic" institutions and reforms. Yet other than by enforcing rigid price controls for mass consumption goods it seems that Rawlings had no clear economic policy and throughout 1982 the fiscal, budgetary and general economic situations continued to deteriorate. According to Hansen (1987) the acute state of the crisis led eventually to a governmental consensus (even including the Marxists) that a significant injection of liquidity was a precondition for any form of economic change and development. Left and right divided only over the preferability of public and private assistance with the left ironically being at the fore of opening discussions with the IFIs (ibid.:197). By early 1983 an Economic Rehabilitation Plan (ERP 1) was drawn up by the Secretary for Finance and Economic Planning, in conjunction with the IFIs. The left's objections to it led to their departure from the government.

ERP 1 embodied a combination of standard IFI prescriptions, some more draconian versions of these prescriptions, and some counter-balancing populist elements (e.g. a selective price control policy). Devaluation and reduction in public expenditure were particularly harsh, while producer price increases were particularly high. In 1987 ERP 2 was introduced. This provided for further producer price increases financed out of further devaluation (6,000 per cent 1983–88) as well as a broad programme of deregulation and privatisation. ERPs 1 and 2 have been supported by approximately US$ 3 bn in loans and grants by donors, the largest amount for any Sub-Saharan African country in the 1980s. In 1990–91 ERP 3 replaced ERP 2. Its main focuss is to be civil service, state enterprise and cocoa sector restructuring, based on rather lower levels of new money (*West Africa*, 21 Jan. 1991).

Both with regard to level of implementation and macroeconomic outturn, adjustment in Ghana has been amongst Africa's more successful—at least until around 1989. GDP per capita increased by about 2 per cent per annum 1983–87, marketed cocoa production increased by about one third 1982–86 (Commander et al., 1989:111), inflation fell from over 50 per cent per annum in the early 1980s to 13.5 per cent in 1988–89 (ECA:A1) while domestic deficit financing was eliminated and revenue collection increased sharply. In 1989 and 1990 however, per capita growth was zero, while inflation climbed first to 25 per cent (1989) and then to 37 per cent (1990) (*West Africa*, 21 Jan. 1991).

Evidence on the social effects of Ghanaian adjustment is mixed, but generally negative. Loxley (1990) states that real wages of urban workers and salaried employees rose sharply (albeit from historically extremely low bases) between 1983 and 1986. At the end of 1990 it was officially conceded that the minimum wage still covered only 20–25 per cent of basic needs requirements (*West Africa*, 24 December 1990). Unemployment of former public sector workers grew sharply as 15000 per annum were laid off between 1986 and 1988 (Commander et al., 111) although this rate of retrenchment has subsequently slowed. A visible deterioration occurred in government services, health facilities virtually ceased to exist and basic infrastructure has remained in poor shape. The benefits of the cocoa boom were confined to the geographically segregated cocoa zone of the West and Central Regions and even here most benefits accrued only to large farmers (ibid.:125). Despite the boom, cocoa production has remained well below the levels of the late 1970s while much of the increase which has occurred is said to have been attributable to changes in regional smuggling patterns. Furthermore, marketed food production actually dropped 20 per cent during 1984–86 as that of cocoa rose (Loxley, 1990). The apparently common phenomenon of greater competition and decreasing returns to labour in the informal sector has also been repeated. Little or no discussion appears to be available on who might have benefitted from adjustment, other than the larger export crop farmers described by Commander et al.

Given the apparently favourable macroeconomic, as opposed to social, record of the Rawlings regime, the low level of new foreign investment in Ghana is of considerable interest. Genuinely new foreign investment during the 1980s is said to have shown no tendency to rise as the decade progressed except towards the end of the decade in the mining sector. The IFIs seem to have blamed this on the Rawlings regime and more particularly on Rawlings personally. Together with the falling off in economic recovery already described this appears to have contributed to a growing disillusion with the "Ghanaian miracle" from early 1990.

Popular disillusion with Rawlings of course dates back much longer. Efforts by the government in the early 1980s to establish and/or support popular democratic institutions bypassing the existing courts and trade unions had long since alienated the Ghanaian TUC, the Churches, the Bar Association and the Association of

Registered Professional Bodies. At the time, the opposition of these forces was largely neutralised by the popular support which Rawlings enjoyed from the unorganised urban poor. In 1988–89 Rawlings made a second attempt to introduce a popular constitutional dispensation which bypassed the traditional institutional forms, when he initiated a system of elected but non-party district assemblies (*Africa Report*, July–August 1989). These District Assemblies brought together the PNDC's own cadres with local chiefs and representatives of local professional groups. Their relative success administratively does not appear to have provided Rawlings with a new base, however. Renewed opposition emerged in which Rawlings' opponents of the early 1980s were supported by the Ghanaian Students' Union, while workers and the poor failed to rally around the government. Under pressure from the IFIs, Rawlings was obliged to concede a public debate on the future of democracy in Ghana.

The immediate effect of the launch of the public debate in July 1990 was to permit broader and more coordinated support to emerge for multipartyism. On 24 July 1990 the Kwame Nkrumah Revolutionary Guard (KNRG), one of the left groups initially closely associated with Rawlings (Hansen, 1987) came out in favour of the release of all political prisoners, pluralism and the election of a constituent assembly to draw up a new constitution (*Africa Confidential*, No. 17, 1990). At the beginning of August a "Movement for Freedom and Justice" (MFJ) was founded, demanding a referendum on multiparty government. MFJ was led by prominent academics and lawyers, as well as by at least one of the leaders of the KNRG while its middle rank cadres were said to include former professional politicians of the Nkrumah and Busia eras (ibid.). According to both *Africa Confidential* and *Financial Times*, further support for MFJ came from Accra's "business and diplomatic communities" (*Africa Confidential*, ibid., *Financial Times*, 22 August, 1990).

The response of the Rawlings regime to MFJ and pressures for democratisation has, like Kaunda's, vacillated between continued pursuit of PNDC's political agenda, repression and concessions. Rawlings has particularly defiantly defended the "right" of the military to "participate in politics" (describing civilian government as a "colonial legacy" (*BBC Summary of World Broadcast*, 3 Jan. 1991)) and has sought to extend the District Assembly system and establish new mass organizations tied to PNDC, for example, the Ghanaian

National Association of Farmers and Fishermen (cf. *West Africa*, 22 April 1991). Meanwhile, MFJ leaders have been subject to regular harassment and the public debate on democratisation was officially wound up in January 1991 with the decision to ask the national Commission for Democracy (which had sponsored the District Assembly system) to look into the future of Ghana's political system. The latter's report, when published, was non-committal and ano҈ dyne. Yet over the same period growing pressures from popular organisations and from donors led to Rawlings having to eventually concede *some* form of democratic change. A "National Consultative Body" on a new constitution, despite being mainly composed of PNDC direct and indirect nominees, was asked by the government to make provision for the formation of parties. Precisely what "partyist" dispensation is intended remains to be seen.

THE INTERNAL POLITICS OF ADJUSTMENT

The final section of this paper will try to sum up and interpret the material described in the case studies, in order to supplement an "external" understanding of adjustment politics with an "internal" one. Three main issues will be focused on in this summing up: how adjustment appears to have impacted on different populations, the circumstances and sources from which "democratisation" has emerged, and the distinguishing conditions of strong popular movements for democratisation.

Adjustment (or, more properly, the stabilisation measures which have normally accompanied adjustment) have everywhere impacted negatively on levels of public service provision. Part of this impact has been the direct result of budgetary restrictions or reductions. Part has been the result of the informalisation process within public service institutions, whereby salaried and wage earning employees have increasingly resorted to moonlighting in order to make ends meet—thus leaving these institutions continuing to exist rather than to function. The results of this have been unevenly distributed with regard to social groups. Peasants, most of whom enjoyed only restricted access to these institutions in the first place, have been relatively weakly effected by their disintegration. At the other end of the spectrum, students—who are totally dependent on the quality of public service provision—have been extremely strongly affected. In both cases, of course, the impact of declines in provision will be subject to blunting depending on the degree of deterioration which existed prior to adjustment.

Besides those highly dependent on public service provision, another population severely effected by adjustment has been those heavily dependent for their reproduction on subsidised consumer and producer inputs. These groups include most of the urban poor, a relatively thin band of peasant producers and some proprietors in import substituting industries. Again, the actual impact of the withdrawal of subsidies would be more or less harsh depending on the extent to which they had already become eroded, either in monetary terms or through non-availability of the subsidised items themselves.

A third population which has been severely hit by adjustment and stabilisation has been those who are primarily dependent on public sector incomes, which of course have everywhere been allowed to float down to levels inadequate for reproduction. As already noted, the principal response of workers to this trend has been for them to "informalise" themselves. This in turn has resulted in increased competition, and probably declining average returns to labour, in the informal sector generally. For most private formal sector workers the picture appears to be broadly similar, although it appears that both some industrial workers and miners in Ghana, and agricultural wage labour elsewhere (Gibbon, 1992) have managed to maintain or even improve on their (albeit historically disastrous) pre-adjustment position. Particular problems have been faced by private employers and employees in import substituting industries.

Despite the fact that agriculture has been the principal intended beneficiary of the adjustment exercise, it appears that in most of the countries described here agricultural growth has not exceeded the rate of economic growth generally. While some better capitalised farmers, particularly in Ghana and Zambia, seem to have been able to take advantage of new opportunities, smaller farmers have simply lacked the resources to do so. In the case of better capitalised farmers it is furthermore questionable how sustainable their recovery is; in Ghana at least it appeared to be slackening off by the end of the period. All peasants have benefitted to some degree from higher prices, better availability of incentive goods and (where introduced) better payment systems, but they have also had to cope with high levels of inflation and, as mentioned, higher input prices. There is no strong evidence that the overall agricultural terms of trade have improved.

Amongst the much smaller group of beneficiaries of adjustment, the most obvious appear to be importers—especially those with "own forex", some proprietors in the service sector—and, related to both phenomena, certain "parallel market" operators whose business operations have now become legitimised. Anecdotal evidence also suggests a degree of movement in the other direction, of members of the state bourgeoisie or party bourgeoisie into a wider range of "black", "grey" or even newly legitimate fields of business activities, as their traditional sources of income have been compromised and as new opportunities have opened up. In Tanzania and Mozambique, elements of the state bourgeoisie have diversified their activities into private trade; indeed in Tanzania the epithet "traders without licenses" has been collectively applied to them (Kiondo, 1988).

On a national comparative basis it would seem that the most profound relative change in living standards has been their downward revision in Zambia, which as late as the end of the 1970s was categorised by the World Bank as a middle-income country. Declines in living standards in Tanzania occurred from a lower base and were probably also more gradual. In Ghana it seems that the high level of funding enjoyed by the adjustment programme has meant that sufficient demand has been created for the living standards of certain popular groups to actually rise. Otherwise the beneficiaries from adjustment have been decidedly narrow in composition.

Turning to the question of the circumstances and sources of democratisation, two quite distinctive trends are evident. In Ghana and Zambia, initiatives for democratisation have come unambiguously from below, and have been at least temporarily strongly resisted from "above". By contrast, the original impetus for democratisation in Tanzania and Mozambique arose within the state apparatuses themselves, although in the case of Tanzania they were subsequently pursued with far more consistency by forces outside the state.

In Zambia, demands for democratisation arose initially from the trade union movement in response to efforts by the state to control its autonomy and subordinate it to the party. These efforts in turn seem to have arisen as the state sought to pass on a very high proportion of the costs of adjustment directly to the urban poor in the form of a withdrawal of the maize subsidy. While economic crisis and decline had severely eroded the economic bargaining power of the unions, they were still considered by the state a potential focus of more generalised protest against its policies. In the event, it turned out that the state lacked the power to bring the unions within its control. While its efforts were not marked by immediate massive popular protests, the failure emboldened opponents of both adjustment policies and other aspects of UNIP politics, and secured a leading role for the unions in ensuing democratic struggles.

In Ghana, a slightly more complex situation emerged. Here the state sought to use some of the goodwill generated by a relatively successful adjustment operation to consolidate a non-party form of political rule. The first step in this process was not to place further restrictions on civil society, but to seek to incorporate local level and partly neo-traditional elites into the state apparatus through introducing a new system of local government. The emergence of this proposal against a popular expectation of a return to civilian rule touched off opposition from a variety of organisations including students' unions, some trade unions, the Bar Association, the Association of Registered Professional Bodies and (episodically) the churches. Some of these constituencies also mobilised opposition to adjustment. Their collective impact was not on the Zambian scale, but they obliged the Rawlings government into a long-term abandonment of its "no-party" option.

In Tanzania and Mozambique, the confinement of organized support for multipartyism to elements within the state apparatus itself reflected the fact that virtually the only organized political forces in these countries were their governments. However, the debate about democratisation led to a loosening up of the political situation in which, in Tanzania at least, popular democratic forces have emerged. On the other hand, a probably more important trend not only in Mozambique but in Tanzania too has been the emergence of struggles around the impact of adjustment. Chissano's "opening from above" has witnessed a wave of strikes over deteriorating living conditions which has yet to see much carry-over into the political sphere (and meanwhile the newly founded opposition parties have been uninterested or unable to link up with these forces). Likewise, in Tanzania, probably the most important public struggle since Nyerere's intervention has been the continuing one at the University of Dar es Salaam. This emerged over protests about the institutions's physical dilapidation but took on more explicitly democratic dimensions as the state sought to clamp down on it in various ways. Even at this stage it did not broaden into a general display of pro-multiparty sentiment, however.

Since a strong popular movement for democratisation exists only in Zambia, distinguishing conditions for them have to be derived from the situation in this country alone. They would seem to include the presence of autonomous secular-democratic institutions outside of the state, widespread but hitherto unorganized popular animosity to state policies, and state efforts to contain this by repression. However, these conditions were also present within Ghana to some extent, implying that there were other factors at work in the Zambian case. Certain of these were probably matters of the extent of the population effected by adjustment and the sharpness with which they were effected. Some though seem to reflect broader differences between the *civil societies* of the two countries, i.e. its set of self-regulating social and political institutions providing focuses for social organization independent of the state. Zambia's "single-partified" civil society in most respects was more similar to Mozambique's and Tanzania's than that to Ghana's. With the *exception* of the unions, there were in fact few genuinely autonomous organizations of any kind (one might even doubt the real autonomy of the unions themselves). By contrast, civil society in Ghana was both more substantial and less dominated by unions, or indeed by secular-democratic institutions generally.

At this point, some tentative conclusions may be advanced concerning the relationship of adjustment and democratisation within the internal politics of adjustment. The first is that there seems to be no evidence to support the optimistic thesis of Diamond et al that the economic beneficiaries of adjustment will be "private bourgeois" and "democratic" and that their growing significance will give backbone to democratic trends. In fact, rather than approaching the issues through the predicted or actual behaviour of interest groups, a more useful procedure may be to look at the constraints which local ruling classes face as a result of adjustment and the subsequent options which are open to them on the one hand, and the character of civil society and the emergent prospects for autonomous democratic development on the other.

For this, it is necessary to introduce one or two new arguments and concepts and to refine others which have been used already in the exposition. The major argument which will be introduced is that alongside and related to dictatorial forms of political rule, the great majority of countries in Sub-Saharan Africa have been characterised during both colonial and post-colonial periods by modes of economic accumulation organized from "above". "Accumulation from above" means a form of state-organized and coordinated extraction of surplus value, in which political means (ultimately resting on force) are routinely employed. These political means may involve forced resettlement/expulsion from land, criminalisation of certain freely-entered into economic relations (e.g. private trade in certain commodities) in order to make participation in other economic relations compulsory, by-laws stipulating minimum acreages, the issuing of "safe conducts" for travel only on condition of meeting production targets; and unpaid participation in certain "development" activities. The resulting accumulation (mainly but not exclusively from peasants) may be either in the form of state property and revenues, or both. This accumulation is typically supplemented by appropriation of revenues from natural resources (e.g. minerals) and by overseas development assistance.

A second argument which will be advanced is that these forms of accumulation and of political domination may be subject to various types of modification or qualification. In the case of the form of accumulation described, important modifications include the extent to which the ruling classes accumulating on this basis are internally differentiated and/or diversified in their sources of accumulation, and the extent to which accumulation from above is accompanied by an accumulation from below, i.e. the development of small private capitals on the basis of freely-entered into economic relations.

Internal differentiation of a bourgeoisie accumulating from above exists where the state-based section of the bourgeoisie operates in partnership with a state-dependent but *privately-constituted* class of bourgeois proprietors. Such a situation is characteristic of some former settler colonies where large-scale private capital exists in the form of landed property or (more rarely) mines. Often the emergent relation is characterised by tensions as well as cooperation. The main point however is that the extension of such differentiation creates a partial limit to the freedom of political and economic manoeuvre of the state-based bourgeoisie. An opposite case is one where all large-scale private proprietors have their enterprises expropriated and only a directly state-based bourgeoisie materialises, as in Mozambique and Tanzania; despite the damaging economic results of this strategy it leaves the state-bourgeoisie, at a later stage, with scope for economic and political concessions to the international financial institutions.

The degree of *diversification* of a state bourgeoisie has a different but also significant bearing on its relationship to the demands of the international financial institutions. Taking the cases of Tanzania and Mozambique again, one finds state bourgeoisies (or, more properly in these cases, petit bourgeoisies) which until very recently have been based rather narrowly on the state machine itself (especially the parastatals and perhaps the armed forces). By contrast, the state bourgeoisie elsewhere in East Africa, notably in Kenya and Malawi, have used their positions in the state to accumulate in formally "private" spheres—in Malawi in the tobacco estate sector, in Kenya in an *extremely* fluid way—in grain growing, the service sector, importing, real estate, business services, etc. The point of this is that where diversification reaches a certain level, it becomes possible for a bourgeoisie to gain from the opportunities adjustment presents, as well as to lose from certain of the restrictions to rent seeking which it threatens. If (as is the case of Malawi) the diversification which occurs is rather narrow and the sector into which diversification has occurred is also subject to reform, the costs to the bourgeoisie may be quite severe. An *absence* of diversification, as in the case of Tanzania and Mozambique, also presents opportunities to a state (petty) bourgeoisie, although using adjustment to take advantage of them here implies the need for a transformation of the traditional basis of their political legitimation.

Together with the degree to which sources of donor support have been diversified, and strategic geo-political position, these characteristics of state bourgeoisies constitute the main parameters of their freedom of manoeuvre vis-à-vis institutions seeking to impose adjustment. Where internal bourgeois differentiation is low and internal diversification is fluid, state bourgeoisies have a chance to internally absorb adjustment. Where, conversely, internal differentiation is present and internal diversification is limited, they may be obliged to transfer its entire costs onto the masses. The extent to and the form in which the latter are mobilised in opposition to adjustment and to adjusting governments is mainly determined by the existing forms of political domination.

The main way in which dictatorial political domination is subject to modification and qualification is through the existence of civil society. Civil societies may be distinguished according to their strength or weakness, which usually dates back to levels of class formation during the colonial period. Countries like Nigeria, with substantial rich peasantries and urban middle classes, subsequently developed far denser and more vibrant civil societies than countries like Tanzania, where pre-independence social differentiation was extremely weak. But civil societies may also be differentiated according to their internal composition. In colonial situations where indirect rule was of major importance, such as Uganda or Senegal, traditional or neo-traditional civil societies were established and were even to a certain extent strong enough to subordinate some elements of the urban middle class to their logic. In colonial situations characterised by concentrations of semi-settled wage labour, by contrast, civil societies of a "modern" type emerged, either on their own or in combination with neo-traditional ones.

Both the density and the internal composition of civil society will determine prospects for opposition to dictatorial regimes. Authoritarian regimes with a dense civil society will be more precarious than those with a "thin" one. Yet where a dense civil society is composed in large part of "traditional" or neo-traditional forces, these may prove amenable to certain forms of state subordination without disturbing the dictatorial form of rule. Secular and modern civil societies are less easily subordinated, except through "corporatist" types of relationships, which adjustment renders impossible. (Of course, terms such as "traditional" and "secular" are shorthands for much more complex dispositions of forces, which can at times also become vehicles for quite "non-traditional" and "unsecular" pressures.)

It may be concluded from these brief reflections that "democratisation from above" in Tanzania and Mozambique represents an effort to provide legitimacy for a new form of ruling class accumulation, based upon a diversification away from purely state-confined channels. The ease with which the latter may be accomplished partly depends on the presence and character of bourgeois forces which are not directly part of the state. In Zambia such a force did exist and was largely powerful enough both to resist a transfer of the costs of adjustment to it and to block one possible accumulative "escape route" for the rent-based forces. It was this which led to the latter's confrontation with a civil society, whose own shape (unlike the Ghanaian case) both concentrated and was conducive to a democratic mobilisation. This is not of course to prejudge the political content either of this democratic movement or of others. At the moment in Zambia, democracy would seem to be an oppositional lowest common denominator.

This paper has suggested some of the international and domestic conditions under which pluralistic democratisation has appeared on the political agendas of the IFIs, African governments and movements of opposition to these governments—with particular reference to the impact of structural adjustment. It has concluded that at the international level, multipartyism has developed in a context where some of the key features of the structural adjustment period—especially the regional roles occupied by the Soviet Union, France and South Africa—have been modified. With regard to the "donor community" it has been argued that pressures for "multipartyist" political conditionality represent in important respects an acknowledgement of the failures of adjustment. In domestic African politics it has concluded that the main effects of structural adjustment have been to oblige at least partial revisions of the repertoire of existing ruling class forms of accumulation. Depending on the space these ruling classes have enjoyed, this has been more or less possible. In circumstances where democratic forms of civil society predominate, the result has been to mobilize political opposition around them; in circumstances where they are not it has still strengthened dispositions within governments to adopt "state craft" as a means of staving off more dramatic changes. There is very little evidence of new domestic bourgeois constituencies for democracy being generated by adjustment, nor perhaps more surprisingly, of any regional tendency toward an exclusive concentration on political repression on the part of embattled states.

These conclusions have themselves been assembled on the basis of a fairly scanty survey, and therefore have a highly provisional character. Further investigation is required to test and develop them. Moreover, they have little directly to say about what will probably be considered a more important set of questions, namely those concerning the medium- and long-term prospects and effects (including the economic effects) of these trends toward multi-partyism, as well as the meaning of current trends in relation to specific political perspectives. In this respect a significant final distinction to be made is that between purely parliamentary democratisation and one which allows the emergence of people's organizations outside of the parliamentary arena. Certainly it is the latter which must be supported if "accumulation from above" is to be replaced by something more progressive and dynamic.

Stick and Carrot: Political Alliances and Nascent Capitalism in Mozambique

Kenneth Hermele

"This is a good carrot",[1] the administrator said, as he munched away on a fresh carrot that he just had picked from the field of a private farmer[2] in the interior province of Niassa, northern Mozambique. The foreign visitors were there, in August 1990, to learn about the needs of the family peasants, but the administrator had preferred to organize a visit to the private farmers of the area. These farmers had managed to occupy the fertile lands along the river, and they all had access to pumps to assure a stable supply of water to their vegetable fields. In addition, most of the private farmers had pick-up trucks, some of them even brand new ones, which had been made available through assistance from USAID and the World Bank.

The private farmers were not annoyed by the fact that the administrator picked as he chose from their fields. On the contrary, before going away they offered him a cardboard box full of vegetables, which he gratefully stacked away at the back of his tattered old jeep before taking off.

Now, did the foreign visitors witness a social coalition between the local administration and the private farmers? Or are they just dependent on each other, albeit in a rather uneven relationship? Or, to put in another way: do the private farmers offer a carrot to the administrator just because he wields the stick of political power, upon which they in turn are dependent for their own survival and possibilities to accumulate?

And also: what other coalitions or alliances are today being formed

---

1. The administrator is the district representative of government in Mozambique. He is appointed by the government and normally also occupies the functions of district party head as well as president of the district people's assembly.
2. "Private farmer" designates in Mozambique a capitalist farmer, employing wage labour and normally practising mechanized agriculture.

in Mozambique? And how are they influenced by and influencing the economic reform programme that is being implemented?

And lastly, what is the interrelationship between the *external* pressures and influences that define the scope for economic policy—a salient feature of the present era of structural adjustment—and the prospects of present and future alliances? Is it the case that a strong, autonomous alliance will only be formed when the state is dependent upon *domestic* social groups to realise its policies? If so, are structural adjustment policies conducive to this end or not?

Since 1987, Mozambique has been going through a structural adjustment programme, known by its Portuguese acronym PRE (Economic Rehabilitation Programme). PRE carries all the customary traits of a World Bank/IMF inspired programme, with one remarkable exception: it is being carried out in a context of a devastating war which obviously leaves its marks on the effects and responses that certain policy measures manage to bring forth. Most noteworthy is the fact that supply responses to any kind of stimulus will be much reduced by the simple fact that most economic activities—and especially long-term, productive investments—are at next to a standstill due to the war and the physical dangers that it entails.

However, the fact that the policies of PRE are implemented in a context of war carries a significance that goes beyond the mere conclusion that "supply responses" are weak or that they are difficult to bring about. I will try to argue that PRE contains elements which reinforce the effects of war and destabilisation. Whereas the war has achieved its major effects in the countryside, the Frelimo government managed to keep the urban population relatively protected through a combination of subsidies, food emergency programmes and continued high priority to the social sectors. With PRE the situation changed, and a drastic decline in living and health standards have been suffered by the majority of the urban population. Hence, destabilisation can be said to have been brought to the cities by PRE. Consequently, it is the *joint* impact of war *and* PRE which has to be the object of study, rather than each of them in isolation.

AN ALLIANCE ESTABLISHED ...

The legitimacy of Frelimo goes back to its foundation in 1962. By joining together three nationalist movements into one front, Frelimo could rightly claim to be the only legitimate representative of the Mozambican people. In 1974, after the *coup d'état* in Portugal, when the victorious Portuguese Movement of the Armed Forces began to negotiate the dismantling of the Portuguese empire, Frelimo managed to have Portugal accept it as the sole representative of the people of Mozambique.[3]

This unique standing was to a great extent achieved during the course of the liberation struggle, where Frelimo de *facto* established a broad alliance in political and social terms with different social strata. These strata were united by their common desire to get rid of the Portuguese. But beneath this common umbrella, very different class projects dwelt. To the peasants, independence meant an end to forced cotton cultivation and the possibility to get better terms of trade and to be treated fairly in terms of extension services, prices, etc. To the middle rural stratum, independence would finally open up the doors to capital accumulation, a door which until then had been kept closed by the colonial administration (Adam, 1986). And to the wielders of traditional and religious power, independence was seen as heralding a new dawn, once the cultural, religious and political monopoly of the Portuguese would be gone.

Therefore, and although Frelimo's policies during the liberation war by necessity basically catered to the interests of the family peasants—the backbone of the armed struggle—nationalists and traditionalists of different brands all gathered around the banner of Frelimo in the hope of realising *their own* projects once independence was achieved.

... AND BROKEN

Upon assuming power, Frelimo opted for a development strategy of rural transformation, which in fact broke the former broad alliance and began to alienate considerable segments of the constituent parties

---

3. Aquino de Bragança, who followed the negotiations with Portugal, tells the story in his paper (de Bragança, 1985).

of the front. The sweeping nationalisations of land and real estate, the more defensive but nevertheless important state appropriations of deserted industrial and agricultural property, the transformation of settler lands into state farms, the ridiculing of traditional and religious leaders and customs—all this contributed considerably to narrowing the political base of Frelimo. The transformation of the *front* into a Marxist-Leninist avant-garde *party* only two years after independence showed the clear intentions of Frelimo to build the new state on a different alliance than the one which had carried the liberation struggle to its successful completion.

The stated objective of Frelimo was to build a new alliance, in the terminology of the Marxist-Leninist party called a "worker-peasant alliance". However, that attempt was soon to founder on the combined effect of the economic and political destabilisation which emanated from South Africa. The South African intervention—a continuation of the South African support of the Portuguese side in the war of liberation—had two important consequences.

Firstly, it reduced the rate of social differentiation by simply taking away most of the openings for such a process. In the south of Mozambique, the process of differentiation lost a good part of its fuel, as the earlier flow of migrant remittances dwindled when South Africa, by unilateral decision, decreased the number of Mozambicans accepted in the mines by two thirds right after independence.[4] Also, the war made long-term efforts almost untenable, as the only secure profit that could be reaped was in trade and transport. As the Frelimo government branded most aspects of private trade and transport as illegal black market activities, the scope for open capital accumulation was also severely restricted.

This effect—the difficulty of accumulation and hence the comparatively low level of class formation—could be seen as a positive outcome by a government set to do without capitalists. However, and this is the *second* consequence, Frelimo's own project of modernisation, collectivisation and industrialisation was also brought to a standstill by the effects of economic and military destabilisation. By the mid-80's, millions of peasants had become internal refugees inside Mozambique, and another million had fled to neighbouring

---

4. For a fuller discussion of the process of differentiation in the countryside, see Hermele, 1988.

countries. It should be easy to see that the project of social transformation that was attempted had been crushed at the outset.

Nevertheless, a case can be made that the destruction of the broad
alliance of the liberation struggle in itself weakened the power base
of Frelimo and in reality left the party without allies when it was
attacked. This attack, as we have seen, was launched from the outside, but the failure of Frelimo's project certainly pleased important
sectors inside Mozambique. As one merchant in Gaza province told
me in August 1990: although the armed bandits had killed his wife
and destroyed all his belongings, he was grateful for one thing—
they had stopped communism in Mozambique. Thus, some of the
former allies of Frelimo—those social groups which were disap-
pointed by the turn that Frelimo had taken upon gaining power and,
hence, by the fact that their social ambitions had been turned down
as illegitimate claims—wanted to see the policies of Frelimo defeated, although they by no means subscribed to the methods which the
armed destabilisation adopted. The break-up of the political alliance
of the liberation struggle had left Frelimo without important allies,
allies that it would have needed to be able to continue to withstand
the pressure from South Africa and the rest of the Western world.

Simultaneously, the fact that the process of social differentiation
in Mozambique—never very pronounced—almost had ground to a
halt, implied a weakening of any national bourgeois development.
With the outside intervention that was to come, this weakening
would prove fatal for the future of Mozambique.

A NEW INTERNATIONAL ALLIANCE EMERGING

In 1984, when Mozambique and South Africa concluded the Nkomati
Accord of Non-aggression and Good Neighbourliness, the accord
was mostly seen as a sign of Mozambican defeat in the face of South
African destabilisation. And, partly, this is correct. But the agreement with South Africa ought also to be seen in relation to the fact
that Frelimo had begun already in the early 1980's to look around for
new allies on the international scene. This need to resolve the alliance problem was brought home by the simple fact that in 1982 debt
servicing absorbed Mozambique's complete export earnings. To get
out of this dilemma, a political offensive was attempted, first with

the Soviet bloc and, later, when that failed to give any palpable results, with the Western countries. It was this latter move which resulted in the Nkomati Accord. Half a year later, Mozambique joined the World Bank and the IMF, thus completing its change of international allies.

The offensive was successful. The boycott of Mozambique by the USA was lifted and Mozambique began to receive great quantities of food aid which until then had been denied by the Western countries. In fact, within a few years Mozambique became one of southern Africa's most favoured aid recipients. The other side of the coin is that Nkomati has come to mean the transformation of Mozambique into an almost completely aid dependent country (see Table 1).

Table 1 shows that whereas at the time of independence Mozambique managed to balance its negative trade account through its service receipts—mostly transit traffic fees from South Africa and Rhodesia and migrant workers' remittances—the situation as of 1980 is completely different. From then on, the trade balance as well as the current account have stayed in the red as the service receipts have turned negative due to growing debt service payments.

The negative current account is made up for by growing aid receipts, new loans and debt rescheduling. In 1989, half of the deficit was covered by grants, whereas the remainder was made up by fresh credits. In the early 1980's, before Nkomati, annual grants did not surpass US$ 100 million; by 1989, the volume of grants had quadrupled.

Table 1. *Mozambique—from service to aid economy 1973–1989, millions of USD*

	1973	1980	1985	1989
Exports of goods	230	281	77	121
Imports of goods	–345	–800	–424	–850
Trade balance	–115	–519	–347	–729
Service Receipts	217	171	107	162
Service Expenditures	–95	–75	–200	–389
Net service receipts	122	96	–93	–227
Current account	7	–423	–440	–956

Source: Hermele, 1990:18

Increasingly, the change of international allies resulted in a growing dependence upon the Western countries and their debt managing institutions, the World Bank and the IMF. Domestically, Frelimo attempted to maintain power claiming that it still represented a wide variety of class positions and projects. In its view, the basic modification needed in Mozambique's alliance system was on the international level, with South Africa and the global financial institutions. The result of this change of allies was not only an increased flow of resources but also a shift in power to the international financial institutions which control these resources, and hence also a shift in the control of Mozambique's economic policy. The shift in allies was symbolised by Nkomati, and the price which had to be paid was PRE.

Domestically, Frelimo did not adopt a broad political agenda to rebuild the broad internal front of the liberation struggle. Could such an internal alliance have been attempted at the same time as a structural adjustment policy package was being implemented? For this to take place, PRE would have needed to be adapted to the concrete situation of Mozambique, recognising the needs to reestablish an alliance which was lost during the first decade of independence, and to devise policies which took into account the situation of war.

As we will see, nothing of this sort happened. On the contrary, PRE in fact aggravated an already serious situation where Frelimo already was losing legitimacy amongst the majority of the peasants as well as amongst the urban population. It is in this sense that PRE and the war of destabilisation can be seen to be working hand in hand.

THE DESTRUCTION OF SOCIAL CONSENSUS

Although PRE in just a few years has managed to initiate a capitalistic transformation of Mozambique, we see few capitalists emerging. And those that do appear on the market are normally not engaging in productive capital accumulation. Rather it is speculative activities, trade, transport, consultancies etc. which have the upper hand. Most of these activities have gained considerably in social legitimacy in wide circles, and it is common knowledge which members of government and the party leadership that now are involved in land grabbing, small businesses, construction of houses, and other forms of private enrichment.

The absence of productive investments is partly linked to the fact that the national bourgeoisie was so poorly developed before independence, and that Frelimo after 1975 did its utmost to avoid its growth. But there is no doubt that a stronger capitalist development would have taken place if PRE had not been coloured by the war of destabilisation.

Whereas the winners are few and rather unproductive, the losers are many and account for most of the productive activities in the country. One indication of the degree of desperation now characterising Mozambican society is the living standards of the majority of the population, in the countryside as well as in the cities. During the first four years of PRE, i.e. until the end of 1990, no protective measures had been established. Table 2 shows a snap-shot of health indicators after a couple of years of PRE.

The data in Table 2 refer to the health status of babies and children, but they are by implication relevant also for the situation of families in general. Although no time-series data are available, the values shown in Table 2 should by themselves be enough to initiate a crash emergency operation for plain humanitarian reasons. Worse, perhaps, is that there are grounds for believing the situation has been deteriorating during the first years of PRE. The situation varies considerably from one district to another (reflecting the development of the war of destabilisation), and some areas have experienced improvements in some of the indicators, especially during the beginning of 1990. But what is new in this situation is that the urban popu-

Table 2.   *Health standards 1988–1989. Percentage share of total population affected*

	Urban	Rural
Low weight at birth	15–17	20–29
Chronic malnutrition	30–45	40–60
Acute malnutrition	3–4	10–48
Insufficient growth	14–28	10–31

Note: Urban areas refers to the cities of Maputo and Tete; Rural areas refers to scattered observations throughout the country.
Low weight at birth: < 2,500 grams
Chronic malnutrition: low weight for age—stunting
Acute malnutrition: low weight for height—wasting
Source: Hermele, 1990:22

lation has become seriously hit. With the budget cuts at the outset of PRE, consumer subsidies disappeared. These subsidies had made about one third of minimum calorie intake available to all sectors of urban society in Maputo and Beira. In money terms, an average urban family (with 8 persons) had to spend one complete minimum wage just in order to acquire one third of its monthly requirements. Now, to meet 100 per cent of its minimum needs, 5–6 minimum wages would be needed to be able to buy the food stuffs on the open market (Ministry of Health, 1990). Furthermore, it should be noted, we have only calculated food requirements; everything else—housing, clothing, transport, school and hospital fees—are additional costs.

It is no exaggeration to state that today two thirds of the population in Mozambique lives below the (very low) poverty line. In the cities, one of the dividing lines separating the vulnerable groups from the less vulnerable is whether a family has access to a family plot (*machamba*) or not. There, some of the basic food stuffs can be eked out while also a small surplus may be grown for the market. The problem is only that an estimated 70 per cent of the Maputo families lack *machamba*. Consequently, the struggle to acquire land, especially around the cities, is increasing as malnutrition affects ever wider segments of the urban population.

In the countryside, the wretched level of living standards can also be seen through the extremely low wage levels which are now being applied throughout Mozambique (see Table 3).

Table 3.　*Wages in the agricultural sector, July–August 1990*

Payment per day 5 hours (7 am–12 noon)	500–700 MT (= 0.5–0.7 USD)
Payment per task furrow of 200 metres; a strong worker finishes 2–3 furrows in 5 hours	200 MT (= 0.2 USD)
Payment in kind 1 capulana, worth 7,000 MT (7 USD) for 5 days x 5 hours' work for strong workers, 10 days x 5 hours for weak; or 20 kg of maize for a week's work	

Note: Established minimum wage for workers is approximately 17,000 MT (17 USD) per month
Source: Field work, August 1990

Summing up, we can conclude that the first years of PRE has put an end to whatever may have remained of the broad alliance of the liberation struggle. Apart from that, and leaving the humanitarian aspects aside for the moment, the situation also raises the question of the possibility of establishing a sound base for economic development: which market should economic agents cater to? As far as *domestic markets* are concerned, the conclusion here seems clear: although some people are getting richer through PRE, no domestic mass market which could sustain a long-term development strategy is emerging. On the contrary, the markets are being destroyed by the draconian measures of PRE: cuts in social expenditures, public sector employment, subsidies, etc. As a consequence, the domestic industrial production frequently ends up being stacked away in warehouses as purchasing power goes down and market outlets simply cannot be found.

What about *export markets*, then, since PRE is commonly described as aiming to foster an export-led growth strategy? Since Mozambique's two dominating export products are cashew nuts and shrimps the prospects are rather dim without a diversification of exports, a step which has yet to be initiated and whose results in any case would take time to materialise. The only available potential export earning activity of importance is the coal mine in Moatize, Tete province, which for a number of years has been unable to export its production through the port of Beira due to war sabotage of the railroad line. As things stand today, only an unprecedented upsurge in donor-related cocktail parties could possibly alter the growing gap between import needs and export earnings (cf. Table 1, above). In fact, the situation may very well grow worse, since the shrimp catch—the lion's share of which is landed by joint ventures or licensed foreign firms—has been outgrowing the carrying capacity of the Mozambican waters, and a temporary moratorium on shrimp catching activities was imposed in 1990 in order to protect the resources and secure them for future exploitation.

Thus, the conclusion seems evident, albeit rather sad: neither domestic nor export markets can perform the necessary functions of stimulating the economy in the short run. Hence, the export-led strategy has run up against an internal contradiction which it appears unable of resolving. Therefore, the contradiction earlier pointed at, that between a weak national capitalistic segment and a growing speculative, easy-buck segment cannot be resolved unless the conditions for long-term accumulation are improved. One condition for this is obviously that the war comes to an end, but that is not enough. Markets must also be created internally and a gradual integration into the world market organised, two conditions to permit an initiation of a process of industrialisation in Mozambique.

INTENTIONAL OR ACCIDENTAL?

The frightening effects of PRE so far give rise to a worry common in many discussions on structural adjustment programmes and their impact on social and economic conditions: are the effects intentional or are they simply accidental? Although it may sound hard to say that PRE created widespread hunger by intention, in the case of Mozambique there are some pieces of information which point in the direction that a more guarded and better adapted version of PRE was turned down in favour of the present hard-hitting variant.

When negotiations between Mozambique and the IMF began a couple years before PRE was set in motion, the Mozambican side had elaborated their own reform design which in two essential respects differed from what was to become the final version of PRE. *Firstly*, social sectors and services were protected and a minimum level of finance reserved in order to guarantee that the national programmes of health and education could be upheld. Also, basic subsidies to the urban population were contemplated. In other words, minimum safeguards were established to avoid further isolating Frelimo from its traditional base.

Secondly, a longer time perspective for completing the transfer from a state-led to a market-directed economy was envisaged. This would have permitted Mozambique to avoid the strong shocks which, as we have seen above, have brought havoc to the majority of the population. In the course of the negotiations these positions had to be relinquished by Mozambique and PRE assumed the dire form that we now know. From the point of view of the international financial institutions, it appears that behind the economic "logic", there existed a political agenda which the present set-up of PRE has managed to realise. This agenda has nothing to do with introducing capitalism as a progressive stage in terms of developing the productive

forces or relations of production. On the contrary, what PRE has
managed to achieve is basically to put an end to state-led development while at the same time terminating—once and for all?—the
legitimacy of Frelimo as well as of the state in the eyes of the majority of the population.

Thus, in the negotiations with international agencies, the effort to
maintain what remained of the former broad alliance with the masses was crushed. Subsequently, PRE has assured that no such alliance
can be revived. On the contrary, the balance of class forces inside
Mozambique has been tilted in favour of speculative and commercial activities whereas urban wage earners and peasants have
been left behind.

This also creates, however, a real problem from the point of view
of the mentors of the structural adjustment programmes: they are
courting domestic protest and rebellion as the burden of the programmes is getting increasingly intolerable[5]. Indeed, in Mozambique strikes and protests have been spreading during the last two
years and have involved a wide spectrum of industrial workers and
civil servants (nurses, teachers, etc.).

A NEW BASIS FOR ALLIANCE POLITICS?

The acceptance by Frelimo of PRE and all that has followed can be
interpreted as the final confirmation of the end of the alliance which
had carried the day during the war of liberation. But the change of
allies also has to be understood in an internal-external dimension:

---

5. It should be emphasized that the level of the tolerance of "hardship" that people
   will accept is not decided by "objective" economic or health factors alone. The
   whole social "atmosphere"—in short, solidarity versus personal enrichment—
   plays a crucial role in establishing the limits for what is permissible in terms of
   "honesty" and "honour" as well as for how much the disfavoured strata are willing to "take" without demonstrating in the streets, engaging in strikes or going
   illegal. Mozambique is a clear case to substantiate this, as the whole social climate
   changed after PRE when it became public knowledge that leading party figures
   like Armando Gebuza were becoming businessmen while other state and party
   figures—or their wives—engaged in land grabbing. It is not that this was illegal—
   it was not even against party regulations after the fifth Frelimo congress of 1989.
   It was simply that it changed people's concepts of where the boundary between
   corruption and fair play lay and, hence, how much sacrifices it was reasonable
   that people accepted.

what Mozambique witnessed was a shift of the relative weight of Frelimo's allies: *domestic* allies were becoming less important as *external* allies came to play the crucial role in securing the financial survival of the indebted state. In short, the World Bank—not peasants—had become essential.

So, Frelimo has found itself trapped (has trapped itself?) in a rather awkward situation. It has become dependent upon an external base which is demanding ever more profound alterations in the historic alliance which carried Frelimo to independence. Simultaneously, Frelimo's own policies has transformed the party into a conglomeration of different class positions and projects, ranging from those segments which want to re-establish the former alliance, to those who wish to give the leading role to a state-led process of accumulation and industrialisation, and to the more simple defenders of "everyone for himself and to hell with the rest".

Therefore, and not surprisingly, policies are not consistent. They oscillate between buying off former allies or politically important groups—e.g. the veterans from the liberation war—by extending credits at favourable terms, on the one hand, and a continuation of the former phases of heavy investment in infrastructure (large-scale irrigation schemes, telecommunications, dams for power generation and irrigation) which totally exhaust Mozambique's limited financial resources, on the other. In agriculture, this anti-peasant bias continues in the three year investment programme 1990–1992 with almost 50 per cent of resources dedicated to large-scale irrigation schemes and sugar plantations (Carrilho et al, 1990).

The outcome of this contradictory situation, so far, is a situation which in Mozambique has been termed "wild capitalism", a kind of unfettered, uncontrolled, short-sighted speculative form of capitalism, where the easy and quick profit always appears to have the upper hand, and where the weakened state loses more and more of its directing power.

One of the reasons for this situation is the unclear class base of Frelimo in the present circumstances: with what allies is the party really intending to play the game? Is the party only a conglomeration of different sectional interests? Has the external alliance taken over all other considerations?

IS THERE A NATIONAL PROJECT TODAY?

Towards the end of 1989, the Frelimo government tried to regain some of the ground it had lost in its initial negotiations with the IMF and the World Bank before the launching of PRE. The negative impact of the reform endeavour had indeed grown so serious and so ominous that the whole venture threatened to throw the country into uncontrollable political turmoil and militant resistance. At the same time, the economic results of the reform programme left much to be desired and some kind of reconsideration was called for.

One indication that the pro-PRE forces had gone too far is that a change of policy was proposed by the government in late 1989 to a so-called Consultative Group meeting in Paris (organised by the World Bank and comprising all the aid institutions active in Mozambique). A resurrection of some of the initial aspects of the home grown reform programme was proposed in the form of adding a social safety net for the continuation of the reform process. From the Mozambican side, a modified reform agenda was proposed as PRES, where the 's' stood for social rehabilitation: from now on the programme was to rehabilitate not only the economy but also the social sectors which it formerly had contributed to destroying. And the donors conceded that PRE had to be complemented with a "social dimension".

In this context, and after more than three years of PRE, the World Bank has undertaken to elaborate a Poverty Reduction Framework Paper (World Bank, 1990), which in fact constitutes a self-criticism of the ruthless policies pursued until then. Here, the need to safeguard the social sectors and to protect the vulnerable groups is underlined. The World Bank now wants to avoid "de-accessing"—to use its own term—people from the social services that rightfully belong to them.

Several comments can be made about this attempt by the World Bank to reduce some of the poverty that has been created in recent years. Firstly, such programmes are invariably devised as an afterthought and do not alter the basic design, nor the main thrust of the reform programmes as such. Secondly, one of their major preoccupations is "visibility"—their design prioritises certain short-run measures to give favourable publicity to donors and governments. Thirdly, and linked to these other characteristics, they are highly selective in the populations they cover. In the World Bank's perspective, the need for poverty reduction is focused on the urban sector, while the impoverishment in the rural areas is neglected. Here, alarming studies by the European Community (European Community, 1989) have indicated that two thirds of the rural population live on or below the poverty line (as measured by calorie intake)—i.e. a situation which is just as serious as in the urban and semi-urban areas.

There are two important differences between the rural and urban areas: *firstly*, that PRE is responsible for creating the emergency in the cities, whereas the war carries a greater part of the burden in the countryside. But even in relation to the peasantry, PRE has been criticised for not improving the rural-urban terms of trade (Stockholm Group for Development Studies, 1989). Therefore, it is an alarming sign that the World Bank poverty reduction paper does not touch on the issue of the peasantry's terms of trade, nor does it suggest that improving terms of trade would be essential in order to eradicate poverty in the rural areas.

The *second* difference between urban and rural areas is that the forms of protest against PRE so far have taken a more prominent form in the cities than in the countryside. This latter difference may explain the World Bank's preoccupation with the impact on the urban population and its neglect of the peasants: it is the vocal opposition which counts and which may endanger the whole reform process in Mozambique.

This may also explain why so little is changing in terms of concrete policy. Irrespective of all good intentions expressed by ministers and party people, time and again, investment plans and projects still to this very day give first priority in terms of money and attention to the modern, large-scale sector, to export crops and to irrigation schemes.

Simultaneously, the party and the state are taking steps to protect their senior staff and secure a smooth transfer to a protected life for the leaders and "responsible" of the state sector in the face of its dismantling. Here, attention is focused upon the social survival of a relatively favoured sector of the population, while the peasants and the majority of the workers as well as rank and file civil servants are left on their own without any special consideration. Special credit schemes and support facilities are now being devised in order to enable former leaders of state farms and state firms, as well as state and party leaders to establish themselves as traders, farmers and capitalists of various shades and vocations.

Meanwhile, in the districts, administrators are fending for themselves. Many have already established local alliances with traders and private farmers, exchanging services of mutual benefit, in this way taking advantage of the carrots and sticks they still may possess. In such local alliances, the administrator may offer a trader or private farmer the possibility of acquiring a tractor or a truck, and in exchange he would receive help to build a house in Maputo or to establish himself in business or agriculture, at times in unofficial joint ventures and partnerships precisely with the same private traders and farmers.

Thus, the administrators who used to be the local representatives of the national project of Frelimo no longer fulfil this role. Most of them are simply out to save their own skin now that they see how the whole project is crumbling. The administrator, who at the beginning of this paper happily ate his carrot, is a case in point. He knew that he soon would lose his political position, as Mozambique is entering a phase with free elections based on a multi-party system. The administrator may then find that when he is losing his stick, his political power, so will he lose the carrot he still is being offered by the propertied classes in the rural setting of Mozambique. That may be one of the explanations to why administrators are now in a hurry to establish themselves as independent entrepreneurs and as owners of real estate: when the stick goes, they may find themselves without carrots.

But if *the* national project is gone, it has been replaced by a number of different projects which have been placed on Mozambique's agenda by social carriers of different origins and with differing goals. To simplify, the basic divide may be expressed as one between a nationalistic capitalist project, where Mozambican capital plays a leading role supported by the Mozambican state, as opposed to one where the basic functions of Mozambique reside in servicing the South African economy with labour, market outlets and investment opportunities. In this latter project, international capital and its financial institutions are crucial actors, whereas the role of the Mozambican state is restricted so that such an integration with South Africa can be accomplished.

AND WHAT NOW?

To sum up: with the end of state-led transformation of Mozambique, *the* national project of Frelimo has disappeared. The party is marginalised, and the state has grown ever more dependent upon external forces while the policies of PRE antagonise ever wider sectors of society. The continuation of this process would clearly lead Mozambique to develop a specific kind of subservient capitalism. In essence, PRE so far has sided with the forces in Mozambique which have opted for a role as junior partners in a game dominated by South Africa. It would appear that today it is this tendency which is the dominating one, and one which has been fostered by PRE.

Further, it should be said that the relative low level of capital accumulation which has taken place in Mozambique and which was discussed earlier, also has contributed to keep Mozambican capital in this dependent, subservient position.

Two social forces are contradicting this tendency, a capitalistic nationalistic offensive force, and a popular defensive one. The offensive one has been hampered by the dominance of the liberal policies of PRE which, as we have seen, have failed to offer a reasonable base—internally and externally—for capital accumulation, by doing away with markets and supportive facilities. Thus, the nationalistic capitalistic project has encountered great difficulties in obtaining even minimum protection and support by the state. This is another way of saying that the nationalist capitalist sector, in spite of its representatives in government and in the leadership of Frelimo, has failed to influence policies to any greater degree.

The popular defensive stance, on the other hand, has had certain successes, symbolised by the modification of PRE into PRES. Widespread deterioration of living conditions has constituted sufficient fuel to create the basis for a common agenda, which could lead to the constitution of a broad front of common interests between peasants and workers and civil servants—all of which have been affected negatively by PRE and its consequences. But so far, very little in terms of common actions and the formulation of joint demands has been taking place. Until today, it is everyone for themselves: peasants around the cities fight to keep their fields out of the hands of the well-positioned land grabbers, civil servants, especially in health and education, take to the streets in opposition to the decline in real income, and workers in industry throughout the country go on strike for better pay. This opposition is only in its infancy, but it is certainly a significant step in the political history of Mozambique. For the first time since independence, open and widespread popular discontent has been voiced and allowed to spread to wide areas of society.

Mozambique has entered a phase where the majority of the people are seeing themselves forced to defend their own interests without being able to count on support from either state or party. Likewise, the nationalistic capitalistic forces realise that the weakness of the Mozambican state and its growing dependence upon foreign agencies both militate against a nationalistic project. Hence, the ground for a common stance exists. The financial institutions probably see PRES as a compromise, necessary in order not to prejudice the whole reform process. Nevertheless, and from the point of view of an alternative base for development, PRES is an essential step. It can be argued that a new alliance can develop by the unification of the offensive and defensive nationalist forces, which need each other in order to be able to have lasting success in their respective projects.

So far, a common struggle belongs to the future, as a possible opening. But the only way to counter the dependence and subordination in relation to South Africa which has been prepared for Mozambique, lies in a joining of forces which until now have not realised that they have a common agenda, which they may only realise if they unite.

Some donor agencies may disavow responsibility for the collapse of the capacity of Mozambican state to fend for its citizens, for the death of the Mozambican nation-state project. But the fact is that there is no force, internal or external, in Mozambique today which carries the same weight as the conditionalities imposed by the international community, through the World Bank and the IMF and by individual agencies. Today, the sticks and the carrots are all controlled by the same actors, actors which are united and motivated by a strong coordinating hand in the shape of the World Bank and the IMF. The struggle for the favours of the system is more and more directed towards outside agencies, while the Mozambican state is relegated to a pawn in the conditionality game.

This game is a formidable problem which a new internal alliance in Mozambique will have to fight. Here lies a great challenge for countries such as the Nordic ones in order to open up the oppressive system of conditionality, so as to at least shift the balance of power in the right direction. Such a change would constitute an important contribution to establishing a new, strong domestic alliance which could begin anew to undertake the arduous task of building a nation-state on the remnants of the state of Frelimo. The alternative, to play along in the conditionality game, would leave Mozambique without a state based on an internal political alliance, a position which certainly would leave the country considerably weakened in the face of the coming struggles to define the future of southern Africa in a post-apartheid perspective.

Structural Adjustment and Multiple Modes of Social Livelihood in Nigeria

Abdul Raufu Mustapha

> Lately in Moscow one of the nastiest curses you can hurl at a person is, "May you live on one salary!" (Remnick, 1990:18–19).

Declining oil revenues from 1981, massive corruption and mismanagement of the economy, and an externally oriented import-substitution industrialisation programme, all combined to plunge Nigeria into a severe economic crisis in the early 1980s. In October 1985, a 15-month national economic emergency was declared, followed in July 1986 with the adoption of a structural adjustment programme (SAP). SAP policies in Nigeria include the abolition of the import licencing system, reduction in public expenditure, reordering capital expenditure, eliminating subsidies (especially on petroleum products) promoting exports, especially agricultural exports, abolishing agricultural commodity boards, reducing the volume of money supply, and deregulating interest rates. Of greatest significance, however, was the managed floatation of the naira under the Second Tier Foreign Exchange Market (SFEM), and the convergence of both foreign exchange windows into the Foreign Exchange Market (FEM); between 1986–90, the naira was allowed to depreciate by 87 per cent relative to the Dollar.

SAP has had fundamental consequences for Nigerian society, politics, and economy. Nowhere are these consequences as profound as in the drastic fall in the living standards of those sections of the population dependent on fixed salaries. Equally affected are some sections of the rural population and urban artisanal groups. This erosion of living standards has spurred many households to seek additional income by engaging in multiple jobs. This paper examines the dynamics and possible implications of this intensified struggle for survival through the pursuit of multiple modes of earning a livelihood.

Multiple modes of earning a livelihood are an aspect of the concept of household survival strategies, which attempts to explain the mutual interactions between domestic units and macro socio-economic structures and processes, especially in periods of rapid change and increased social stress. These concepts represent an attempt to move beyond the static analysis of "marginality" and the "informal sector", and aim at the introduction of the dynamism of human agency into the analysis of changing forms of production, and the resultant activities of domestic groups, in their attempts to meet immediate material needs (Redclift, 1986). The analysis of survival strategies therefore facilitates the comprehension of both macro trends and micro-level market and non-market responses.

Discussions of survival strategies usually commence with an examination of either the household or the economy. Proceeding from the latter invariably structures the analysis in terms of the dichotomies between "urban" and "rural", or "industrial" and "agrarian" (Redclift, 1986:223). Beginning from the household has the advantage of a greater capacity for generating empirical data, while an economy-focused analysis is better able to capture the dynamic of shifting macro trends. The former is essentially quantitative analysis, while the latter is basically qualitative. The economic focus of this paper is therefore biased towards qualitative analysis.

But the choice of primary focus—household or economy, and quantitative or qualitative—is not the only analytic problem. It has been claimed by Wolf that the conceptualisation of some phenomena as "household survival strategies" is often a figment of researchers' fertile imagination. She asserts that unwarranted assumptions about individuals and households often lead to a misrepresentation of intra-household behaviour, and the distortion of stratifications based on gender and generation. Contrary to most "survival strategies" analysis, she conceptualises the household as both a cooperative and conflictual unit, within which the "survival" of some may be at the expense of others (Wolf, 1990). Considerations of issues of gender and generation are therefore important in uncovering the reality of the household and its "survival strategies".

In the Nigerian context, these pose a number of difficult analytical problems. Independent incomes of wives has always played a major role in the sustenance of most Nigerian households, and it is therefore difficult to specify precisely what constitutes a "living wage" for the working classes, against which the need for additional "survival strategies" can be assessed. Furthermore, are wives' trading incomes to be considered as part of their households' "survival strategies", even when they may have exclusive control over them, and only specified household obligations?

Though the concept of multiple modes derives most of its meaning from the concept of survival strategies, there may still be the need to specify its salient characteristics. Firstly, multiple modes of earning a livehood should primarily be seen as a process of income-generation (Castells and Portes, 1989:12), since poverty, crisis, and survival are not absolute terms. Secondly, unlike informal sector activity, multiple modes of earning a livelihood may systematically include "criminal" activities.[1] However, in reality, most activities falling under the multiple modes of earning a livelihood may simply be quasi-illegal or non-legal, like informal sector activity.

Thirdly, the contemporary intensification of the multiple modes dynamic is an international phenomenon, consequent on structural and technological changes going on in the world economy. Nannake Redclift and Mingione, for example, have examined changes in post-industrial societies, and the attendant "struggle for livelihood" at the household and community levels. They highlight the European discovery or rediscovery of the world of work "outside" capitalist relations of production (Redclift and Mingione, 1985). Similarly, Thurman and Trah point out the increasing tendency towards part-time work in industrialised societies (Thurman and Trah, 1990) while Michael Redclift examines the nature of survival strategies in rural Europe, pointing out that British data suggests that full-time farmers "have largely been replaced" by part-timers with little previous experience in agriculture (Redclift, 1986:225) However, within the context of SAP in a developing society, these global tendencies take on an added potency.

---

1. Castells and Portes differentiate between informal and criminal activities by pointing out that "Those labeled 'criminal' specialize in the production of goods and services socially defined as 'illicit', while informal activity is characterized by being unregulated by the institutions of society, in a legal and social environment in which similar activities are regulated" (1989:12, 15).

Informal activities produce socially accepted goods and services, but often through non-legal means, while criminal activities like the drugs trade produce illegal goods by illegal means.

Finally, unlike most European and Latin American analyses, it is argued here that the contemporary relevance of the multiple mode concept in Nigeria transcends the levels of the individual, households, and communities. Public and private institutions are equally involved in the process. For example, declining subsidies and revenues have forced the Nigerian Airports Authority (NAA) to go into commercial agriculture, involving the preparation and leasing of the tracts of land within airport perimeter fences (*Business Concord*, 2 June 1987:1, and 12 June 1987:12). Similarly, universities are now establishing not only consultancies but holding companies which engage in such activities as running petrol stations and bakeries.[2] Not even the church is immune from the process. In the face of dwindling individual contributions, the Celestial Church of Christ launched a series of "industrial projects" in the hope of augmenting its income (*Business Concord*, 19 April, 1989:3).

What is the economic and social context for the intensification of the multiple mode of earning a livelihood in Nigeria? What are its impacts on different social classes? What is its "political economy"? Can it contribute to sustainable adjustment? What are its impacts on the exercise of state power?

SOCIO-ECONOMIC CONTEXT: UNEMPLOYMENT, SELF-EMPLOYMENT, AND INFLATION

The adoption of SAP in Nigeria was accompanied by the setting of various macro-economic targets. The budget deficit was to be reduced to under 3 per cent of the GDP; non-statutory transfers to all economic and quasi-economic parastatals were to be confined to not more than half of their 1985 levels; public sector employment was to be frozen; wages were to be increased at less than the rate of inflation through the maintenance of wage controls (A. Alhaji, Minister of State, Budget and Planning, *Business Concord*, June 27, 1989:7); and an annual growth rate of about 6.8 per cent was envisaged (Central Bank of Nigeria, 1987:11).

---

2. For an example of the University of Ibadan holding company, see *Business Concord*, October 27, 1987:5.

The attempt to control the budget deficit took the form of cutting public expenditure. But this was not an across-the-board approach; some sectors were more affected than others. Social services, specifically education and health, suffered drastic cuts while the security services and the financial institutions did much better.

Tables 1 and 2 highlight changes in percentage shares in the federal government's recurrent and capital expenditures by sector, from 1986 to 1989. It is important to note that with the devaluation of the naira from 1986, and the intensification of the inflationary pressures in the economy, total budgetary allocations after 1986 diminished in real terms. Increased shares in the budget for education and health in 1988 may therefore continue to represent a fall, in real terms, from

Table 1. *Recurrent Expenditure of the Federal Government:*
1986–1989 (% share)

	1986	1987	1988	1989
ADMINISTRATION	34.8	38.6	29.8	24.1
General Admin.	19.7	19.0	18.4	14.3
Defence	9.5	12.6	6.9	6.5
Internal Security	5.6	7.0	4.5	3.3
ECONOMIC SERVICES	6.7	7.0	6.3	5.5
Agric. & Water Res.	0.5	0.5	0.4	0.6
Construction	3.7	4.1	3.6	1.9
Trans. & Comm.	1.2	1.8	1.2	1.1
Others	1.3	0.6	1.1	1.9
SOCIAL SERVICES	11.2	3.0	10.9	16.3
Education	6.3	2.3	7.5	11.6
Health	3.2	0.4	2.2	2.2
Others	1.7	0.3	1.2	2.5
TRANSFERS	47.3	51.4	53.0	54.1
Debt Charges	39.0	39.5	47.6	51.0
(1) Internal	32.1	24.4	21.7	23.1
(2) External	6.9	15.1	25.9	27.9
Pensions	8.0	1.0	4.9	2.7
Total Exp. (N Million)	7,697.0	15,646.0	19,409.0	25,994.0

Sources: Central Bank of Nigeria, Annual Report, 1988 (p. 86) and 1989 (p. 88)

Table 2. *Capital Expenditure of the Federal Government:*
1986–1989 (% share)

	1986	1987	1988	1989
ADMINISTRATION	2.9	28.5	22.8	17.4
General Admin.	2.0	24.2	14.3	12.4
Defence	0.8	2.9	4.6	3.6
Internal Security	0.1	1.4	3.9	1.4
ECONOMIC SERVICES	12.1	33.9	25.5	22.9
Agric. & Water Res.	4.1	7.0	7.9	11.5
Manufacturing etc.	1.5	15.8	9.2	5.6
Trans. & Comm.	3.1	8.5	5.6	3.7
Others	3.4	2.6	2.8	2.1
SOCIAL SERVICES	7.2	9.7	20.7	12.3
Education	4.3	1.5	3.9	2.6
Health	0.7	0.9	1.9	1.5
Housing	–	–	9.3	8.0
Others	2.2	7.3	5.6	0.2
TRANSFERS	77.8	27.9	31.0	47.4
Capital Repayment	65.0	20.9	25.0	40.1
(1) Internal	–	1.9	1.6	0.9
(2) External	–	19.0	23.7	39.2
Total Exp. (N Million)	9,077.0	6,373.0	8,340.0	15,034.0

Sources: Central Bank of Nigeria, Annual Report, 1988 (p. 87) and 1989 (p. 89).

the 1986 levels.[3] Furthermore, the relative increase in the resources for general administration after 1987 is hardly a reflection of the healthy state of the main civil service; the increases were largely to finance two new states created in 1987, and a plethora of new governmental agencies like the mass mobilisation agency (MAMSER). Similarly, new resources committed to agriculture did not go to the ministries of agriculture, but to a new rural development agency, the Directorate for Food, Roads and Rural Infrastructure. Partly because of the continued significance of a statist orientation within Nigerian ruling classes, funds channelled to parastatals rose rather than diminished (*Business Concord*, June 27:1989).

---

3. The increases may have been precipitated by the charge, by the former Head of State, General Obasanjo, that SAP lacked "the milk of human kindness".

Meanwhile, despite the selective cuts in public expenditure, the budget deficit remains a problem, as Table 3 illustrates; and the 6.8 per cent annual growth has remained a mirage. But some SAP targets were met: real wages were brought down and public sector employment was frozen, natural wastage notwithstanding. Official Nigerian labour statistics are completely unreliable, and cannot form even a rudimentary basis for assessing unemployment trends. However, it would seem that within the civil service, embargoes on the filling of existing vacancies were used to block new appointments. Within parastatals and the private sector, similar embargoes have been accompanied by retrenchment drives aimed at those already in employment; in the first half of 1987 alone, the organised manufacturing sector was reported to have shed 14 per cent of its labour force. (*Monthly Business and Economic Digest, MBED,* July 1987; United Bank for Africa, Lagos: 3).[4] Many jobs have been lost, in a situation in which new employment opportunities are rare.

The generation of public and private sector unemployment which was an aspect of the pre-SAP economic crisis, has continued under SAP, and has influenced the tendency towards multiple modes of livelihood. Firstly, the unemployment trend is closely associated with the casualisation or re-casualisation of some of the labour still in employment (Andrae and Beckman, forthcoming). Secondly, sacked workers, being more desperate, have tended to initiate forms

Table 3. *Nigeria: Budget Deficits, 1986–90, as % of GDP*

Year	%
1986	10.3
1987	4.2
1988	8.5
1989	2.9
1990	4.4*

* % of Gross National Expenditure (The GDP figure is higher)
Sources: Central Bank of Nigeria, *Annual Reports* (various), and *Business Concord,* Aug. 15, 1989:15 and Jan. 9, 1990:16.

---

4. In 1988, a prominent labour economist, T.M. Yesufu, claimed that 4 million unemployed youths were roaming the streets of the country (*MBED*, Ibid., Nov. 1988:5).

of survivalist economic activities—the conversion of personal motor-bikes into "express taxis" is but one example—which soon spread to the ranks of the poorly paid still in employment. Thirdly, the potential threat to the SAP project, and indeed the regime, arising from the unabated tide of unemployment, prompted the initiation of many self-employment and open apprenticeship schemes under the National Directorate of Employment (NDE). These schemes made available some technical and financial assistance to the self-employed, and coupled with the emphasis on developing a "maintenance culture" in the country, created many possibilities of moonlighting by various categories of workers.

The government hopes that its unemployment problem will be largely solved through the vigorous promotion of self-employment. By the end of 1987, 100,000 youths were expected to have gone through the open apprenticeship scheme (*MBED*, Oct. 1987:3). And contrary to the previous situation under which university graduates looked for jobs in the public sector, parastatals, and the organised private sector, the new drive was to get at least 20 per cent of the graduates of 1987 involved in self-employment. It was hoped that this figure would rise to 60 per cent by 1992 (*MBED*, June 1987:7). This deliberate de-institutionalisation of employment and economic activities (Castells and Portes, 1989) is a crucial "enabling environment" for the intensification of moonlighting and other multiple modes of earning a livelihood.

Consequently, the informal sector, which is the primary focus of multiple mode activities in Nigeria, is changing under the impact of new entrants. It has been claimed that this sector occupies between 50 per cent and 70 per cent of the urban working population in many developing societies (Cornia, 1987:93). In the late 1970s, a study of Lagos estimated that the informal sector in the city occupied about 50 per cent of the city's working population (Fapohunda, 1985:5). Lagos is likely to have the largest formal and informal sector economies in Nigeria. Under SAP, however, it is likely that a larger proportion of the working population is now dependent on informal sector activities, possibly pushing the percentage in most Nigerian cities to close to 70 per cent of the working population. This possible expansion in the personnel involved in the informal sector is coupled with decreasing economic opportunities under SAP. The result is likely to be a general reduction in returns, and an increasing uneveness in the distribution of the returns. Employment conditions may also have deteriorated, especially for women and children.

Apart from unemployment and self-employment, another socio-economic factor which forms the context for understanding the logic of the multiple modes tendency in Nigeria is an inflationary spiral, which ceaselessly reduces even the waged to the level of the barest "hand-to-mouth" existence. SAP was predicated on a rate of inflation of about 16 per cent per annum. But as Table 4 shows, even the contested official statistics[5] indicate that the situation is far worse. While official figures indicate that the rate of inflation in 1986 was a mere 5.4 per cent, the then Minister of Information was reported to have claimed that the prevailing rate was 300 per cent (*MBED*, Dec. 1986:7). Whatever the true figure may be, the fact is that since the introduction of SAP, workers on restrained wages, and others on fixed incomes are caught in the "scissors" between a massively depreciated currency on the one hand and spiralling prices on the other.

In the pre-SAP period between 1975 and 1985, civil service real wages in Nigeria fell by about 58 per cent for the lowest basic salary earners, and by about 78 per cent, for the highest basic salary earner (Robinson, 1990:377; Chew, 1990:1013). These falls were also reflected in the private sector. These long-term declines in urban in-

Table 4. *Nigeria: Changes in Composite Consumer Price Index in %, 1982–1989.*

Year	%	Year	%
1982	7.7	1986	5.4
1983	23.2	1987	10.2
1984	39.6	1988	38.3
1985	5.5	1989	47.5

Sources: Central Bank of Nigeria, *Annual Report* (various)
The *Nigerian Economist*, Feb. 19, 1990:32.

---

5. Professor Dotun Phillips, Director General of Nigeria's premier social science research institute has accused the Federal Office of Statistics (FOS) of putting out dubious and unrealistically low inflation figures.

comes in most of Sub-Saharan Africa have seriously eroded the urban-rural income divide (Jamal and Weeks, 1988). However, the additional hardships caused by the post-1985 adoption of SAP has led to some measures, allegedly tailored to compensate for falling real wages. Salary scales have been "elongated", and a "SAP relief package" involving additional allowances has been promised, though not always paid, to all wage earners. But these increments have been miniscule, compared to the rate of inflation, and the depreciation of the currency. Real wages continue to fall, and between 1986 and 1990, it is possible that real wage rates have declined by at least 25 per cent.[6]

Against the above background, government-sponsored charades like the 1986 "Campaign Against Rising Cost of Living" are neither convincing, nor effective (*MBED*, Vol. 9, No. 12). Many workers are compelled to find ways of augmenting their income if they and their households are not to go under. And invariably, it is a question of running in order to keep still.

Multiple modes of earning a living were always a feature of the Nigerian economy and the economic crisis of the early 1980s has only added more dynamism to the tendency. But SAP has also fundamentally modified the process. Firstly, it has intensified the process of informalisation within the economy. Secondly, SAP policies have also encouraged a tendency of decreasing and uneven returns within the expanded informal sector. While some sectors are booming, many others are hardly adequate for ekeing out a living. Thirdly, working conditions within the informal sector have deteriorated. Many Nigerian newspapers are filled with sorrowful stories of little children who have been withdrawn from school by their parents, so that these children can join in petty-trading and roadside vending. Fourthly, in pre-SAP times, the multiple modes tendency was largely limited to the working and artisanal classes, and sections of the peasantry. But with the erosion of the incomes of professional classes, many of them are now involved in the dynamic; SAP has led to the widening of the social base of the multiple modes dynamic. Finally, there seems to be an increase in socially harmful activities, such as part-time prostitution, within the multiple modes dynamic.

---

6. This is a guesstimate. After months of negotiations with unions and employers, the government agreed to raise the minimum wage in January 1991. The unions have accused the government of reneging on the agreement.

URBAN SOCIAL GROUPS AND THE MULTIPLE MODES TENDENCY

The reality of the multiple modes tendency differs from one social group to the other, depending on their location within the economy, the skills, assets, and connections at their disposal, and their overall ability to profitably convert these variables into an income-generating dynamic. With regard to urban social groups, differences between the working class, professional classes, and youths and artisans will be examined here.

The working class

The history and psychology of the Nigerian working class has tended to move it in the direction of the multiple modes tendency. The process of proletarianisation from the end of the 19th century was fiercely resisted (Hopkins, 1979). Wage labour was associated, not with "free" labour and the contract, but equated with servitude. The ambition of many workers was the accumulation of enough capital to "regain their freedom" through recourse to trading (Williams, 1980). Straddling between waged employment and the informal and agrarian economies was pervasive. Often, workers took temporary industrial employment during the dry season, only to return to their farms in the rainy season (Main, 1985). Though wage rates up to about 1983 roughly guaranteed a "living wage", it was often the case that the acquisition of luxury items, educational fees for the children, remmittances to kin, and even basic sustenance within the household depended also on the independent incomes of wives, earned through activities like petty trading. Therefore, the multiple mode of earning a livelihood has deep roots in the Nigerian working class.

From the mid-1970s, however, changes were taking place in this process of proletarianisation. Formal sector employment became increasingly valued, and many workers would hold on to formal sector jobs on a much more permanent basis; there emerged a noticeable preference for full proletarianisation. Such was the growing attachment to urban, working class values, that even retrenched migrant workers sometimes refused to return to rural life and farming (Main, 1985). The depreciation of rural incomes in the oil-boom years, and the simultaneous appreciation of urban ones, tended to lead therefore to the consolidation of a distinct and fairly stable working class identity, (Lubeck, 1986) based roughly on a "living wage". The renewed emphasis on the multiple modes tendency within the working class under SAP may therefore be seen as a process of deconstructing an evolving working class identity.

How have the crisis and the multiple mode tendency manifested themselves within the working class? Under Shagari, (1979–83) the economic crisis affected the working class through the inability of many employers to pay their workers promptly at the end of the month. The nationalist and repressive Buhari regime (1983–85) eliminated subsidies, raised the cost of social services, retrenched many workers, and unilaterally imposed many "development levies" on the working class. Some states, such as Imo and Niger, even suggested the adoption of the infamous "Imo Formula", under which the governments unilaterally assumed the right to revise a worker's wage at the end of month. Workers wages were thereby to be determined, not by their contracts, their productivity, or the cost of living, but by the whims of state bureaucrats whose major corncern was the cash-flow crisis of the states. (*MBED*, Jan.–Feb., 1985:4; Aug., 1985).[7]

Under Babangida, (1985–present) an initial effort was made to continue with overtly authoritarian measures aimed at bringing down the wage bill. The National Economic Emergency declared in October 1985 was accompanied by compulsory deductions from workers wages. In 1987, an attempt was made to modify the Minimum Wage Act in such a way that would exclude many workers from the provisions of the Act. But in the final analysis, the major instrument the Babangida regime has used to curtail workers income has been the exchange rate.

The urban working class wage is no longer adequate to support the average family, and not even the trading activities of wives can guarantee continued access to minimum levels of sustenance. For millions of Nigerian workers, the answer is to engage in multiple modes activities; not only are working class wives enmeshed in the informal sector, the workers themselves must engage in second, or even more occupations.

---

7. In January 1991, the Federal Government dismantled the unified salary structure of the civil services of the Federation. Henceforth, local and state governments are free to negotiate and fix whatever wage rates they deem fit.

Some of the mechanisms of this process are as follows. Firstly, private assets and skills are commercialised. Private motorcycles are periodically converted to taxis called "express" in Kaduna, "ina zaki" (where are you going?) in Sokoto, and "achaba" in Kano. The Kano term has a slight connotation of the dishonest pursuit of gain. In Gusau, workers in a textile mill have consistently refused to do overtime work on Sundays despite increased incentives; they claim that they make more from their "express taxis".

Secondly, many other workers, lacking in private assets and skills, simply take a more serious interest in farming. Despite workers' resistance to a return to semi-proletarianisation, many have effectively regressed from proletarians to peasant-proletarians. They may be "permanently" employed, but there is no doubt that their interest in their jobs has become episodic. Thirdly, those lacking access to farmland take to petty trading; clerks and other lower level bureaucrats engage in petty corruption. Every survivalist stratagem permitted by the circumstance is utilised. Some combine different types of multiple mode activities.

This "new" tendency towards the multiple mode is not completely identical with the similar process which characterised the initial constitution of the working class. Then, workers "straddled" many modes of income-generation sequentially rather than simultaneously. Straddling was a strategy for containing the rigours of proletarianisation; excessive demands by the colonial state were thwarted by exit from or reversion to peasant status. The "new" straddling always combines wage employment with other activities, reflecting both the working class commitment to proletarianisation, and its inability to secure a "living wage" as a class. It amounts to a last-ditch defence mechanism by a working class on its knees, while the "old" straddling was an assertion of the worker's limited control over his life. By presenting him with an alternative, it enhanced his bargaining position within industry. On the other hand, the "new" straddling implies an intensified form of self-exploitation for survivalist ends.

The professional classes

The professional classes, like the working class, exist under the ravages of unemployment and inflation characteristic of SAP. Even wives of officers of the ruling military establishment claim that their husbands' salaries are no longer enough for maintaining their households in the style they are accustomed to. Consequently, officers' wives are said to have abandoned their traditional role as homemakers, and embarked on strategies for acquiring additional incomes. Some take on office jobs, while others with fewer educational qualifications, take to sewing, hair-dressing and trading.[8] Additionally, many sections of the professional classes have complained about the inability of the state and other employers to maintain the minimum standards necessary for the proper execution of their duties. Similarly, others have complained about increased state repression and authoritarianism (Jega, 1989). The pay levels, and the conditions of service are therefore alienating many professionals from continued concentration on paid employment.

However, the logic informing the increased participation of professional classes in multiple modes of earning a livelihood is essentially different from that of large sections of the working class. For most members of the latter class, engagement in multiple modes activities is critical to individual and household survival. This is directed at reversing reduced levels of nutritional intake, and the inability to meet medical, educational and utility bills. For the professional classes, however, the threat to survival is not that stark and dire. Access to housing, medical, educational, and nutritional resources, albeit at an increasingly falling standard, are tenuously maintained. For these classes, multiple mode activities are seen essentially as means of containing, and possibly reversing the obvious slide in their living standards, which, within the context of a developing society, can be said to be "middle class". Between 1984 and 1987, there was a boom in the number of people taking out life policies with insurance companies (*Business Concord*, Sept. 4, 1987:5). Most of those involved are likely to have been professional people. This phenomenon is graphically illustrative of the uncertainties and fears unleashed under SAP; especially the fear that one's household was somehow threatened with the possibility of sinking into the ranks of the "new poor".

Another important distinction between the involvement of the

---

8. Cf. Speech by Mariam Abacha (wife of the Defence Minister and Chairman, Joint Chiefs of Staff), entitled "SAP and Army officers' wives", *Business Concord*, May 31, 1988:7.

working and professional classes in the multiple modes strategy is that while the former are largely confined to labour-intensive, capital-scarce, and low-returns operations on the margins of the economy, the latter have better financial and political resources which they can put to more effective income-generating use. The income differential between senior and junior workers in 1986 was reported to be 1:27 and 1:10 in the private and public sectors respectively (*Business Concord*, March 14, 1989:15). The professional groups also have better access to banks and political networks. They are therefore able to invest in small-scale manufacturing units, installed at the back of the house, or in their garages. They are also better able to make the political connections necessary for the procurement of the needed raw materials.

Thirdly, by virtue of their training, the professional classes tend to have better business ideas when engaged in multiple modes of earning a livelihood. Refuse collection is packaged as "environmental sanitation"; sewing mistresses give way to "fashion designers"— a social group which has grown enormously in Nigeria. Essentially, the professional classes tend to have a better idea of what they have, and what income they may be able to generate therefrom. An advert appeared in a business journal, stating that a young man wanted to start a *garri* processing project. He did not have the N 10,000 capital needed, but had a second-hand car. The purpose of the advert was to solicit a loan of N 1000 with which to repair the car, which he intended to run as a *kabukabu* (unlicenced and unpainted taxi). He hoped that this *kabukabu* business would then pay off the N 1000 loan, and also constitute the basis for accumulating the N 10,000 which was really his primary objective (*Business Concord*, Dec. 16, 1988:8). The professional classes are also more conscious of their supposed contributions to "economic recovery" and they expect, or demand, government recognition and assistance.

Sectorally, the participation of professional classes in the multiple modes dynamic is heavily biased towards small-scale manufacturing—the proverbial "cottage" industry, commercial (and subsistence) farming, and moonlighting of all types, including *kabukabu* business. The tendency towards small-scale manufacturing is encouraged, not just by the resource base of the professional classes, but also by the nature of the organised manufacturing sector which hitherto had been largely reliant on imported inputs. Rising costs of capital and foreign exchange, and administrative and other over-heads have eroded capacity utilisation, and also pushed up the prices of the finished products to well beyond what the average Nigerian is willing to pay. The Nigerian consumer is now prepared to purchase the cheaper, but poorer quality products of the small-scale sweat-shops owned and managed by members of the professional classes. It would seem that the favourite sub-sectors appear to be food processing, soap and cosmetics, and candle-making in that order of importance (*Business Concord*, March 18, 1988:10).

Nigerian professionals have become more involved in farming, and many of them are now big-time farmers. Many university academics run big farms whose output is partly for consumption, but also for profit. This pronounced profit motivation differentiates the farming businesses of professional classes from the more subsistence-oriented working class farming. Some professional class farmers have even established a measure of forward integration; their food processing establishments use the proceeds of their farms. The more common model is to run the farm largely from hired labour (although family labour is also important, especially for mobilising inputs and supervising farming operations). Many academics-cum-farmers even procure specialised skills (e.g. for making particular yam mounds) from places hundreds of miles from their abode. Such is the commercial dimension to this dynamic that some academics specialise in land preparation and leasing. Even in crowded Lagos, the increasing interest in farming is noticeable; the putrid jungles bordering the highways leading into the city have fallen under cultivation:

> Such developments in market-gardening are becoming commonplace. Every evening, civil servants bring their children to the grounds in their cars to tend their spaces for the fortunes that lay inside the soil. The discovery [of civil servants] in the Badagry and Ajao farms creates an impression that most Nigerian top workers are now into farming while at the same time keeping their jobs in Lagos.... They are absentee farmers, trying to strike gold by using full-time labourers... (Ogbuile, 1990, B1).

The moonlighting skills of the professional classes are most graphically illustrated in the story of the *kabukabu*. As a Lagos observer noted:

> Until the late 80s, unregistered and unlicensed cab operators—otherwise called kabukabu—were a rarity. Those who operated kabukabu did it as a pastime, there were no hassles and the person hiking a ride paid only a token usually less than half of the usual fares, just enough to support main-

tenance savings. But all that has changed. From a casual pastime, kabukabu became a part-time [job] for hard-pressed civil servants ... (*The Guardian* (Lagos), June 30, 1990:12)

Another keen Lagos observer also pointed out that:

... kabukabu is virtually on every route. In fact, kabukabu rules some routes, constituting the only fair means of transport. No painted taxis, no public buses; kabukabu holds sway....Young clearing and forwarding agents supplement lean times by hauling passengers from Ikeja [airport] all the way to Apapa Wharf, while middle-aged couples secure the day's sustenance on the road via kabukabu. (*Business Concord*, Oct. 16, 1987:8)

It is hardly surprising that in April 1990, the Lagos State Government was reported to be considering the legalisation of the *kabukabu*; and the Federal Road Safety Corps are planning to bring motorcycle "express taxis" under regulation.

Youths

P. Bauer long ago pointed out the critical importance of trading within the Nigerian economy (Bauer, 1955). About 20 per cent of the GDP is derived from trading activities. Much of this trading—especially at the "petty" trading end—is dominated by women, youths, and even small children. This system of trading has historically been marked by the multiple modes tendency, as seasonality in the supply of goods forces traders into different branches of commerce, or momentarily out of commerce entirely. A survey of traders in Samaru in 1989 revealed that only 45 per cent of the traders interviewed were full-time traders. 55 per cent combined trading with other activities, such as farming, teaching, sewing, typing, mechanical repairs, and schooling (Yaro, 1989:24). 46 per cent of all the traders interviewed had a weekly turnover of about N25 (US$3), reflecting the extremely marginal nature of much of petty trading. Most of the petty traders were youths, and a high proportion of them were women.

SAP may have intensified the search for income through a combination of petty trading and other activities, but it is doubtful if it has improved the prospects for accumulation or even economic survival through such activities. What is clear is that increasingly, many Nigerian women and youths are gravitating towards other forms of generating income. On the positive side, there is the increasing proliferation of "fashion homes" for designer clothes, sometimes run by those still in employment. The sporadic growth of these fashion homes has been cited as a major source of problems for organised manufacturers of garments. On the other side, there is a noticeable increase in prostitution and drug trafficking by largely young and female clerks, traders, housewives, students, etc. Nigeria is now acknowledged as a leading courier country in the international drugs trafficking circuit.

THE RURAL ECONOMY AND MULTIPLE MODES

Location within the national economy—urban or rural—and social class have so far been the main organising variables in this examination of the multiple modes dynamic in Nigeria. However, these two variables are insufficient for explaining the relationship between the rural economy and multiple modes of earning a living. Unlike workers or professionals who exhibit broad similarities, different peasantries relate differently to the multiple modes dynamic. It is therefore necessary to be more specific and localised when analysing the relationship of peasant societies to the multiple modes dynamic; ethnicity, history, and cropping systems all become relevant factors. These issues can be illustrated by brief summaries of the histories of the cocoa-growing Yoruba peasantry in southwestern Nigeria on the one hand, and the grain-growing Hausa peasantry of Kano on the other.

The nature of rural Yorubaland was dramatically transformed in the 1890s by three factors: the end of the Yoruba Civil War, the imposition of British colonialism, and the introduction of cocoa. Cocoa became the single most critical factor in the countryside. A peasantry evolved, completely tied to the fortunes of cocoa, and accumulation from cocoa cultivation was used to expand cocoa fields, to maintain the household, and to educate the children of cocoa farmers (Agboola, 1980; Berry, 1975). The dynamic of multiple modes of accumulation—either as the simultaneous combination of farming and other activities, or as the development of a complementary nonfarm sector—was not crucial to the cocoa-growing peasantry. From the 1960s, however, the cocoa industry went into decline. Peasant accumulation, and even survival, through cocoa cultivation was put under severe stress. In response, peasant households diversified into petty trading and other service activities to maintain their livelihood. The recourse to the multiple modes strategy amongst the cocoa-growing peasantry is therefore a reflection of the failure of continued accumulation through agriculture (Berry, 1985).

Fieldwork in rural Kano in 1986—just before SAP—revealed that almost all members of the rural Hausa village of Rogo included in the sample were engaged in own-farming. A few rich farmer-traders maintained large farms through hired labour and the help of supervisory farm-servants, while some artisans engaged in small-scale farming through the use of hired labour. The prevalence of farming was, however, matched by the equal prevalence of subsidiary occupations; most household heads in the sample had two or more subsidiary occupations. Non-agricultural income was 18 per cent of the total cash income of the rich peasantry in the sample.[9] The same figures for the middle and poor peasants in the sample were 50 per cent and 85 per cent respectively (Mustapha, 1990).

Research elsewhere has also noted that no Hausa peasant depends exclusively on agrarian cultivation, farming being often mixed with as many as four other supplementary occupations (Hill, 1972). Indeed, such has been the centrality of supplementary occupations to the Hausa peasantry, that a colonial official denied in 1925 that there was any large "agricultural class" in Kano Emirate (National Archives Kaduna, Kanprof., 1708A–Taki Assessment and Revenue Survey–Kano Province). Clearly, the simultaneous combination of farming and allied subsidiary activities, and the development of a complementary non-farm sector, are both pronounced aspects of agrarian accumulation in rural Hausaland.

If the multiple mode dynamic represents a downward spiral in the accumulation process of the Yoruba peasantry, the reverse is the case for the grain-growing Hausa peasantry for whom the multiple modes logic has historically been a central aspect of the accumulation process. Here, it represents an upward, not a downward spiral; farming creates the basis for branching out into more lucrative activities. It is therefore impossible to generalise about the role of the

9. The 18 per cent is undoubtedly an underestimate. It is possible that the rich peasant household heads were reluctant to disclose the full extent of their non-farm incomes.

multiple modes logic within the peasantries of Nigeria; neither is it possible to generalise about the impact of SAP on that role. The comments that follow are therefore limited to the grain-growing Hausa peasantry of rural Kano.

The intimate connection between farm and nonfarm production in rural Kano demands an examination of both sub-sectors if the impact of SAP on one form of production is to be understood. That SAP is "good" for agriculture has since passed from the realms of official propaganda into popular myth. In reality, however, it is too early to draw conclusions; contradictory tendencies abound (Mustapha, forthcoming) and more time is needed for them to work themselves out. Some aspects of SAP, like increased local sourcing by industry and the banning of wheat and rice imports, have boosted the demands for (and prices of) agricultural products. Farmers have responded to these incentives; the aggregate index of agricultural production is on the increase, from 3.5 per cent in 1988 to 6.1 per cent in 1989 (*New Nigerian*, June 20, 1990:3).

A limited re-survey of Rogo in July 1990 revealed that this positive aspect of SAP is clearly noticeable. Some rich peasants have expanded their holdings by about 20 per cent between 1986 and 1990. These rich peasants describe a general improvement in their farming operations in the region of 50 per cent. Some have actually doubled their plough-teams and fertiliser use. But even these rich peasants who appear to benefit from SAP have had to make some adjustments in their farming operations; some now appear to place a greater emphasis on improved seeds which are more pest-resistant. This is clearly a strategy to confront the escalating cost of pest-control chemicals. Others have dropped labour-intensive crops like pepper; again, a move dictated by the need to contain rising labour costs.

But underlying these positive trends are counter-trends which question the sustainability of agrarian improvements under SAP. The Central Bank itself stated that improved production in 1989 was due to favourable weather, increased hectarage cultivated, and improved storage facilities. It also pointed out that there were "severe shortages" in inputs—fertilisers, chemicals, and tools (*New Nigerian*, June 20, 1990:3). Government monitoring agencies have also collected evidence which suggests that fertiliser use may be on the decline, and that increased fertiliser costs may be cutting into farmers' profit margins (Wedderburn, 1988). For its part, the Nigerian

Agricultural and Co-operative Bank (NACB) has pointed out that
SAP "seriously hinders" agricultural mechanisation, because of extremely high costs of capital and tools (*Business Concord*, Aug. 28
1987:16). This squeezing of the input base of agriculture—remi-
niscent of colonial economic policy which concerned itself with balancing the budget at the expense of developmental investments—
suggests that much of the increased production may be from the
expanded hectarage. Given the low level of production technology,
and population pressure, it is doubtful if this model of agrarian
accumulation—"on the cheap"—can be sustained for very long
without serious environmental and productivity consequences.

Indeed, these negative aspects of SAP are manifest in Rogo. A rich
peasant who used 140 50 kg bags of fertiliser in 1986 could only
obtain 20 in 1990. Many denounced the increasing subjection of fertiliser distribution to patronage networks, and its escalated price;
from N 10 (official) and N 17 (market) per 50 kg bag in 1986, to
N 80—N 100 in 1989, and N 47—N 50 in 1990. Labour costs have also
increased by about 120 per cent between 1986 and 1990; tractor-
hiring costs by about 500 per cent. Agricultural expansion in Rogo
from 1983 has been based on the cultivation of high-yielding, but
input-intensive varieties of maize and beans. Maize will not do well
without fertiliser; beans are prone to pests, and need chemicals.
There has therefore been a noticeable recent decline in the cultivation of these crops, as farmers return to local varieties of guinea-corn
and millet, which need less fertiliser and chemical inputs. But this
shift in crops grown reduces agricultural productivity, and cannot
address the problem of escalating labour costs and general inflation.

Whether SAP is really "good" for agriculture remains a debate-
able point which cannot be categorically answered for now. What is
clear, however, is that it is beginning to affect the supplementary
activities of many peasants. A rich peasant who combined farming
with selling fertiliser, trading in grains, selling firewood, and running a transport business now claims to be in dire straits; he cannot
get fertiliser to sell, profitability of the grain trade is reportedly down
because of high production costs, and many ordinary peasants now
prefer to go into the bush for their own firewood, rather than waste
their limited financial resources on firewood purchases. Only the
transport business appears to be unscathed. On the other hand,
another rich peasant is apparently sufficiently well-to-do to recently

open a vehicle spare-parts shop, a line of business usually dominated by Igbo traders.

Some members of the rural semi-proletariat may also have benefited from higher labour prices; one has been able to buy some land
between 1986 and 1990. Some others complain that inflation has can-
celled out all their gains from increased monetary wages. Rural artisans, too, may be affected by the increasing production of cheap and
poor quality household goods in the urban informal sector, for there
has always been an intimate connection between urban and rural
artisanal production (Jaggar, 1973). For now however, Rogo artisans
appear to have a greater volume of business, but complain about
greater difficulty in getting inputs like scrap metal. They also complain about costs.

CONCLUSION: MULTIPLE MODES AND SUSTAINABLE ADJUSTMENT

It is clear from the Nigerian evidence that the very survival of many
households under SAP depends on their ability to augment their
formal sector wages through informal sector activities; the Moscovite
curse, referred to at the beginning of this paper is equally potent in
Nigeria. SAP's impact on informal sector activities of the multiple
modes type has helped to release the "creative imagination" of the
Nigerian public; and far from being marginal activities, some of
them are actually dynamic (Meagher, 1990a). Some multiple modes
activities may also be said to be socially relevant; the Lagos *kabukabu*
plays a crucial role in the city's transport system. Based on these
arguments, it is tempting to conclude that multiple modes activities
contribute to "economic recovery" and may form the basis for
renewed growth in the future. However, there are other economic
and socio-political considerations which suggest that, in the long
run, multiple modes activities may be counter-productive and anti-
developmental.

The economic issues which demand attention when considering
the relevance of multiple modes to sustainable adjustment are: the
relationship between wage rates and productivity levels; work standards and morale; profitability; macro and micro linkages.

Considering the problems confronting Nigerian workers under

SAP, it is hardly surprising that those sympathetic to the trade union movement are arguing that "the price of labour should reflect the cost of producing it" (Bello, 1989:9). Expressing a contrary opinion, a senior member of the business community, Dr. Omolayole, called upon the government "... not to link disposable incomes, especially salaries to the present cost of living, but on the level of productivity" (*Business Concord*, April 11, 1989:10). This tension between demands for a living wage and demands for higher productivity lies at the heart of the economic basis of the multiple mode. Some members of the business community expect productivity increases from workers who are not paid a living wage, and who are therefore obliged to survive out of increased self-exploitation. This seems to be expecting too much, and the history of forced labour in colonial Africa suggests that labour, paid below the "standard wage", is neither cooperative nor efficient. Because the multiple modes tendency is premised on the neglect of "garrinomics",[10] it undermines any possibilities for sustained productivity increases from formal sector labour.

Secondly, it may even be the case that the multiple modes tendency is not only compromising future productivity increases, but erodes present levels of efficiency and productivity by undermining work standards and morale. The civil servant farmers of the Lagos swamps are still on their farms well after the commencement of office hours in the morning. And though academics from agricultural science and related discplines may benefit from the welcome opportunity to relate theory to practice, it is also the case that tight farming schedules compete with the demands of students and other academic pursuits. The government is allegedly worried about the extent of the involvement of university teachers in private businesses, and the National Universities Commission (NUC) has accused such teachers of "double dealing" (*The Guardian*, Lagos, Nov. 8., 1990:1). It is equally noteworthy that while Nigerian academics are complaining about under-staffing and lack of autonomy, the NUC is advocating a policy of complete autonomy for university-run consultancy companies. These companies, the NUC argues, should be allowed to move out of university premises, and take relevant university staff along with them on secondment (*Business Concord*, Nov. 6, 1987:5, 7).

---

10. Garri is a basic staple.

Thirdly, it cannot be said that all multiple mode activities are profitable. Some people, fearful of sitting still whilst the economic system is crumbling, jump into activities of dubious profitability. In this particular regard, lack of specialisation is not a virtue conferring a measure of flexibility, but a decisive handicap. For example, many bureaucrats and academics from Kano have established farms around Dambatta, using the peasants of that area as farm supervisors and labourers. It is said that many of the peasants are now to be heard, asking their friends: wawanka nawa? (How many fools have you got?). Apparently, the peasants divert the farm inputs supplied by the urban-based absentee-farmers, whom they regard as fools, to their own farms (Personal communication, Shehu Yahaya). For many people, multiple modes activities may not amount to more than a frantic, but futile, psychological attempt to escape from threatened destitution.

Finally, economic analyses of informal sector activities like the multiple modes type are often at the micro level, without any attempt to explore their relation to the over-arching macro economic climate. Furthermore, micro-level analyses sometimes reflect more of ideological prejudice—like the unbridled belief in local sourcing—than economic reality. This may sometimes result in disaster. Some experiences in Nigeria illustrate this point. The Nigerian Association of Small Scale Industrialists (NASSI) has pointed out that 720 small businesses had collapsed in Lagos State alone, between January 1987 and June 1988. The association was obliged to try to correct the "general impression that local raw materials could be sourced anywhere at little or no cost" (*Business Concord*, Aug. 2, 1988:1, 7). Similarly, when farmers complained about escalating cost of cutlasses, the World Bank representative in Nigeria, Mr. Tariq Husain, urged the farmers not to worry; he opined that the cutlass they bought in 1988 would last for 5 to 10 years, and further advised that instead of buying expensive, imported flat steel cutlasses, the farmers should use cutlasses made from locally available scrap. In response, a farmer pointed out that "...The type of cutlass Mr Husain is talking about does not last. They can not even withstand the rigours of farming because they bend easily" (*Business Concord*, March 14, 1989:11).

It is this same uncritical—and economically naive—belief in local sourcing which led some analysts to praise the ingenuity of some local motor refurbishers who are converting old trucks into public transport buses, called molue. The refurbishers were hailed as "automobile doctors", and their products were praised as being "deceptively new" and "specially built for Nigerian roads" (Ekwegbalu, 1987). By 1990, however, the same molues were being described as a "menace" to the public; in Lagos alone, the buses are said to have sent over 2000 people to their early graves (*National Concord*, June 22, 1990:16). In 1990, an editorial in a Lagos newspaper aptly summed up the issue: "Today, the commuter is left at the mercy of cheap metal constructs masquerading as buses; often, a seven-tonne body is knitted and painted onto a five-tonne chasis" (*Daily Times*, June 30, 1990:6).

To be a viable source of economic growth on a long-term basis, the informal sector—including many multiple modes activities—must overcome the problems of duplication of businesses, poor quality products, and lack of standardisation.[11] As Jolly points out, micro-level approaches of the survival strategies type will never form an adequate basis for tackling the problem of poverty in the long run (Jolly, 1988). And Cornia has also observed that though survival strategies can be useful as "buffering mechanisms" in times of economic crisis, they are not merely inexpensive laissez-faire solutions, and their negative or doubtful effects deserve appropriate attention. Support for survival strategies should therefore be seen as complementary to, and not substitutes for, macro-economic policies aimed at growth and equity within the formal sector (Cornia, 1987).

Survival strategies also have important political ramifications. In Nigeria, there are two major issues involved. The first is the increased individualisation and personalisation of some aspects of public life, and related problems of clientelism and corruption. The second deals with the role of repression, and the prospects for democracy.

At the household and community levels, economic crisis can often generate survival strategies aimed at pooling resources between households, thereby expanding the scope for community cooperation. In barrios of Lima such as Huaycan, poor households are

---

11. In 1990, the sale of defective paracetamol syrup resulted in the death of about 100 children all over the country. In January 1991, press reports suggest that table salt contaminated with toxic substances, have found their way into the Nigerian market.

reported to be pooling together their feeding and child-care responsibilities in the face of a worsening economic crisis. The families chip in to buy the minimal things needed to keep a soup kitchen going. The same spirit of community cooperation has been reported for Kenyan women, who have responded to the crisis by forming many womens' and church self-help groups (Personal communication, Adhiambo Odaga). In Nigeria, a similar spirit of community cooperation existed before SAP; in Lagos for example, attacks by armed robbers led to the formation of many street and neighbourhood associations, for the mutual protection of lives and property. In Zaria, academics joined together in "meat clubs" for getting cheaper meat through bypassing the middlemen and buying live cows for slaughter.

However, since SAP and the deepening of the general and economic crisis of the Nigerian state, it would seem that the new, and more dynamic, forms of cooperation are not those organisations based on neighbourhoods or streets, but a resurgence of particularistic ethnic and religious groupings who not only help their members to cope with the crisis, but also help ultimately to fragment the collective spirit or identity of the neighbourhood or community. There is the distinct impression that inclusive community based organisations have been weakened by the economic and political-cum-religious crisis of the Nigerian state. The "meat clubs" of Zaria later all but disappeared, and many womens' savings societies (*adashi*), as in the rural Kano village of Diribo, have collapsed (Personal communication, Ayesh Imam). But some forms of community based cooperation still persist; farmers joining together to hire water-pumps, families and households exchange gifts and food, and community resources are mobilised for the building of village utilities. There is even the claim that womens' groups are being formed under the government-sponsored Better Life For Rural Women programme; it is however unclear if this claim is correct, or just another publicity gimmick. Occassionally, disparate social groups and forces would come together temporarily in anti-SAP riots.

At the level of trade unions and professional organisations, the impact of economic crisis and its attendant survival strategies are often more distinctly disruptive. Trade unions are always weakened by a convergence of economic crisis and high unemployment; scope for union gains narrow, and union activity becomes oriented towards the protection of past gains, rather than the advancement of present needs. Even this defensive position may be untenable. Workers invariably resort to a personal struggle for survival through survival strategies and seek new access to needed resources, thereby further eroding the collective commitment of the union. This access may be through the agency of familial, township, ethnic, regional, "old-boy", or religious organisations.

Collective union consciousness is increasingly undermined by competing particularistic ties. It is not an accident that such particularist organisations have become prominent within the professional classes in Nigeria in the late 1980s. The quest for personal advantage and survival also undermines the bureaucratic ethos in many public and private sector bureaucracies. Favouritism, clientelism, and corruption are intensified, as any observer of contemporary Nigeria would note. The tendency towards state failure is enhanced by poor wages and the recourse to "survival strategies" (Klitgaard, 1989).

The above dynamic may also affect the peasantry. In Rogo, political power was monopolised by the traditional aristocracy between 1903 and 1966, largely under British colonial tutelage. From the late 1960s, there was an increasing opening up of the rural political process to other social groups. Consequently, rich farmer-traders have tended to wield considerable political influence in the countryside, and mediate the political and economic interaction between town and country. This "gate-keeper" role is performed within the context of the dominance of a populist ideology, and a clear orientation towards political calculation on the part of most peasants (Mustapha, 1990). Increased clientelism and corruption in the state, parastatal, and commercial bureaucracies in the country may affect this urban/ rural economic and political interface by putting more pressures on the farmer-traders. Complaints about the personalisation of fertiliser distribution and increased favouritism are rife in the village.

These connections between structural adjustment, survival strategies, and the nature of the African state have been the subject of recent academic speculation. The role of repression, and the prospects for democracy are other central concerns. Redclift and Mingione have noted the paradox that under late capitalism, organisational decentralisation of capitalist enterprises is accompanied by increasing concentration of capital, and its hegemonic hold over society (Redclift and Mingione, 1985). A similar paradox exists under

SAP; increasing economic liberalisation is accompanied by increased political repression.[12]

Herbst has sought to explain this linkage between structural adjustment and repression. He argues that African politics was essentially the institutionalisation of patron-client relationships. Pre-structural adjustment politics were based on the use of various resources by the leader to buy political support. Under SAP, he argues, the government is obliged to change its constituency; from those dependent on state patronage, to those reliant on market forces, as the ability of the state to hand out patronage diminishes. This weakening of the patronage system will weaken the state's power structure, and make it "less flexible" in dealing with political crisis. The change in constituency is closely followed by a change in control mechanism; the absense of patronage leads to increased repression (Herbst, 1990).

Defending an opposing position, Bratton argues that the control of the African state over society has historically been weak. Economic crisis and subsequent liberalisation leads to the "contraction" of the state. This "retreat" of the state, he argues, will, "willynilly", enlarge the political space for democratic intervention by popular associations in civil society (Bratton, 1989a). Some other theorists have elaborated the dynamic which transforms structural adjustment into increased democracy. They argue that as the state withdraws from many economic activities, the ruling class learns to live through non-state activities, while non-ruling class groups gravitate towards survival strategies, independent of state patronage. Increasingly, the ruling class, free of the pervasive grip of the state, has less need for the zero-sum logic of much of African politics, and increasingly gravitates towards the rational and democratic resolution of intra-ruling class problems. Through survival strategies, non-ruling class groups also break out of patronage networks and press for more autonomy, rationality, and democracy.

The major problem with both approaches in associating structural adjustment and survival strategies with the political process is that they rely, not so much on a study of the reality of African politics under SAP, but on a mechanistic association of economic trends with particular political possibilities.

---

12. The Buhari regime sought to undermine and disband many organs of civil society—the news media, trade unions, students unions, and professional associations. Babangida's regime has continued, if not intensified, this trend.

Herbst's argument rests on a number of false assumptions. African politics is completely subsumed under a patron-client dynamic, ignoring other impulses, such as the role of associational life in civil society. Contrary to the Nigerian experience, he asserts that SAP will do away with the patronage system; but the diminishing resource base of the patronage system does not mean that the whole system will disappear. It may even be that diminishing resources within the patronage system may lead to increased favouritism and factionalism as the struggle for the little resources left intensifies. In Nigeria, the Central Bank was accused of patronage in the distribution of scarce foreign exchange in pre-SAP days. It was felt that "market forces", working through the decentralised commercial banks, will eliminate this patronage system. In reality, however, reports in the Nigerian media show clearly that the commercial banks have since spun their own patronage and racketeering webs.

The argument that structural adjustment and survival strategies will lead to increased democratisation is equally based on abstract logical deductions, unrelated to reality. Under SAP, the ruling class is no less dependent on the state, and national politics does not look any cleaner; involvement in survival strategies by non-ruling class groups does not lead to a break out of patronage networks. Involvement in such networks may even intensify in the struggle for survival.

The reality of political life under SAP is the intensification of repression and the "contraction" of democratic political openings, (Ibrahim, 1986; Yau, 1986; and Mustapha and Othman, 1987) not as a result of the need by the state to fill the void created between erstwhile patrons and clients as Herbst argues, but because the adoption of SAP as state policy contains within it an unstated predisposition towards the incorporation or dismantling of associations in civil society whose members are likely to bear the brunt of SAP policies. Repression occurs not because people demand the continuation of patronage, but because they want to defend their livelihood against swinging cuts on their standard of living. SAP has closed, not opened up, democratic space; but it will still have to contend with civil society.

In the face of SAP, many individuals and households in Nigeria have adopted survival strategies including the multiple modes tendency, and it is only to be hoped that the nation, and its composite individuals, households, and institutions will survive this phenomenon.

References and Bibliography

Adams, H.R., 1991, *The effects of international remittances on poverty, inequality, and development in rural Egypt*, International Food Policy Research Institute, Research Report 86.

Adams, J., 1991, "The rural labour market in Zimbabwe", *Development and Change*, Vol. 22.

Adam Y., 1986, *Cooperativização agrícola e modificações das relações de produção no período colonial em Moçambique*, Eduardo Mondlane University, Maputo.

Adepoju, A., 1991, "South-North migration: The African experience", *South-North migration*, Vol. xxix, No. 2, June.

Agboola, S., 1980, "Agricultural changes in Western Nigeria: 1850–1910", in Akinjogbin, I. and S. Osoba, (eds.), *Topics on Nigerian Economic and Social History*, University of Ife Press, Ile-Ife.

Ake, C., 1987, "The Nigerian state: Antimonies of a periphery formation", in Ake, C., (ed.), *The Political Economy of Nigeria*, Longman.

AKUT, 1990, "The report of the AKUT Group 1987–1990 and the plans for 1990–1993", *AKUT* 42, (Uppsala: AKUT—Working Group for the Study of Development Strategies).

Akwetey, E., 1990, "State, unions and structural adjustment: A comparative study of Ghana, Tanzania, and Zambia. Project proposal submitted to SAREC", University of Stockholm: Department of Political Science.

Althusser, L., 1969, *For Marx*, Allen Lane, London.

Amanor, D.E., 1991, "Cape Verde: The economy", *Africa South of the Sahara, Yearbook*, London.

Andrae, G., "Urban workers as farmers: Agro-links and livelihood of Nigerian textile workers in the crisis of the 1980s", in Baker, J. and P. O. Pedersen, (eds.), *The Rural-Urban Interface in Africa*, Nordiska Afrikainstitutet, Uppsala (forthcoming).

Andrae, G. and B. Beckman, 1991, "Workers, unions, and the crisis of the Nigerian textile industry", in Brandell, I., (ed.), *Workers in Third World Industrialization*, Macmillan, London.

Anyang' Nyong'o, P., 1988a, "Political instability and the prospects for democracy in Africa", *Africa Development*, Vol. xiii, No. 1.

Anyang' Nyong'o, P., 1988b, "Democracy and political instability: A rejoinder to the comments by Thandika Mkandawire", *Africa Development,*. Vol. xiii, No. 3.

Asobie, H.A., 1991, "Economic crisis, structural adjustment and the middle classes in Nigeria", Paper presented at the Workshop on the UNRISD Research Project on Crisis, Adjustment and Social Change, Lagos, March.

ASUU (Academic Staff Union of Universities), 1984, "How to save Nigeria".

Azarya, V. and N. Chazan, 1987, "Disengagement from the state in Africa: Reflections on the experience of Ghana and Guinea", *Comparative Studies in Society and History*, Vol. 29, 1.

Babangida, I., 1989, "Address to the nation on the outcome of the deliberations of the AFRC on 6/10/89", *BBC Summary of World Broadcasts*, 10/10/89, ME/0583 B/1.

Bangura, Y., 1986, "Structural adjustment and the political question", *Review of African Political Economy*, 37.

Bangura, Y., 1988, "The crisis of underdevelopment and the transition to civil rule: Conceptualizing the question of democracy in Nigeria", *Africa Development*, Vol. xiii, No. 1.

Bangura, Y., 1989a, "Crisis, adjustment and politics in Nigeria". Outline of a research programme, *AKUT* 38, Uppsala.

Bangura, Y., 1989b, "Crisis and adjustment: The experience of Nigerian workers", in Onimode, B., (ed.), *The IMF, the World Bank and the African Debt*, Vol. 2, Social and economic impact, ZED and IFAA, London.

Bangura, Y., and B. Beckman, 1991, "African workers and structural adjustment. With a Nigerian case study" in Ghai, D., (ed.), *IMF and the South: Social Impact of Crisis and Adjustment*, London, Zed Books, also in Olukoshi, A., (ed.), *The Politics of Structural Adjustment in Nigeria*, (forthcoming).

Barraclough, S., 1990, "Dilemmas of agrarian transformation. The state, the peasant question and democracy in the Third World", Paper at Third World Forum's seminar on Democracy, Socialism and Development, Zimbabwe, June.

Bates, R., 1981, *Markets and States in Tropical Africa: The Political Basis of Agricultural Policies*, Berkeley, University of California, Los Angeles.

Bates, R., 1986, *Government Policies Toward Agriculture in Africa: The Prospects for Reform*, Duke University Program in International Political Economy, Working Paper No. 4.

Bathilly, A., 1987, "Senegal's fraudulent 'Democratic Opening'", in Institute for African Alternatives, *Africa's Crisis*, London.

Bathilly, A., 1989, "Political development in Senegal", *Journal of African Marxists*, Issue 11, February.

Bauer, P., 1955, "The trader in peasant economies", *New Commonwealth*, April 18.

Beckman, B., 1988a, "When does democracy make sense? Problems of theory and practice in the study of democratisation in Africa and the Third World", Paper to AKUT Conference on Democracy, Uppsala, October.

Beckman, B., 1988b, "The post-colonial state: Crisis and reconstruction". *IDS Bulletin*, 19:4; also in University of Edinburgh, Centre of African Studies, *African Futures: 25th Anniversary Conference.*

Beckman, B., 1988c, "Comments on Göran Hydén's State and Nation under Stress", in Swedish Ministry of Foreign Affairs, *Recovery in Africa: A Challenge for Development Cooperation in the 90s*, Stockholm.

Beckman, B., 1988d, "Bistånd och Demokrati: En kritik av den nya interventionismen", (Aid and Democracy: A critique of the new interventionism), *DebattSida* 2/88, Stockholm, SIDA.

Beckman, B., 1989, "Whose democracy? Bourgeois versus popular democracy in Africa", *Review of African Political Economy* 45/46.

Beckman, B., 1990, "Structural adjustment and democracy: Interest group resistance to structural adjustment and the development of the democracy movement in Africa. Research proposal submitted to SAREC", University of Stockholm, Department of Political Science.

Bello, M., 1989, "Economics of garri, or garrinomics", *Business Concord*, Jan. 20.

Bennell, P., 1990 "Corporate attitudes to investment in Sub-Saharan Africa", *Development Policy Review* Vol. 8.

Berg-Schlosser, D., 1985, "On the conditions of democracy in third world countries", Paper to the International Political Science Association World Congress, Paris.

Bernstein, H., 1990 "Agricultural modernization in the era of structural adjustment", *Journal of Peasant Studies*, Vol. 17, No. 4.

Berry, S., 1975, *Cocoa, Custom, and Economic Change in Rural Western Nigeria*, Clarendon, Oxford.

Berry, S., 1985, *Fathers Work for Their Sons: Accumulation, Mobility, and Class Formation in an Extended Yoruba Community*, University of California Press, Berkeley.

Bhagwati, J.N., 1982, "Directly unproductive profit seeking (DUP) activities", *Journal of Political Economy*, Vol. 90.

Bienefeld, M., 1986, "Analysing the politics of African state policy. Some thoughts on Robert Bates' work", *IDS Bulletin*, 17:1.

Bienen, H., 1990, "The politics of trade liberalisation in Africa", *Economic Development and Cultural Change*, Vol. 38, No. 4, July.

Bienen, H.S. and M. Gersovitz, 1985, "Economic stabilisation, conditionality, and political stability", *International Organisation*, 39, 4, Autumn.

Bobbio, N., 1988, "Gramsci and the concept of civil society", in Keane, J., (ed.), *Civil Society and the State*, Verso, London.

Booth, D., 1990, "Structural adjustment in socio-political context: Some findings from a local study in Tanzania", Paper delivered to Development Studies Association Conference, mimeo.

Bratton, M., 1989a, "Beyond the state: Civil society and associational life in Africa", *World Politics*, Vol. XLI, No. 3.

Bratton, M., 1989b, "The politics of government-NGO relations in Africa", *World Development*, April.

Bratton, M., 1990, "Non-governmental organisations in Africa", *Development and Change*, Vol. 21, No. 1, January.

Buchanan, J., 1980, "Rent seeking and profit seeking", in Buchanan, J.M., R.D. Tollison and G. Tullock, (eds.), *Towards a Theory of Rent-Seeking Society*, Texas A. and M. University Press.

Callaghy, T.M., 1989, "Toward state capability and embedded liberalism in the Third World: Lessons for adjustment", in Nelson, J.M., (ed.), *Fragile Coalitions: The Politics of Economic Adjustment*, Transaction Books.

Callaghy, T.M., 1990, "Lost between state and market: The politics of economic adjustment in Ghana, Zambia, and Nigeria", in Nelson, J.M., (ed.), *Economic Crisis and Policy Choice: The Politics of Economic Adjustment in the Third World*, Princeton University Press.

Camdessus, M., 1988, "The IMF: Facing new challenges: An interview with Michael Camdessus, Managing Director of the IMF", *Finance and Development*, June.

Campbell, B., 1989, "Structural adjustment and recession in Africa: Implications for democratic process and participation", Paper to the 1989 African Studies Association Meeting, Atlanta.

Carrilho, J., et al, 1990, *An Alternative Strategy for Agricultural Development*, by Carrilho, J., M. Martins, J. Trindade, L.E. Birgegård, and M. Fones-Sundell, Maputo.

Carter, A., 1989, "Industrial democracy and the capitalist state", in Duncan, G., *Democracy and the Capitalist State*, Cambridge University Press.

Castells, M. and A. Portes, 1989, "The world underneath: The origins, dynamics, and effects of the informal economy", in Portes, A., M. Castells, and L. A. Benton, (eds.), *The Informal Economy: Studies in Advanced and Less Developed Countries*, The Johns Hopkins University Press, Baltimore.

Cawson, A., 1989, "Is there a corporatist theory of the state?", in Duncan, G., *Democracy and the Capitalist State*, Cambridge University Press.

Central Bank of Nigeria (CBN), *Annual Report and Statement of Accounts*, (various).

Chazan, N., 1983, *An Anatomy of Ghanaian Politics: Managing Ghanaian Political Recession, 1969–1982*, Westview, Boulder.

Chazan, N., 1988, "Ghana: Problems of governance and the emergence of civil society", in Diamond, L., et al., (eds.), *Democracy in Developing Countries, Vol. 2, Africa*, Lynne Rienner, Boulder.

Cheng, T-J., 1989, "Democratising the quasi-Leninist regime in Taiwan", *World Politics*, XLI, No. 4, July.

Chew, D., 1990, "Internal adjustments to falling civil service salaries: Insights from Uganda", in *World Development*, Vol. 18, No. 7.

Chourci, N., 1986, "The hidden economy: A new view of remittances in the Arab World", *World Development*, Vol. 14, June.

Cliffe, L., 1987, "The debate on African peasantries", *Development and Change*, No. 18 (4), October.

Coleman, J. and R. Sklar, 1985, "Preface" to Bender, G., J. Coleman, and R. Sklar, *African Crisis Areas and U.S. Foreign Policy*, University of California Press, Berkeley.

Collier, R.B., 1982, *Regimes in Tropical Africa: Changing Forms of Supremacy, 1945–1975*, University of California Press.

Commander, S., J. Havell, and W. Seine, 1989, "Ghana 1983–87" in Commander, S., (ed.), *Structural Adjustment and Agriculture: Theory and Practice in Africa and Latin America*, ODI/James Curry, London.

Cornia, G., 1987, "Adjustment at the household level: Potentials and limitations of survival strategies", in Cornia, G., R. Jolly and F. Stewart, (eds.), *Adjustment with a Human Face*, Clarendon, Oxford.

Cornia, G.A. and F. Stewart, 1990, "The fiscal system, adjustment and the poor", *Innocenti Occasional Papers* No. 11, November.

Coulon, C., 1988, "Senegal: The development and fragility of semi-democracy", in Diamond, L., J.J. Linz and S.M. Lipset, *Democracy in Developing Countries, Vol 2, Africa*, Lynne Rienner, Boulder.

Cowen, M. and K. Kinyanjui, 1977, "Some problems of class formation in Kenya", IDS, University of Nairobi (mimeo).

Crook, R., 1990, "State, society and political institutions in Côte d'Ivoire and Ghana", *IDS Bulletin*, Vol. 21, No. 4.

Crook, R., 1991, "Decentralisation and participation in Ghana and Côte d'Ivoire", in Crook, R. and A.M. Jerve, (eds.), *Government and Participation: Institutional Development, Decentralisation and Democracy in the Third World*, CMI Report 1991:1, Chr. Michelsen Institute, Bergen.

Dahl, R., 1971, *Polyarchy: Participation and Opposition*, New Haven.

Dahl, R., 1985, *A Preface to Economic Democracy*, University of California Press.

de Bragança Aquino, 1985, "Independence without decolonisation: The transfer of power in Mozambique 1974–1975. Some background notes", Paper presented to the Conference on Transfers of Power in Africa, Harare 1985, (also published in *Portuguese in Estudos Moçambicanos*, No. 5/6, 1986).

de Soto, H., 1989, *The Other Path: The Invisible Revolution in the Third World*, I.B. Taurus & Co, London.

Diamond, L., 1987, "Class formation in the African state", *Journal of Modern African Studies*, Vol. 25, No. 4.

Diamond, L., 1988a, "Roots of failure, seeds of hope" in Diamond, L., J. Linz, and S. Lipset, *Democracy in Developing Countries, Vol. 2, Africa*, Lynne Rienner, Boulder, Colorado.

Diamond, L., 1988b, *Class, Ethnicity and Democracy in Nigeria: The Failure of the First Republic*, Macmillan.

Diouf, M. and M.C. Diop, 1989, "La revanche des élèves et étudiants sur l'état et la société civile 1978–1988", Paper to AKUT Conference, Uppsala.

Donaldson, T., 1990, "The ethics of conditionality. International debt and the problem of 'Good Medicine'", (mimeo).

Dutkiewicz, P. and G. Williams, 1987, "All the king's horses and all the king's men couldn't put Humpty Dumpty together again", *IDS Bulletin*, 18:3.

ECA (Economic Commission for Africa), 1987, *The Abuja Statement: The Challenge of Economic Recovery and Accelerated Development*, Abuja.

ECA, 1988, "The Khartoum declaration: Towards a human-focused approach to socio-economic recovery and development in Africa", in *ECA Annual Report*, New York, UN.

ECA, 1990, *Economic Report on Africa 1990*, Addis Ababa.

ECA, 1991, *Report to the conference of African ministers of industry at its tenth meeting on industrial development in Africa in the 1980s*, Dakar, Senegal, June.

Eke, P., 1975, "Colonialism and the two publics in Africa: A theoretical statement", *Comparative Studies in Society and History*, Vol. 17, No. 2.

Ekuahare, B., 1984, "Recent patterns of accumulation in Nigeria", *Nigerian Journal of Political Science*, Vol. 3, No. 1.

Ekwegbalu, E., 1987, "SAP ushers in motor refurbishing", *Business Concord*, Nov. 6.

European Community, 1989, "Current conditions of consumption and production of the rural population of Mozambique" (mimeo), Maputo.

Fadahunsi, A., 1984, "Oil, industrialisation and the state in Nigeria", Centre for Social and Economic Research, Ahmadu Bello University, Zaria, Nigeria, CSER Reprint No. 14.

Fapohunda, O., 1985, *The Informal Sector of Lagos*, University Press, Ibadan.

Finer, S.E., 1985, "The retreat to the barracks: notes on the practice and the theory of military withdrawal from the seats of power", *Third World Quarterly*, 1, January.

Food and Agriculture Organisation (FAO), 1990, *The State of Food and Agriculture: World Regional Review, Structural Adjustment and Agriculture*, Rome.

Galli, R., 1990, "Liberalisation is not enough: Structural adjustment and peasants in Guinea-Bissau", *Review of African Political Economy*, No. 49.

Getzel, C., 1984, "Dissent and authority in the Zambian one-party state, 1973–80" in Getzel, C., C. Bayliss, and M. Szeftel, (eds.), *The Dynamics of the One-Party State in Zambia*, Manchester.

Ghai, D. and C.H. Alcántara, 1991, "The crisis of the 1980s in Africa, Latin America and the Caribbean: An overview", in Ghai, D., (ed.), *The IMF and the South*, Zed Book, London.

Gibbon, P., 1991, "Towards a 'Political Economy' of the World Bank 1970–90", Paper given at the Scandinavian Institute of African Studies, Africa Days Workshop, Uppsala, April, (mimeo).

Gibbon, P., 1992, "Agriculture and Structural Adjustment in Ghana and Kenya", *Journal of Peasant Studies*.

Griffith-Jones, S., 1990, "Cross-conditionality from the recipient's point of view", Paper delivered to IDPM Conference on Policy-Based Lending, (mimeo).

Gutto, S.B., 1988, "Social revolutions—the preconditions for sustainable development and people's power in Africa. A contribution to the Anyang' Nyong'o/Mkandawire debate", *Africa Development*, Vol. xxx, No. 4.

Gyimah-Boadi, E., 1989, "Economic recovery and politics in the PNDCs Ghana", *Conference Paper*, IDS, Sussex, April.

Habermas, J., 1973, *Legitimation Crisis*,. Heineman, London.

Haggard, S. and R.R. Kaufman, 1989, "Economic adjustment in new democracies", in Nelson, J.M., (ed.), *Fragile Coalitions: The Politics of Economic Adjustment*, Transaction Books.

Hansen, A., 1990, "Refugee settlement versus settlement on government schemes: The long-term consequences for security, integration and economic development of Angolan refugees (1966–1989) in Zambia", *UNRISD Discussion Paper*, 17, November.

Hansen, E., 1987, "The state and popular struggles in Ghana", in Anyang' Nyong'o, P., (ed.), *Popular Struggles for Democracy in Africa*, Zed Books, London.

Helleiner, G.K., 1990, "Structural adjustment and long-term development in Sub-Saharan Africa", *QEH Development Studies Working Papers*, No. 18, Oxford University, March.

Herbst, J., 1990, "The structural adjustment of politics in Africa", in *World Development*, Vol. 18, No. 7.

Hermele, K., 1988, *Land Struggles and Social Differentiation in Southern Mozambique*, Research Report 82, Uppsala, the Scandinavian Institute of African Studies.

Hermele, K., 1990, *Mozambican Crossroads. Economics and Politics in the Era of Structural Adjustment*, Report 3, Chr. Michelsen Institute, Bergen.

Hill, P., 1972, *Rural Hausa: A Village and a Setting*, CUP, Cambridge.

Himmelstrand, U., 1989, "Mamdani versus Hydén—Analysis of a Debate. Working Paper for the Project, 'In Search of New Paradigms for the Study of African Development'", Nairobi.

Holm, J.D., 1988, "Botswana: A paternalistic democracy", in Diamond, L., et al., *Democracy in Developing Countries, Vol 2, Africa*, Lynne Rienner, Boulder.

Hopkins, A., 1979, "The Lagos strike of 1897: An exploration in Nigerian labour history", in Cohen, R., P. Gutkind and P. Brazier, (eds.), *Peasants and Proletarians*, Hutchinson, London.

Huntington, S.P., 1968, *Political Order in Changing Societies*, Yale University Press, New Haven.

Huntington, S.P., 1984, "Will more countries become democratic?", *Political Science Quarterly*, 99.

Hutchful, E., 1987, "The crisis of the new international division of labour. Authoritarianism and the transition to free-market economies in Africa", *Africa Development*, 12:2.

Hydén, G., 1988, "State and nation under stress", in *Recovery in Africa: A Challenge for Development Cooperation in the 1990s*, Swedish Ministry for Foreign Affairs, Stockholm.

Hyden, G., 1983, *No Shortcuts to Progress. African Development Management in Perspective*, London, Heinemann.

Ibrahim, J., 1986, "The political debate and the struggle for democracy in Nigeria", *Review of African Political Economy*, No. 37.

Ibrahim, J., 1988, "From the primitive acquisition of power to the primitive accumulation of capital", (mimeo), Zaria.

Ibrahim, J., 1989, "The state, accumulation and democratic forces in Nigeria", Paper to AKUT Conference, Uppsala.

Ibrahim, J., 1990, "Expanding Nigerian democratic space", (mimeo), Bordeaux.

Ibrahim, J., "The transition to civil rule: Sapping democracy", in Olukoshi, A., (ed.), *The Politics of Structural Adjustment in Nigeria*, (forthcoming).

IMF, 1988, *IMF Survey*, June, Washington, D.C.

International Labour Office (ILO)/JASPA, 1988, *African Development Report*, Addis Ababa.

International Labour Office (ILO)/JASPA, 1991, *The Dilemma of the Informal Sector: Report of the Director General*, Addis Ababa.

Iyayi, F., 1986, "The primitive accumulation of capital in a neo-colony: Nigeria", *Review of African Political Economy*, No. 35.

Jaggar, P., 1973, "Kano City blacksmiths: Precolonial distribution, structure and organisation", *Savanna*, Vol. 2, No. 1.

Jamal, V. and J. Weeks, 1988, "The vanishing rural-urban gap in Sub-Saharan Africa", *International Labour Review*, Vol. 127, No. 3.

Jamal, V., 1991, "Inequalities and adjustment in Uganda", *Development and Change*, Vol. 22.

Jaycox, K., 1990, "Public lecture by the World Bank Vice President for Africa", SIDA's U-Forum, Stockholm, 18 April.

Jega, A.M., 1989, "Professional associations and SAP in Nigeria", Paper to ROAPE Conference on Democracy in Africa, University of Warwick, (forthcoming in Olukoshi, A., (ed.), *The Politics of Structural Adjustment in Nigeria*).

Jolly, R., 1988, "Poverty and adjustment in the 1990s", in Lewis, J., et al., *Strengthening the Poor: What Have we Learned*, Transaction Books, Oxford.

Kahler, M., 1989, "International financial institutions and the politics of adjustment", in Nelson, J.M., (ed.), *Fragile Coalitions: The Politics of Economic Adjustment*, Transaction Books, Oxford.

Kahler, M., 1990, "External influence, conditionality and the politics of adjustment", San Diego, University of California, (mimeo).

Kasfir, N., 1986, "Are African peasantries self-sufficient?", *Development and Change*, No. 17 (2).

Keane, J., 1988a, "Remembering the dead: Civil society and the state from Hobbes to Marx and beyond", in Keane, J., *Democracy and civil society*, Verso, London

Keane, J., 1988b, "Despotism and democracy: The origins and development of the distinction between civil society and the state, 1750–1850", in Keane, J., *Civil Society and the State*, Verso, London.

Kiondo, A., 1988, "The politics of economic liberalisation in Tanzania", Unpublished Ph.D. Thesis, University of Toronto.

Klitgaard, R., 1989, "Incentive Myopia", *World Development*, Vol. 17, No. 4.

Kraus, J., 1989, "The impact of Ghana's stabilisation and structural adjustment programmes upon workers and trade unions", Paper presented to the 1989 African Studies Association Meeting, Atlanta.

Kydd, J., 1989, "Zambia in the 1980s. The political economy of adjustment", in Commander, S., (ed.), *Structural Adjustment and Agriculture: Theory and Practice in Africa and Latin America*, ODI/James Currey, London.

Lal, D., 1983, *The Poverty of "Development Economics"*, London, Institute of Economic Affairs, Hobart Paperback 16.

Lal, D., 1987, "The political economy of economic liberalisation", *World Bank Economic Review*, Vol. 1, No. 2.

Lankester, T., 1990, "Verbal contribution to round table on prospects for policy-based lending in the 1990s", IDPM Conference on Policy-Based Lending, Manchester, September.

Lawrence, P., 1989, "The state and legitimation. The work of Jorgen Habermas", in Duncan, G., (ed.), *Democracy and the Capitalist State*, Cambridge University Press.

Legum, C., 1990, "The coming of Africa's second independence", *The Washington Quarterly*, Winter issue.

Lemarchand, R., 1991, "The political economy of informal economies", University of Florida, (mimeo).

Lindstrom, L., 1989, "The working class and democratisation in South Korea", *AKUT Conference Paper*, Uppsala, October.

Lipset, M., 1983, *Political Man: The Social Basis of Politics*, Heineman, London.

Lipton, M., 1977, *Why Poor People Stay Poor. Urban Bias in World Development*, Temple Smith, London.

Lofchie, M.F., 1975, "Political and economic origins of African hunger", *The Journal of Modern African Studies*, Vol. 13, December 4.

Lofchie, M., 1989, *The Policy Factor: Agricultural Performance in Kenya and Tanzania*, Lynne Rienner, Boulder.

Loxley, J., 1987, "The IMF, the World Bank and Sub-Saharan Africa. Policies and politics", in Havnevik, K., (ed.), *The IMF and the World Bank in Africa: Conditionality, Impact and Alternatives*, the Scandinavian Institute of African Studies, Uppsala.

Loxley, J., 1990, "Structural adjustment programmes in Africa: Ghana and Zambia", *Review of African Political Economy*, No. 47.

Loxley, J., 1991, "Ghana's recovery: An assessment of progress, 1987–1990", Ottawa, University of Manitoba, for the North-South Institute, (mimeo).

Lubeck, P., 1986, *Islam and Urban Labour in Northern Nigeria: The Making of a Muslim Working Class*, CUP, Cambridge.

MacGafee, J., 1983, "How to survive and become rich amidst devastation: The second economy in Zaire", *African Affairs*, Vol. 82, 328.

MacGafee, J., 1987, *Entrepreneurs and Parasites: The Struggle for Indigenous Capitalism in Zaire*, Cambridge.

Machiavelli, N., 1968, *The Prince*, Everyman ed., London, J.M. Dent.

Maghimbe, S., 1990, "Rural development policy and planning in Tanzania", Ph.D. Thesis, University of London.

Main, H. A. C., 1985, "Responses to inequalities: Workers, retrenchment and urban-rural linkages in Kano", Commonwealth Geographical Bureau Workshop, Bayero University, Kano.

Mamdani, M., 1985, "A great leap backward", *East African Social Science Review*, Vol. 1, No. 1.

Mamdani, M., 1986, "Peasants and democracy in Africa", *New Left Review*, 156.

Mamdani, M., 1987, "Extreme but not exceptional: Towards an analysis of the agrarian question in Uganda", *The Journal of Peasant Studies*, Vol. 14, No. 2.

Mamdani, M., 1991, "Uganda: Contradictions in the IMF programme and perspective", in Ghai, D., (ed.), *The IMF and the South*, Zed Books, London.

Mamdani, M., T. Mkandawire and E. Wamba-dia-Wamba, 1988, *Social Movements, Social Transformation and the Struggle for Democracy in Africa"*, CODESRIA, Dakar.

Manufacturers' Association of Nigeria, 1987, *Sample Survey of the Nigerian Manufacturing Sector*, January-June, Lagos.

Manufacturers' Association of Nigeria (MAN), 1989, *Half-Yearly Economic Review*, Lagos.

Marshall, J., 1990, "Structural adjustment and social policy in Mozambique", *Review of African Political Economy*, No. 47.

Martins, L., 1986, "The 'liberalisation' of authoritarian rule in Brazil", in O'Donnell, G., P.C. Schmitter and L. Whitehead, *Transitions from Authoritarian Rule: Latin America*, Johns Hopkins University Press.

Martinussen, J., 1980, "Social classes and forms of state and regime in peripheral societies", *AKUT 24*, Uppsala.

McCleary, W.A., 1989, "Policy implementation under adjustment lending", *Finance and Development*, March.

Meagher, K., 1990a, "Informalization and economic crisis in Africa: A reassessment of the development potential of the informal sector", (mimeo), Zaria.

Meagher, K., 1990b, "The hidden economy: Informal and parallel trade in northwestern Uganda", *Review of African Political Economy*, No. 47.

Meagher, K., 1991, "Limits to labour absorption: Conceptual and historical background to adjustment in the urban informal sector", Paper presented to the Workshop on UNRISD's Project on Crisis, Adjustment and Social Change, Lagos, March.

Ministry of Health, 1990, "Análise da capacidade de compra do salário mínimo para os alimentos básicos, setembro de 1990", (mimeo), Maputo, 1990.

Mkandawire, T., 1988a, "The road to crisis, adjustment and de-industrialisation: The African case", *Africa Development*, Vol. xiii, No. 1.

Mkandawire, T., 1988b, "Comments on democracy and political instability", *Africa Development*, Vol. xiii, No. 3.

Mkandawire, T., 1991a, "Crisis and adjustment in Sub-Saharan Africa", in Ghai, D., (ed.), *IMF and the South: Social Impact of Crisis and Adjustment*, Zed Books, London.

Mkandawire, T., 1991b, "Fiscal structure, state contraction and political responses in Africa", Paper presented to CODESRIA Conference on the Politics of Adjustment, Dakar, Senegal, (mimeo).

Molokomme, A., 1989, "The multi-party democracy in Botswana", *Southern African Political Economy Monthly*, September.

Moore, B., 1966, *Social Origins of Dictatorship and Democracy: Lord and Peasant in the Making of the Modern World*, Beacon, Boston.

Moore, M.P., 1984, "Political economy and the rural-urban divide, 1767–1981", *Journal of Development Studies*, 20, 3:5–27.

Mosley, P., J. Harrigan and J. Toye, 1991, *Aid and Power, The World Bank and Policy-Based Lending in the 1980s*, Routledge, London, 2 vols.

Moyo, J., 1989, "Zimbabwe: A critical appraisal of the ZUM challenge", *Southern African Political Economy Monthly*, Vol. 2. No. 11.

Mustapha, A.R., 1988, "Ever decreasing circles: Democratic rights in Nigeria, 1978–1988", Paper for CODESRIA Project on Nigeria, St Peter's College, Oxford.

Mustapha, A.R., 1990, "Peasant differentiation and politics in rural Kano 1900–1987", Ph.D. Thesis, University of Oxford.

Mustapha, A.R., 1991, "From boom to bust: Structural adjustment and the cocoa industry in Nigeria", Paper presented to the UNRISD Workshop on Crisis, Adjustment and Social Change, Lagos, March.

Mustapha, A.R., "Structural adjustment and agrarian change in Nigeria", in Olukoshi, A., (ed.), *The Political Economy of Structural Adjustment in Nigeria*, James Currey, London, (forthcoming).

Mustapha, A.R., and S. Othman, 1987, "The idea of democracy", *West Africa*, 28 September.

NANS (National Association of Nigerian Students), 1984,"*The Students' Charter.*

Ncube, P., M. Sakala and M. Ndulo, 1987, "The IMF and the Zambian Economy: a case study", in Havnevik, K., (ed.), *The IMF and the World Bank in Africa*, the Scandinavian Institute of African Studies, Uppsala.

Nelson, J., 1990a, "Consolidating economic adjustment: Aspects of the political economy of sustained reform", Paper delivered to IDPM Conference on Policy-Based Lending, (mimeo).

Nelson, J., 1990b, "Prospects for political conditionality and adjustment lending to Eastern Europe", Verbal contribution to *IDPM Conference on Policy-Based Lending*.

Nelson, J.M., 1989, "The politics of pro-poor adjustment", in Nelson, J.M., (ed.), *Fragile Coalitions: The Politics of Economic Adjustment*, Transaction Books, New Brunswick.

Neocosmos, M., 1991, "The agrarian question in Africa and the concept of 'Accumulation from below'", Paper given at the Scandinavian Institute of African Studies, Africa Days Workshop, Uppsala, April, (mimeo).

Ng'ethe, N. and J.G. Wahone with G. Ndua, 1989, "The rural informal sector in Kenya: A study of micro-enterprises in Nyeri, Meru, Uasin Gishu and Siaya districts", *IDS Occasional Paper*, No. 54, IDS, University of Nairobi.

Ninsin, K., 1991, *The Informal Sector in Ghana's Political Economy*, Freedom Publications, Accra.

NLC (Nigeria Labour Congress), 1985, *Towards National Recovery: Nigeria Labour Congress' Alternatives*, Lagos.

Nordic Office, 1986, "Nordisk Meddelelse 86/325, Nordisk Kontor, World Bank, Washington", Telex to SIDA, Stockholm, 17 October.

Nordman, C., 1979, "Prelude to decolonisation, 1964–1970", Ph.D. Thesis, Oxford.

Nyerere, J., 1967, *Socialism and Rural Development*, Dar es Salaam.

O'Connor, J., 1973, *The Fiscal Crisis of the State*, St. Martins Press, New York.

O'Donnell, G.A., 1973, *Modernisation and Bureaucratic-Authoritarianisation: Studies in South American Politics*, Institute of International Studies, University of California.

O'Donnell, G.A., P.C. Schmitter, and L. Whitehead, 1986, *Transitions from Authoritarian Rule: Prospects for Democracy*, Johns Hopkins University Press, Baltimore.

OAU (Organization for African Unity), 1980, *Lagos Plan of Action for the Implementation of the Monrovia Strategy for the Economic Development of Africa*, Addis Ababa.

ODC (Overseas Development Council), 1987, "Should the IMF withdraw from Africa?", *Policy Focus*, No. 1.

Ogbuile, N., 1990, "Fortunes in the swamps", *The Guardian*, Lagos, July 1.

Olson, M., 1982, *The Rise and Decline of Nations: Economic Growth, Stagflation and Social Rigidities*, Yale University Press, New Haven.

Olukoshi, A., 1989, "Impact of the IMF-World Bank programmes on Nigeria", in Onimode, B., (ed.), *The IMF, the World Bank and the African Debt. The Economic Impact*, IFAA and Zed Books, London.

Olukoshi, A., 1991, "The politics of structural adjustment in Nigeria", Paper presented to the Scandinavian Institute of African Studies, Africa Days Workshop, Uppsala, April.

Olukoshi, A., "Nigerian Marxist responses to the formation of the Nigerian Labour Party (NLP)", in Neugebauer, C., (ed.), *Philosophy, Ideology and Society in Africa*, Munich and Kinshasa, African University Press, (forthcoming).

Osoba, S., 1978, "The deepening crisis of the Nigerian national bourgeoisie", *Review of African Political Economy*, No. 13.

Othman, S., 1987, "Power for profit: Class, corporatism and factionalism in the Nigerian military", Paper for the Conference on West African States since 1976, School of Oriental and African Studies, University of London, June.

Parfitt, T., and S. Bullock, 1990, "The prospects for a new Lomé Convention", *Review of African Political Economy*, No. 47.

Pelczynski, Z.A., 1988, "Solidarity and the rebirth of civil society", in Keane, J., (ed.), *Civil Society and the State*, Verso, London.

Please, S., 1984, *The Hobbled Giant*, Lynne Rienner, Boulder.

Please, S., 1990, Verbal contribution to round table on prospects for policy-based lending in the 1990s, IDPM Conference on Policy-Based Lending, Manchester, September.

Pletcher, J.R., 1986, "The political uses of agricultural markets in Zambia", *The Journal of Modern African Studies*, Vol. 24, 4.

Portes, A., M. Castells and L. Benton, 1989, *Informal Economy: Studies in Advanced and Less Developed Countries*, Johns Hopkins University Press.

Powell, G.B., 1982, *Contemporary Democracies: Participation, Stability and Violence*, Harvard University Press.

Pye, L.W. and S. Verba, (eds.), 1965, *Political Culture and Political Development*, Princeton University Press.

Rawls, J., 1972, *A Theory of Justice*. Oxford University Press, Oxford.

Redclift, M., 1986, "Survival strategies in rural Europe: Continuity and change", *Sociologia Ruralis*, Vol. XXVI-3/4.

Redclift, N. and E. Mingione, 1985, (eds.), *Beyond Employment: Household, Gender and Subsistence*, Blackwell, Oxford.

Reinikka-Soininen, R., 1990, *Theory and Practice in Structural Adjustment: The Case of Zambia*, Helsingin Kauppakorkeakoulin Julkaisuja D-126, Helsinki.

Remnick, D., 1990, "Millions of Soviet lives pervaded by poverty", *Guardian Weekly*, London, June 10.

Robinson, D., 1990, "Civil service remuneration in Africa", *International Labour Review*, Vol. 129, No. 3.

Roitman, J.L., 1990, "The politics of informal markets in Sub-Saharan Africa", *Journal of Modern African Studies*, Vol. 28, No. 4.

Rotchild, D. and N. Chazan, (eds.), 1988, *The Precarious Balance: State and Society in Africa*, Boulder, London.

Rudebeck, L., 1989, "The politics of structural adjustment in a West African village", *AKUT 41*, Uppsala.

Rudebeck, L., 1990a, "Conditions of people's development in post-colonial Africa", *AKUT 43*, Uppsala.

Rudebeck, L., 1990b, "The effect of structural adjustment in Kandjadja, Guinea-Bissau", *Review of African Political Economy*, No. 49.

Rugumisa, S., 1990, "A Review of the Tanzanian Economic Recovery Programme 1986–89", *Tadreg Research Report, No. 1*, Dar es Salaam.

Russell, S.S., 1986, "Remittances from international migration: A review in perspective", *World Development*, No. 14, June.

Sandbrook, R., 1985, *The Politics of Africa's Economic Stagnation*, Cambridge, CUP.

Sandbrook, R., 1986, "The state and economic stagnation in tropical Africa", *World Development*, 14, 3:319–332.

Sandbrook, R., 1991, "Economic crisis, structural adjustment and the state in Africa", in Ghai, D. (ed.), *The IMF and the South: The Social Impact of Crisis and Adjustment*, Zed Books, London.

Sano, H.-O., 1990, *Big state, small farmers: The search for an agricultural strategy for crisis-ridden Zambia*, Centre for Development Research, Copenhagen.

Sanyal, B., 1991, "Organising the self-employed: The politics of the urban informal sector", *International Labour Review*, Vol. 130, No. 1.

Sender, J. and S. Smith, 1990, *Poverty, Class and Gender in Rural Africa. A Tanzanian Case Study*, Routledge, London.

Shivji, I., 1986, "The transformation of the state and the working people" in Shivji, I., (ed.), *The State and the Working People in Tanzania*, Codesria, Dakar.

Shivji, I., 1989, "The pitfalls of the debate on democracy", *Codesria Bulletin*, Nos. 2, 3.

Sidell, S.R., 1988, *The IMF and Third World Instability: Is there a Connection?*, St Martin's Press.

Stewart, F., 1987, "Should conditionality change?", in Havnevik, K., (ed.), *The IMF and the World Bank in Africa*, Scandinavian Institute of African Studies, Uppsala.

Stewart, F., 1990, "The 1980s—decade of inhuman adjustment", *UNICEF Intercom*, No. 58, October.

Stockholm Group for Development Studies, 1989, "Market Intervention and Price Policies for Agricultural Marketing in Mozambique", (mimeo), Stockholm.

Strickland, R.S., 1991, "Stabilisation strategies of the International Monetary Fund and the effects on income and welfare: The case of Zambia", Ph.D.Thesis, University of Sussex.

Tandon, Y., 1982, (ed.), *Debate on Class, State and Imperialism*, Tanzania Publishing House,

Taylor, A.B., 1989, "The debt problem of Sub-Saharan Africa", *European Journal of Development Research.*, No. 2, December.

Taylor, L. and H. Shapiro, 1990, "The state and industrial strategy", *World Development*, Vol. 18, No. 6.

Therborn, G., 1977, "The rule of capital and the rise of democracy", *New Left Review*, No. 103.

Thurman, J., and G. Trah, 1990, "Part-time work in international perspective", *International Labour Review*, Vol. 129, No. 1.

Törnquist, O., 1985, "Class and democracy in South and South East Asia: Some critical notes", *Cooperation and Conflict*, xx.

Törnquist, O., 1988, "Rent capitalism, state and democracy: A theoretical proposition". Revised version of paper to the *Thirteenth Indian Social Science Congress*; and the *Conference on State and civil society in Indonesia*, Monash University, Melbourne, November.

Toye, J., 1987, *Dilemmas of Development. Reflections on the Counter-Revolution in Development Theory and Policy*, Blackwell, Oxford.

Toye, J., 1989, "Can the World Bank resolve the crisis of developing countries?", *Journal of International Development*, Vol. 1, No. 2.

Toye, J., 1990, "The year of liberal revolution: a survey of 1989", *World Economic and Business Review*, Blackwell, Oxford.

Toye, J., 1991, "Is there a new political economy of development?", in Colclough, C. and J. Manor, *States or Markets? Neo-Liberalism and the Development Debate*, Oxford University Press, Oxford.

Toyo, E., 1985, "Neocolonialism, primitive accumulation and third world orientations", *Nigerian Journal of Political Science*, Vol. 4, Nos. 1 and 2.

Turner, T., 1982, "Nigeria: Imperialism, oil technology and the comprador state", in Nore, P. and T. Turner, (ed.), *Oil and Class Struggle*, ZED Books, London.

Turner, S., 1991, "Lesotho: The economy", *Africa South of the Sahara, Yearbook*, London.

UNDP (United Nations Development Programme), 1990, *Human Development Report*, Oxford.

Vanhanen, T., 1989, "The level of democratisation related to socio-economic variables in 147 states in 1980–85", *Scandinavian Political Studies*, Vol. 12, No. 2.

Wangwe, S., 1987, "The impact of the IMF/World Bank philosophy: The case of Tanzania", in Havnevik, K., (ed.), *The IMF and the World Bank in Africa*, the Scandinavian Institute of African Studies, Uppsala.

Waterbury, J., 1989, "The political management of economic adjustment and reform", in Nelson, J.M., (ed.), *Fragile Coalitions: The Politics of Economic Adjustment*, Transaction Books.

Waterman, P., 1983, *Aristocrats and Plebeians in African Trade Unions? Lagos Port and Dock Worker Organization and Struggle*, The Author, The Hague.

Wedderburn, S., 1988, *Nigeria: Key Issues in Formulating Fertilizer Policy*, APMEPU, Kaduna.

Weissman, S.R., 1990, "Structural adjustment in Africa: Insights from the experiences of Ghana and Senegal", *World Development*, Vol. 18, No. 12.

Williams, G., 1980, *State and Society in Nigeria*, Afrografika Publishers, Ibadan.

Williams, G., 1987, "Primitive accumulation: The way to progress?", *Development and Change*, Vol. 18, No. 4, October.

Wolf, D., 1990, "Daughters, decisions and domination: An empirical and conceptual critique of household strategies", *Development and Change*, Vol. 21.

World Bank, 1981, *Accelerated Development in Sub-Saharan Africa: An Agenda for Action*, Washington.

World Bank 1989a, *Sub-Saharan Africa From Crisis to Sustainable Growth. A Long-Term Perspective Study*, Washington.

World Bank 1989b, *Africa's Adjustment and Growth in the 1980s*, Washington.

World Bank, 1989c, *World Development Report*, Washington.

World Bank, 1990a, *Tanzania: Tanzania/World Bank Relations 1961–87, Vol. I, Overview*, Report No. 8329, Washington.

World Bank, 1990b, *Tanzania: Economic and Financial Policy Framework 1989/90 – 1991/92*, Ref. Sec. M 90–83.

World Bank, 1990c, *Mozambique*, Poverty Reduction Framework Paper, Washington.

Wright, G., 1989, "U.S. foreign policy and destabilisation in Southern Africa", *Review of African Political Economy*, No. 45/6.

Yaro, H.P., 1989, "Petty trading in Samaru, Zaria local government area in Kaduna State", B.A. Thesis, Dept. of Geography, Ahmadu Bello University, Zaria.

Yau, A., 1986, "Repression and students' protests in Nigeria", (mimeo).

Yesufu, T.M., 1982, *The Dynamics of Industrial Relations: The Nigerian Experience*, University Press Limited.

Zack-Williams, A.B., 1990, "Sierra Leone: Crisis and despair", *Review of African Political Economy*, No. 49.

Zwingina, J., 1987, "The crisis of hegemonic decline: U.S. disinterest in Africa", *Review of African Political Economy*, No. 38.

NEWSPAPERS AND PERIODICALS

Africa Confidential, London
Africa Economic Digest, London
Africa Report, London
BBC Summary of World Broadcasts, London
Business Concord, Lagos
Daily News, Dar es Salaam
Daily Times, Lagos
Economist Intelligence Unit, Quarterly Reports, London
Financial Times, London
The Guardian, Lagos
The Guardian, London
Monthly Business and Economic Digest (MBED), Lagos
Mozambique File, Maputo
National Concord, Lagos
New Nigerian, Lagos
Newswatch, Lagos
The Nigerian Economist, Lagos
Sunday News, Dar es Salaam
West Africa, London

Notes on the Contributors

Yusuf Bangura is a Research Fellow at the United Research Institute for Social Development (UNRISD). He was formerly a lecturer in Political Science at Ahmadu Bello University, Zaria, Nigeria and a visiting research fellow at Stockholm University and AKUT*, University of Uppsala, both in Sweden. He was educated at the London School of Economics and Political Science, and has published widely on the socio-political context of the African crisis and on the effects of adjustment policies on Nigerian workers.

Björn Beckman is a SAREC**-funded Associate Professor of Development Studies in the Department of Political Science, Stockholm University, Sweden. He taught Political Economy at Ahmadu Bello University, Zaria, Nigeria from 1978 to 1987 and is currently a Research Associate of Bayero University, Kano, Nigeria. His first African research experience was in Ghana (1967–1971). He is an overseas editor and frequent contributor to the *Review of African Political Economy*. Major publications include *Organising the farmers: Cocoa Politics and National Development in Ghana* (NAI, 1976), and with Gunilla Andrae, *The Wheat Trap: Bread and Underdevelopment in Nigeria* (Zed, 1985), and *Industry Goes Farming* (NAI, 1987). Current research is on interest group politics and structural adjustment, including a study of the Nigerian textile unions, also with Andrae.

Peter Gibbon was trained as a sociologist and political scientist. He is currently a Research Fellow at Nordiska Afrikainstitutet (the Scandinavian Institute of African Studies), Uppsala, Sweden, where he coordinates a research programme on the social and political context of structural adjustment. He has worked in Ireland, Britain and Tanzania. His publications include *The State in Northern Ireland 1921–72* (Manchester University Press, 1979), *Thurcroft: A Village and the Miners' Strike* (Spokesman Press, 1986) and "Towards a Political Economy of African Socialism" (with M. Neocosmos) in H. Bernstein and B. Campbell (eds) *Contradictions of Accumulation in Africa* (Sage, 1985).

---

* Arbetsgruppen för studier av Utvecklingsstrategier (the Working Group for the Study of Development Strategies)
** Swedish Agency for Research Cooperation

Kenneth Hermele is an economist who is currently a Research Fellow with AKUT at the University of Uppsala, Sweden. In 1983–86 he worked in the Ministry of Agriculture in Mozambique. At AKUT he codirects a research project on democracy and structural adjustment with special reference to Latin America and Africa. His publications include *Land Struggles and Social Differentiation in Southern Mozambique* (NAI, 1988), and *Mozambican Crossroads: Economics and Politics in the Era of Structural Adjustment* (Chr. Michelsen Institute, Bergen, 1990).

Abdul Raufu Mustapha is a Senior Lecturer in the Department of Political Science, Ahmadu Bello University, Zaria, Nigeria, where he teaches Political Economy and Nigerian Politics. He is a graduate of Ahmadu Bello University and Oxford University, England and has at different times been a member of the Editorial Working Group and an overseas editor of the *Review of African Political Economy*. His current research interests are the interaction between society and ecology in rural Hausaland, and the sociology of cocoa farming households in the Nigerian cocoa belt.

Arve Ofstad is a Development Economist, and has been a Research Fellow at Chr. Michelsen Institute in Bergen since 1976. He worked two years (1979–80) for UNDP in Mozambique, and was affiliated (1987–88) to the Institute of Economic Growth in Delhi, India. His research includes work on poverty alleviation policies, intra-regional trade in Southern Africa, and Norwegian aid policies and practices in India and Mozambique. He is currently the coordinator of the CMI research programme on Southern Africa.

John Toye is a development economist with special interests in public finance, commodity markets, the evaluation of foreign aid and theories of development. He has taught at the Universities of Cambridge and Wales and is currently Director of the Institute of Development Studies and a Professorial Fellow of the University of Sussex, England. His recent publications include *Dilemmas of Development*, (with Michael Lipton) *Does Aid Work in India* and (with Paul Mosley and Jane Harrigan) *Aid and Power*.

Seminar Proceedings
from the Scandinavian Institute of African Studies

1. *Soviet Bloc, China and Africa.* Eds. Sven Hamrell and C.G. Widstrand. 173 pp. Uppsala 1964. (Out-of-print)
2. *Development and Adult Education in Africa.* Ed. C.G. Widstrand. 97 pp. Uppsala 1965. (Out-of-print)
3. *Refugee Problems in Africa.* Ed. Sven Hamrell. 123 pp. Uppsala 1967. SEK 30,-
4. *The Writer in Modern Africa.* Ed. Per Wästberg. 123 pp. Uppsala 1968. SEK 30,-
5. *African Boundary Problems.* Ed. C.G. Widstrand. 202 pp. Uppsala 1969. SEK 30,-
6. *Cooperatives and Rural Development in East Africa.* Ed. C.G. Widstrand. 271 pp. Uppsala 1970. (Out-of-print)
7. *Reporting Africa.* Ed. Olav Stokke. 223 pp. Uppsala 1971. SEK 30,-
8. *African Cooperatives and Efficiency.* Ed. C.G. Widstrand. 239 pp. Uppsala 1972. SEK 60,-
9. *Land-locked Countries of Africa.* Ed. Zdenek Cervenka. 368 pp. Uppsala 1973. SEK 80,-
10. *Multinational Firms in Africa.* Ed. C.G. Widstrand. With an introduction by Samir Amin. 425 pp. Uppsala 1975. (Out-of-print)
11. *African Refugees and the Law.* Eds. Göran Melander and Peter Nobel. 98 pp. Uppsala 1978. SEK 50,-
12. *Problems of Socialist Orientation in Africa.* Ed. Mai Palmberg. 243 pp. Uppsala 1978 (Out-of-print)
13. *Canada, Scandinavia and Southern Africa.* Eds. D. Anglin, T. Shaw and C.G. Widstrand. 190 pp. Uppsala 1978. SEK 70,-
14. *South-South Relations in a Changing World Order.* Ed. Jerker Carlsson. 166 pp. Uppsala 1982. SEK 90,-
15. *Recession in Africa.* Ed. Jerker Carlsson. 203 pp. Uppsala 1983. SEK 95,-
16. *Land Management and Survival.* Ed. Anders Hjort. 148 pp. Uppsala 1985. SEK 100,-
17. *Religion, Development and African Identity.* Ed. Kirsten Holst Petersen. 164 pp. Uppsala 1987. SEK 110,-

18. *The IMF and the World Bank in Africa: Conditionality, Impact and Alternatives.* Ed. Kjell J. Havnevik. 179 pp. Uppsala 1987. SEK 110,-
19. *Refugees and Development in Africa.* Ed. Peter Nobel. 120 pp. Uppsala 1987. SEK 110,-
20. *Criticism and Ideology. Second African Writers' Conference—Stockholm 1986.* Ed. Kirsten Holst Petersen. 221 pp. Uppsala 1988. SEK 150,-
21. *Cooperatives Revisited.* Ed. Hans Hedlund. 223 pp. Uppsala 1988. SEK 170,-
22. *Regional Cooperation in Southern Africa. A Post–Apartheid Perspective.* Eds. Bertil Odén and Haroub Othman. 243 pp. Uppsala 1989. SEK 170,-
23. *Small Town Africa. Studies in Rural–Urban Interaction.* Ed. Johathan Baker. 268 pp. Uppsala 1990. SEK 170,-
24. *Religion and Politics in Southern Africa.* Eds. Carl Fredrik Hallencreutz and Mai Palmberg. 219 pp. Uppsala 1991. SEK 170.-
25. *When the Grass is Gone. Development Intervention in African Arid Lands.* Ed. P.T.W. Baxter. 215 pp. Uppsala 1991. SEK 170,-
26. *Authoritarianism, Democracy and Adjustment. The Politics of Economic Reform in Africa.* Eds. Peter Gibbon, Yusuf Bangura and Arve Ofstad. 236 pp. Uppsala 1992. SEK 230,- (hard cover), SEK 145,- (soft cover)